Foundations
and
Public Policy

SUNY series in Radical Social and Political Theory

Roger S. Gottlieb, editor

Foundations
and
Public Policy

The Mask of Pluralism

Joan Roelofs

State University of New York Press

Published by
State University of New York Press, Albany

© 2003 State University of New York

For information, address State University of New York Press,
90 State Street, Suite 700, Albany, NY 12207

Production by Michael Haggett
Marketing by Patrick Durocher

Library of Congress Cataloging-in-Publication Data

Roelofs, Joan.
    Foundations and public policy : the mask of pluralism / Joan Roelofs.
      p. cm. — (SUNY series in radical social and political theory)
    Includes bibliographical references and index.
    ISBN 0-7914-5641-2 (alk. paper) — ISBN 0-7914-5642-0 (pbk. : alk. paper)
      1. Endowments—United States. 2. Policy sciences—Research grants—United States. 3.
Political planning—United States. I. Title. II. Series.

HV97.A3 R64 2003
320'.6'0973—dc21
                                                                                    2002029232

10 9 8 7 6 5 4 3 2 1

Contents

Acknowledgments

For their encouragement, inspiration, and/or enlightenment, I wish to thank the following people: Robert Arnove, Edward Berman, Simi Berman, Erkki Berndtson, Carolyn Chute, Gerard Colby, Mary Anna Colwell, Charlotte Dennett, Bill Domhoff, Mark Dowie, Daniel Faber, Donald Fisher, Peter Dobkin Hall, Bill Harbaugh, Stanley Katz, Peter Kellman, Frances Kunreuther, Michael Mandel, Ward Morehouse, Gretchen Muller, Stephan Nikolov, Jim O'Connor, Susan Ostrander, Teresa Odendahl, Jon Pratt, Adolph Reed, Carmelo Ruiz, Brian Tokar, Jon Van Til, Stephen Viederman, Victor Wallis, and Betty Zisk. This book also has benefited greatly from my experiences as a board member of the Haymarket People's Fund, as a National Endowment for the Humanities Fellow at the University of Virginia, and as a participant in the National Issues Forums at the New England Center for Civic Life, Franklin Pierce College. For invaluable help, I would like to thank Keene State College librarians Lois Merry and Patrick O'Brien and social sciences administrative assistant Nancy Gitchell. Keene State College, using the fair procedures negotiated by the Keene State College Education Association (KSCEA), provided me with a sabbatical leave to write this book.

Thanks to State University of New York Press for an efficient and a friendly publication process.

Finally, I appreciate the sustenance I receive from my homegrown cheering squad, Cora and Daniel Roelofs.

The following journals have granted permission to include in this book material adapted from my previously published articles:

Telos, for "Foundations and the Supreme Court" (winter 1984–1985), pp. 59–87.

Critical Sociology, for "Foundations and Social Change Organizations: The Mask of Pluralism" (fall 1987), pp. 31–72. (The journal's title was then *The Insurgent Sociologist.*)

New Political Science, <http://www.tandf.co.uk>, for "Foundations and Political Science" 23 (1992), pp. 3–28.

Permission has been granted to use quotations in epigraphs from the following sources:

Alejandro Bendaña, "Which Way for NGOs?" *Interhemispheric Resource Center Bulletin* (October 1998), <http://www.fpif.org/>.

Samuel Hayes, "The Politics of Reform in Municipal Government," *Pacific Northwest Quarterly* (October 1964), pp. 157–169.

Max Lerner, "The Divine Right of Judges," *The Nation* (January 29, 1936), pp. 379–81.

Preface

For the last twenty years I have been studying philanthropic foundations, with a particular focus on the large "liberal" ones that seek to influence public policy. My approach has been critical, in the tradition of power structure research. Foundations play a major part in producing consensus, yet their role has been unduly obscured. Exposés of conservative foundations are more common, but their authors rarely investigate the provenance of ideas being "pushed to the right." Radical foundations also exist. To explore their potential for promoting social change, I served as a board member of an alternative foundation. It was time to incorporate my studies and experience into a book-length work.[1]

My major goal has been to persuade other political scientists that a realistic accounting of the political world must acknowledge the activities of foundations and their grantees, which include think tanks, advocacy groups, cultural institutions, social service providers, and others. These institutions have frequent and significant interactions with corporations, governments, and international organizations. Political scientists hardly ever take notice of either the official or critical literature about philanthropy and its spawn.

Some examples of omissions follow. Scholars note the interaction of "interest groups" with the U.S. Supreme Court but not the foundation grants creating both that particular universe of groups and the Court's intellectual milieu, such as clinical legal education. Political scientists (unlike sociologists) tend to see political phenomena in atomistic, individualistic terms and focus on partisan or personality characteristics, ignoring the networks.

Research on money and politics understandably emphasizes campaign contributions, but generally ignores the funding of ideas. Political scientists rarely study the origin and dissemination of their own disciplinary paradigms or mainstream political ideology, as they are assumed to be common sense or holy writ. Critical political scientists are few and obscure, and their empirical findings are not assimilated into political knowledge, yet it surely matters to democratic theory that the "marketplace of ideas" may be rigged.

Another example follows: Sidney Tarrow and Adam Przeworski, writing in *PS,* state that political scientists could not predict the collapse of communism in the Soviet Union and Eastern Europe.[2] Had the profession been observing foundation initiatives for co-opting elites, according to the rationale proposed by fellow political scientist Zbigniew Brzezinski, it might have had some clues.[3]

Foundations had a major role in creating the United Nations (UN), and they continue to finance selected UN programs. Even the International Criminal Court for the former Yugoslavia receives substantial private funding from the Rockefeller Foundation and George Soros.[4] What are the implications for the study of political power and influence?

Another largely neglected puzzle is a question that in 1967 gave rise to the Caucus for New Political Science: To what extent do foundations determine the research agenda for political scientists? A few studies provide some hints, yet a systematic look at political scientists as *objects* of power might be in order. Oddly enough, while foundations plan research through their satellite or "buffer" organizations, such as the Social Science Research Council, those with critical perspectives rarely study the political world collaboratively. This book will provide research tips for uncovering these neglected sources of power and influence. No normal-size book could give a complete account of foundation activities; they are vast. Thus I am providing an overview of issues particularly important to political science, along with other material that indicates the ubiquity of foundations.

My evidence includes primary sources (e.g., foundation and organization reports, grants listings); secondary sources (e.g., investigations based on archives, and official and critical studies); field research (e.g., participant-observer studies); and experiences and communications in the "nonprofit researchers" network. I have included numerous quotations, indicating how much my work owes to previous researchers. Many critical voices have been muted; they deserve the publicity that our media withhold.

My philanthropy studies have been financed entirely by my position as professor at Keene State College (including two one-semester sabbatical leaves, in 1986 and in 2001), except for a National Endowment for the Humanities Summer Seminar at the University of Virginia in 1982. Under the circumstances (including a teaching load of eight courses each year), this work may be incomplete, and there may even be some errors. However, there often are major errors in well-funded establishment political science. For example, Przeworski notes that specialists in Eastern Europe were so enthralled by "totalitarian" theory that they could not imagine, and did not look for, evidence of conflict in communist systems.[5] I would add that, unlike many political scientists, I would not call an election "free" if it is conducted under threats of massive destruction and economic sanctions (should the current government be reelected), and if millions of dollars have been donated by foreign sources to opposition parties, the press, and supporting organizations (e.g., Nicaragua and Yugoslavia). I hope that any incompleteness and inaccuracies in this book will prompt others to corrective research. That is how political science should evolve.

My purpose is not to "demonize" foundations. They are vastly influential institutions, yet their power is understated by most researchers and by the foundations themselves. Through their "gatekeeper" and funding roles, they discourage criticism of themselves and the organizations they sponsor, and they marginalize critical studies.

On the other hand, what the foundation network actually has promoted and institutionalized cannot be summarily judged. It is clear that it does many good things, and some bad things; predicting what the world would be like without foundation initiatives is beyond my analytic skills. Only this seems clear: for whatever reason it is that we study power, it is wrong to ignore foundations and their networks.

1

Introduction

> A part of the bourgeoisie is desirous of redressing social grievances, in order to secure the continued existence of bourgeois society. To this section belong the economists, philanthropists, humanitarians, improvers of the condition of the working class, organizers of charity, members of societies for the prevention of cruelty to animals, temperance fanatics, hole-and-corner reformers of every imaginable kind.
> —Marx and Engels, *The Communist Manifesto*

Antonio Gramsci's theory of hegemony suggests a conceptual framework useful for understanding foundations. Gramsci, an Italian socialist imprisoned by the Fascists, argued that any political system, such as democratic capitalism, is maintained in two ways. The more obvious is the political realm, or "the state," which controls through force and laws. It is complemented by subtle but overarching system maintenance performed by "civil society," or the private realm, which produces consent without the resort to force.

> These two levels correspond on the one hand to the function of "hegemony" which the dominant group exercises throughout society and on the other hand to that of "direct domination" or command exercised through the State and "juridical" government. The functions in question are precisely organisational [sic] and connective.
>
> The intellectuals are the dominant group's "deputies" exercising the subaltern functions of social hegemony and political government.[1]

Gramsci's category of "intellectual" is a broad one; he maintained that all men [sic] were intellectuals, although they do not all perform that function in society. Those who did included artists and scholars, the clergy, teachers, journalists, political party and other activists, engineers, administrators, doctors, lawyers, social workers, and professional reformers. Gramsci did not discuss foundations; there were few in the Italy of his day, although there were corporate grants for ameliorative projects. The Catholic Church was the dominant structure in the Italian nongovernmental world.

To elaborate on Gramsci, in the modern foundation we find the domain of intellectuals par excellence. Furthermore, a central group of liberal foundations exerts "hegemonic" power over civil society, including all of these intellectuals and their institutions, and it has a large role in shaping governmental policies. Hegemony now operates on a global scale, facilitating the globalization of both political and civil society.

Gramsci meant by "the dominant group" what is generally called "the ruling class," or the owners of major productive resources. Intellectuals act on their behalf, whether or not they are members of "ruling class" families. System maintenance, according to Robert Michels, requires attractive positions for ruling class scions not needed to direct industry.[2] Political systems are most secure when all educated, artistic, and ambitious people can find interesting, well-rewarded work; the defection of intellectuals is the chief destabilizing factor.[3]

Foundations provide an institutional basis for the hegemonic function. They appear distant from their corporate origins and support, so they may claim a neutral image. Unlike universities, they are not hobbled by disciplinary traditions or professional qualifications, so they can include anyone and can fund all kinds of projects.

Incorporation of the restless and cheeky is one function of our vast "third" or nonprofit sector. Michels thought that government employment would do the trick, but nongovernment employment is even better as a stabilizer, for reasons we will see later. Marx and Engels probably never imagined that whether or not reformers fixed anything, capitalism would be solidified by their operations. Nonprofits are a reliable source of employment that does not build up the unsettling pile of surplus manufactured goods.

Hegemonic institutions elicit consent by the production and dissemination of ideology that appears to be merely common sense. Deviations from the central myths are considered "extremism," "paranoia," "utopianism, " "self-defeating dogmatism," and the like. Dissent is thereby neutralized, often ridiculed, but dissenters are welcomed and may be transformed. Raymond Williams observed that hegemonic control is so invincible because it is a dynamic process, creatively incorporating emergent trends.[4]

Intellectuals are attracted to these institutions because they offer prestige, power, perks, and/or social mobility; access to resources needed for their own creations or the "good work" they are doing; and legitimation. Technological changes have upped the ante for doing most anything, whether artistic, scholarly, or activist; consequently, control of resources becomes even more influential.

We also may understand foundations using the power elite theory of C. Wright Mills, later developed and empirically supported by G. William

Power Elite

Corp. rich suppl.
their small #s
by dev.
of npos & think

policy netwk

Domhoff and others. Domhoff argues that the corporate community dominates the federal government, local governments, and all significant policy-
making institutions.

> The corporate rich and the growth entrepreneurs supplement their
> small numbers by developing and directing a wide variety of nonprofit
> organizations, the most important of which are a set of tax-free charita-
> ble foundations, think tanks, and policy-discussion groups. These spe-
> cialized nonprofit groups constitute a *policy-formation network* at the
> national level (emphasis in the original).[5]

What we will see in the following pages is how corporate-created institutions not
only dominate but also tend to supplant governmental ones, local to international. Today there is no replay of the heated debate in our early Republic, when
all corporations, including "voluntary associations," often were regarded as a
threat to democracy.[6]

Domhoff identifies the power elite as the leadership group in society. However, it is not coextensive with the "corporate rich."

> The concept of a power elite makes clear that not all members of the
> upper class are involved in governance; some of them simply enjoy the
> lifestyle that their great wealth affords them. At the same time, the
> focus on a leadership group allows for the fact that not all those in the
> power elite are members of the upper class; many of them are high-level
> employees in profit and nonprofit organizations controlled by the cor-
> porate rich. . . . The power elite, in other words, is based in both own-
> ership and in organizational positions.[7]

My studies also have been guided and inspired by educational theorist
Robert Arnove's anthology, *Philanthropy and Cultural Imperialism,* and its contributors.[8] Arnove maintains that:

> . . . [F]oundations like Carnegie, Rockefeller, and Ford have a corrosive
> influence on a democratic society; they represent relatively unregulated
> and unaccountable concentrations of power and wealth which buy tal-
> ent, promote causes, and, in effect, establish an agenda of what merits
> society's attention. They serve as "cooling out" agencies, delaying and
> preventing more radical, structural change.[9]

The scholars in the Arnove book are sociologists or educational theorists;
there are no political scientists. Their research provides detailed evidence for their
theories and serves as a fine model for political science scholarship. Yet foundations, and most of the nonprofit sector, are largely ignored by political scientists,

except for studies of parties and pressure groups, or the administration of public welfare by private agencies.[10]

One prominent political scientist who argues for a "power elite" interpretation of U.S. politics is Thomas Dye.[11] From him, I have learned a great deal; his evidence is compelling. However, he is not especially critical of elite dominance and barely discusses the elite's international activities. This is a serious omission, because the "cultural imperialism" described by Arnove and others refers both to the hegemony over U.S. society and the more common understanding of imperialism: earth-circling ideas and institutions that facilitate political, economic, and military domination.

Historians Barry Karl and Stanley Katz acknowledge and document the vast power of the foundations, both in providing essential services to the polity, such as planning, and in training elites for efficient and enlightened leadership.

> The creation of the modern foundation and its legitimation as a national system of social reform—a privately supported system operating in lieu of a governmental system—carried the United States through a crucial period of its development: the first third of the twentieth century.[12]

They generally approve of these interventions and do not probe the contradictions to both "free enterprise" and democratic theory implied by the need for extra-constitutional planners.

Resource mobilization theory has illuminated the fate of social change movements—why they live, grow, die, or are transformed. Resources are crucial for all forms of political action, far beyond the campaign and lobbying funding emphasized in "money in politics" studies. Sociologist J. Craig Jenkins, who takes particular notice of foundations, states:

> The foundations have been political "gatekeepers," funding the movement initiatives that were successfully translated into public policy and institutional reforms. In the process, they have also selected the new organizations that became permanent features of the political landscape.[13]

This applies as well to foundation funding of political parties, governmental factions, and overthrow movements. Although illegal in the United States, such grants are considered quite proper when foreigners are recipients.

Zbigniew Brzezinski is a political scientist as well as a preeminent figure in our national security establishment. His works are particularly useful in understanding the "globalization of hegemony." He observes that, "Cultural domination has been an underappreciated facet of American global power."[14] Brzezinski long ago predicted that communism would be defeated not by the force of atomic bombs but by the politics of knowledge (and information technology), which would transform "professional elites." Meanwhile, the allure of U.S. mass culture would convert all others.[15]

> As the imitation of American ways gradually pervades the world, it creates a more congenial setting for the exercise of the indirect and seemingly consensual American hegemony. And as in the case of the domestic American system, that hegemony involves a complex structure of interlocking institutions and procedures, designed to generate consensus and obscure asymmetries in power and influence.[16]

Of course, Brzezinski believes this hegemony to be an excellent thing, the only alternative to "international anarchy."[17] However, he fears that "America's global power" will not last:

> A genuinely populist democracy has never before attained international supremacy. The pursuit of power and especially the economic costs and human sacrifice that the exercise of such power often requires are not generally congenial to democratic instincts. Democratization is inimical to imperial mobilization.[18]

Whether one views cultural imperialism as salutary or destructive clearly depends on one's value system and/or position in society. There may be broader agreement that at least from a scholarly perspective, the invisible must be made visible.

By the following scheme I hope to document the foundations' power and reach. Chapter 2 explains what foundations are, how they have been viewed by critics and supporters, and their dominance over the "third sector." Chapter 3 describes the hegemonic role of foundation ideology, propagated via think tanks, academic disciplines, and the media. Chapters 4 through 8 illustrate foundation interventions to reform, ameliorate, and make the system "work," or to look as though it is working. Yet we may wonder after all whether it is live democracy or merely the embalmed corpse of it. Perhaps what is called "democratic capitalism" is more accurately some variant of "social engineering."

Foundation initiative in major governmental reforms, local, national, and international, is the focus of chapter 4. Chapter 5 indicates how the market has been supplemented to provide a suitable array of somewhat affordable arts and culture. Chapter 6 illustrates some nonmarket solutions devised by elites to mitigate persistent poverty, economic insecurity, inadequate investment, and other failures of the invisible one to play its hand. Chapter 7 documents the large role of foundations in litigation strategies for civil rights and other major issues, especially during the Warren Court era. Chapter 8 describes ways that foundations neutralize dissent and prevent alternatives from developing credibility, especially by channeling social change organizations away from criticisms of the corporate economy and its global penetrations. Chapter 9 discusses the global initiatives of foundations and their export of domestic social engineering techniques. Finally, chapter 10 offers conclusions and questions for further research, with a special plea for the serious political study of foundation power.

2

What Are Foundations?

The domination by the men in whose hands the final control of a large part of American industry rests is not limited to their employees, but is being rapidly extended to control the education and "social service" of the nation. This control is being extended largely through the creation of enormous privately managed funds for indefinite purposes, hereinafter designated "foundations," by the endowment of colleges and universities, by the creation of funds for the pensioning of teachers, by contributions to private charities, as well as through controlling or influencing the public press.
—U.S. Congress, Commission on Industrial Relations, *Report*

HISTORY AND EARLY RECEPTION

The great foundations arose in the early twentieth century when the new millionaires sought a systematic way to dispose of their fortunes. There was more than enough to leave to their families, and handling voluminous charitable requests required a bureaucracy. There were other motives. The Carnegie Corporation, for broad educational purposes, was chartered by New York State in 1911. Then John D. Rockefeller decided ". . . to establish one great foundation. This foundation would be a single central holding company which would finance any and all of the other benevolent organizations, and thus necessarily subject them to its general supervision."[1] The Rockefeller Foundation failed to obtain a congressional charter due to the odium of the name, but it was chartered by New York State in 1913.

"Another motive for establishing the foundation, to which Rockefeller gave high priority, was a desire to show socialists that capitalism was capable of promoting the greatest 'general good'."[2] Many in the early twentieth century did not view capitalism, or their "Supermen," the "Robber Barons," in a favorable light. The Progressive movement (before World War I) was strongly peppered with socialists and populists. Public opinion had been outraged by the Ludlow Massacre, in which a strike at the Rockefeller copper mine in Colorado ended with the deaths of miners and their families.

The Russell Sage and Cleveland foundations, Baron de Hirsch Fund, and others were created at about this time. The Ford Foundation was established in 1936 and funded Michigan charities:

> When the old man died in 1947, the Foundation acquired nearly 90 percent of the company's stock in the form of nonvoting shares, while the family retained the (voting) balance. Some $300 million in inheritance taxes thus shrank to a few million, and it was arranged for the Foundation to pick up even this modest tab; no FMC stock had to be put up at public auction.[3]

With the increasing value of the Ford stock, the Foundation's wealth outgrew its local focus—for many years it was the wealthiest foundation—and prompted its search for purposes both national and international in scope.

Tax evasion and public relations have motivated most foundations (along with indeterminable quantities of guilt and benevolence). However, their greatest threat to democracy lies in their translation of wealth into power. They can create and disseminate an ideology justifying vast inequalities of life chances and political power; they can deflect criticism and mask (and sometimes mitigate) damaging aspects of the system; and they can hire the best brains, popular heroines, and even left-wing political leaders to do their work.

There is considerable agreement among (nonfoundation-sponsored) observers, whether of the Right or Left, on how foundations function in our society. Robert Arnove (see chapter 1), regards them as prime determiners of the public agenda. On the other side, Birchite Gary Allen observes:

> The terrible part of this business is that the economic fraud permitted the Rockefellers through their foundations—though maddening to the middle-class taxpayers who are aware of it—is the least malignant part of the foundation picture. It is the political and social impact of these foundations which is devastating.[4]

These also were the views of early-twentieth-century, middle-class Progressive reformers. A congressional investigation was undertaken in 1915, prompted especially by the Rockefeller Foundation, which was regarded as a snow job to dispel nationwide horror at the Ludlow Massacre. The inquiry was headed by Progressive Senator Frank Walsh, who gave the report its name. The Walsh Commission concluded:

As regards the "foundations" created for unlimited general purposes and endowed with enormous resources, their ultimate possibilities are so grave a menace, not only as regards to their own activities and influence but also the numbing effect which they have on private citizens and public bodies, that if they could be clearly differentiated from other forms of voluntary altruistic effort, it would be desirable to recommend their abolition.[5]

The Commission challenged the very concept of the foundation: a self-perpetuating corporation, which could use its resources for practically unlimited purposes. It also had taken testimony on early foundations' operations. Witnesses suggested that if Rockefeller and Carnegie wanted to improve human welfare, they might pay their workers more.

The Walsh Commission report is still relevant to the study of foundations. However, like much early-twentieth-century anti-capitalist critique, its recommendations were forgotten after the First World War. The mood of the country had changed, and the foundation's image was improving. This can be partly attributed to grants for fighting diseases and providing war relief. Another mollifying development was the increasing coverage of the college professors' pension plan, established in 1905 by the Carnegie Foundation for the Advancement of Teaching.[6] Furthermore, foundation methods became more subtle. The American Council of Learned Societies (1919) and Social Science Research Council (1924) were created as academic holding companies to distribute research funds slightly laundered of the Rockefeller and Carnegie stains. These "buffer" organizations may appear neutral to activists and academics, and to the general public their provenance generally is hidden.

By the eve of World War II, foundations were more acceptable. Margaret Sanger, once a member of the socialist-anarchist "Reds" crowd, was working hand in glove with the Rockefeller Foundation birth-control subsidiaries.[7] Thus a movement for liberation becomes entangled with and supported by the elite, whose interest in population control stems from other motives.

By the late 1940s, many socialist intellectuals were part of the foundation orbit. Congressional committees began accusing foundations of promoting communism![8] This was because they identified communism not with proletarian revolution or the overthrow of capitalism but with the concept of social engineering. René Wormser, counsel to the Reece Committee investigating foundations, viewed with alarm a vast bureaucracy composed of the major foundations and their satellite organizations (Social Science Research Council, American Council of Learned Societies, American Council on Education, etc.): "The ideas and concepts of this bureaucracy are based heavily on the assumption of a cultural lag—the need to adjust law, values, and human affairs in general to a tempo dictated by our rapid technological progress."[9]

This perception is accurate as far as it goes, but the right-wing critics did not focus on the goals of the foundations: to preserve the power and wealth of the present ownership class and to make whatever social and political changes were necessary to ensure this. This might require economic planning and even some redistribution of wealth and power. To the unsophisticated, the "welfare state" might look like socialism. Indeed, one socialist theory, Fabianism, argued that the surest path to socialism was through gradualism, so the idea of "creeping socialism" had some basis. However, others might regard foundation-supported ameliorative measures, such as Social Security and farm price supports, as inoculations preventing socialist challenges.

The elite embraces such "radical" ideas as economic planning, world federalism, social responsibility of corporations, social responsibility of the legal profession, and racial integration to promote stability and forestall radical change. On the other hand, the foundations do not sponsor research or issue pamphlets on the desirability of supplanting the multinational corporations with collective or cooperative ownership.[10] On the contrary, they have made respectable the idea that public "seed" money should be provided to revitalize capitalism (e.g., the Ford Foundation's Community Development Corporation model). As a former president of the Carnegie Corporation, Alan Pifer stated: ". . . foundations should anticipate the streams of social change and facilitate the adaptation of major institutions to such change."[11]

The objectives and operations of foundations are not confined to the United States. This became clear when the Ford Foundation announced its goals for the future of mankind in 1949.[12] Ford has intervened in grassroots political movements at home and abroad, and it seeks to shape institutions and influence public policy from above and below. Foundations have played a large part in the Cold War and are well camouflaged by their neutral and benevolent clothing. This has been their role since the earlier "cold war": the attack by populists and socialists on the "robber barons."

CRITICS AND SUPPORTERS

Critical studies of foundations have appeared from time to time; they receive less and less attention as the years go by. Perhaps this is because the general public reads less, and specialists read fewer works outside of their field. There also has been a well-organized public relations effort on philanthropy's behalf.

In addition to the scholarly studies discussed previously, there have been some notable popular works. Horace Coon's *Money to Burn* emphasized the interlocking directorates and financial interests of foundation trustees.[13] He aimed especially well at the war industries represented on the Carnegie Endowment for International Peace board. Ferdinand Lundberg, a journalist turned academic, included foundations in his more general critiques of capitalism in *America's Sixty Families, The Rich and the Super-Rich,* and *The Rockefeller Syndrome.*[14]

David Horowitz, a leftist turned rightist, published an excellent, well-documented series on foundations in *Ramparts* magazine.[15] Ben Whitaker, a British journalist, produced a fine study, *The Foundations*.[16] Both were inspired by the 1967 revelations that foundations were fronting for Central Intelligence Agency (CIA) projects. Whitaker observed:

> The political territory throughout the world which is principally prized and sought by the CIA is what it usually calls the NCL (the Non-Communist Left). Its policy is to infiltrate—and, if possible, take over the leadership of—moderate reform movements to prevent them from moving further leftwards, and in this way to safeguard American interests—not excluding the economic ones. Hence its field of interest has a useful overlap with the catchment-area of foundations.[17]

An outstanding study of a foundation-supported think tank, the Council on Foreign Relations, is *Imperial Brain Trust*, by Lawrence Shoup and William Minter.[18]

Criticism also comes from liberals who do not object to the hegemonic role of foundations. Their ire is directed at those that exist merely to evade taxes, or those active in right-wing causes. They often complain that the large "progressive" foundations are not doing enough. At a 1973 congressional investigation of foundations, the director of the Tax Reform Research Group, (Naderite) Thomas Stanton, asked: "Are we, the American people, really getting our money's worth for the immense tax subsidies which we grant to foundations and donors?"[19] He approved of the well-staffed, active, big foundations.

In recent years, critical works have emanated from conservatives. Far Right John Birch Society books such as John Stormer's *None Dare Call It Treason* see foundations as part of a plot by the Establishment to create a socialist world order.[20] They have many of the details right, but their conclusions would be judged "extremist." The Capital Research Center provides a more moderate conservative critique. Its major concerns are that foundations are violating the values of their founders and donors, and/or destroying capitalism, by funding performance artists, environmental organizations, and other Leftists.[21]

None of these evaluations has penetrated much into public opinion or political science in recent years. Money in elections takes the spotlight, although G. William Domhoff argues that the campaign funders are important only for narrow issues, such as tax breaks and regulation, rather than systemic matters.[22]

The strongest defenders of foundations argue from functional and pragmatic premises. Burton Weisbrod, in a work sponsored by the Ford Foundation, maintains that:

> We have shown that there are likely to be both efficiency and equity failures in the private market, and we have suggested that government,

which might be expected to correct such failures, is not always able to do so. . . . Failures in the government sector, might give rise to a need for a voluntary sector, . . .[23]

Barry Karl and Stanley Katz conclude that both social justice and technological change engendered the foundations.

> What made the combination of charity and technology unique in American society was the tradition of federalism—the unwillingness of Americans to give their national government the authority to set national standards of social well-being, let alone to enforce them.
>   Into the gap created by this impasse stepped the modern foundation, a system of national philanthropy—privately devoted to increasing the welfare of mankind.[24]

Karl adds that foundations have a special function in creating and training democratic elites; that such leadership is essential in modern society; and that it is not based on class, wealth, or race, as were traditional elites. Twentieth-century philanthropy, unlike traditional charity, sought not to give alms to the poor but to use social science to eliminate the causes of poverty and other afflictions of humanity.[25]
  Jon Van Til invokes Karl Polanyi, who argued that making "the market" the supreme principle of society leads to the destruction of civilization's social and humanitarian protections, whether their source is government, guild, religion, charity, community, or family. Polanyi had said:

> Our thesis is that the idea of a self-adjusting market implied a stark utopia. Such an institution could not exist for any length of time without annihilating the human and natural substance of society; it would have physically destroyed man and transformed his surroundings into a wilderness.[26]

Van Til argues that we need a substantial counterweight to these destructive forces; the "third sector," in which foundations play a guiding role, can provide balance and give us hope for banishing humankind's maladies.[27]
  Other defenders claim that foundations can innovate by breaking through creaky political machinery and unenlightened public opinion. James Joseph, president of the Council on Foundations, argued:

> [Foundations] have the unique advantage of being somewhat insulated from public opinion and political constituencies. Consequently, grantmakers can take pride in their ability to fund innovative programs and work on the frontlines of social problems without concern for popular opinion or building political mandates.[28]

LEGAL STATUS

Foundations did not enjoy a distinctive legal status until the Tax Reform Act of 1969. Before that, most received charters from states as charitable or nonprofit organizations and were subject to whatever the states' requirements and privileges were for such entities. When they applied for and received federal income tax exemption, they were treated much the same as any charitable 501 (c) (3) entity (the numbers indicate the location in the tax law).

The first permanent federal income tax, the Revenue Act of 1913, exempted corporations "organized and operated exclusively for religious, charitable, scientific, or educational purposes, no part of the net income of which insures to the benefit of any private stockholder or individual."[29] Thus what is distinctive about nonprofits is not their abstention from profitable activities but how these gains are utilized; they must not accrue to individuals or stockholders. Later laws prohibited all of these organizations from propaganda, lobbying, or participating in political campaigns.

In 1943, financial reports were required of tax-exempt organizations, with the exception of various specified types (religious, schools, public charities, etc.). Private foundations were not among those exempt from this requirement. Congress enacted further regulations in 1950, aimed at any exempt organization that operated a business on the side as a source of revenue. This was a reaction to the New York University Law School case, which had acquired the Mueller spaghetti company as a feeder. Most of these early regulations expressed Congress' concern with the use of charities, including foundations, for self-dealing and other financial scams. In the tax laws of 1954 and 1964, donations to ordinary charities were given more favorable treatment for tax deductibility purposes than those to private foundations.

Starting in the 1950s, there was considerable congressional scrutiny of foundations. To some extent, this reflected a populist reaction against the corporate-liberal-internationalist thrust of the "Eastern Establishment"; congressional leadership was Southern during these years. Investigations chaired by Representatives E. E. Cox of Georgia and Carroll Reece of Tennessee raised suspicions of "subversive" activities and expressed uneasiness with support for "behavioralism" in the social sciences. Because their critique went off the rails at times, it was lumped with "McCarthyism" and had little credibility as a serious examination of foundations.

Representative Wright Patman of Texas began investigations in 1961; his committee's concerns included the power of foundations, their competition with small businesses, their use for scams, and their international activities. The Ford Foundation's grants to members of Robert Kennedy's staff (after his assassination) and to Cleveland Congress of Racial Equality (CORE) for voter registration prompted further congressional scrutiny. A 1969 Senate investigation questioned the honoraria and travel payments to judges, federal and local officials, and congresspeople who participated in foundation conferences, task forces, and the like. The investigators also were concerned about the "revolving door," whereby officials would go back and forth between government and foundation positions.[30]

The foundation witnesses claimed that they were being singled out unfairly. At the time, businesses and trade associations were lavish with honoraria and travel expenses. When the inquisitors said that foundations were different because they were tax exempt, the rebuttal was that speakers at college graduations often are government officials, and that they receive honoraria.[31] Many examples given by the witnesses revealed the great importance of foundation-supported think tanks and policy networks, for example, the Council of State Governments, to the education and socialization of government officials.

McGeorge Bundy, then president of the Ford Foundation, stated that it had only one federal judge on its board of directors, and that:

> I have been out of the Government 3 years now but I did come straight from government to a foundation. Our vice president for international affairs . . . came to us straight from . . . Director of the AID.
>
> Dean Rusk . . . went straight from Assistant Secretary of State to the presidency of the Rockefeller Foundation and when he left the office as Secretary of State he received a senior appointment again at the Rockefeller Foundation. . . . Cabinet officers seek out some of our program officers or vice presidents and ask them if they are available for service. . . . We had a representative in one part of Latin America who accepted an appointment as an Ambassador under the Johnson administration.[32]

The ensuing regulations did not interfere with any of these arrangements; in recent years, the Pew Charitable Trusts has been sponsoring "civility" retreats for the entire U.S. House of Representatives at the Greenbrier Resort.[33] Although foundations were henceforth forbidden to ". . . persuade members of legislative bodies or government employees to take particular positions on specific legislative issues, except in the course of technical advice or assistance rendered in response to a written request," they could fund occasions or institutions of general influence without penalty.[34]

The Tax Reform Act of 1969 Act imposed a 4 percent excise tax on foundations' net investment income, ostensibly for administrative purposes, put restrictions on self-dealing and business operations, and required them to spend at least 6 percent of net investment income (changed to 5 percent of investment assets in 1981). The last provision addressed concerns that foundations might grow interminably without serving their charitable purposes. More disclosure was required, in an annual report to be filed with the Internal Revenue Service (IRS) and to be made available to citizens at the foundation's office.[35]

The Act established detailed definitions of foundations and distinguished three types for tax purposes and donor tax deductibility. Private foundations were grant-making institutions that existed primarily on investment income. Operating foundations were those that spent at least 85 percent of their income directly for programs related to the foundation's purpose (e.g., Colonial Williamsburg). Under some circumstances, primarily grant-making institutions might fit into this category (e.g., learned societies). Public charities were those that received no more than one-third of support from investment income and more than one-third of support from the public, "in the form of gifts, grants, contributions, membership fees, and gross receipts from admissions and other related activities."[36] The latter category receives the most favorable tax treatment, and it includes the Boy Scouts and the like, as well as many community foundations. An organization's name does not always indicate its status, although the term *fund* often is used in preference to "foundation" by "public charities." More to the point, political restrictions similarly applied to all of these organizations. However, the Act singled out private foundations, because that is where abuses were anticipated.

Foundations may not spend money for lobbying, electioneering (including for referenda), or "grassroots" campaigns (i.e., inducing the public to lobby). On the other hand, the "examination of broad social, economic and similar problems" and "making available the results of nonpartisan analysis, study or research" was specifically permitted. Thus the conferences, publications, institutes, advocacy organizations, and Web sites, which are major channels of foundation influence, were specifically legitimated. Also allowed was testifying before legislatures on matters affecting the status of foundations, and all litigation remained permissible. Voter registration drives were restricted, but permitted under certain circumstances. The Act required foundations to supervise their grantees to ensure against forbidden activities. In addition, all grants to individuals had to be both "deserved" and had to require a specific product or achievement—the latter directed at the RFK staff debacle.

Despite these restrictions, which caused much moaning in the foundation world, the hegemonic power of foundations was in no way threatened. If anything, the law assigned a specific charitable "niche" to foundations: expertise on broad social, economic, and governmental problems.

Congressional scrutiny and legislation stimulated the nonprofit sector to become better organized. A Commission on Private Philanthropy and Public Needs was created in 1973, chaired by John H. Filer, CEO of the Aetna Insurance Company, funded by foundations and corporations and endorsed by both the U.S. Treasury Department and Chairman Wilbur Mills of the US House Ways and Means Committee. The Commission's six-volume report included a recommendation that there be a government agency for philanthropy.[37] This did not happen, but private institutions emerged. Independent Sector, a trade association, was created, which undertook public relations and provided statistical information. Academic centers for philanthropy studies were initiated, the first being the Program on Non-Profit Organizations at Yale. Peter Dobkin Hall maintains that because of the Filer Commission

> for the first time all charitable tax-exempt agencies, from giant grant makers through grassroots activist organizations, were treated as part of a unified nonprofit sector. More than merely reporting on the current state of American philanthropy and voluntarism, the Filer Commission succeeded in creating a new language and a new conceptual framework, which would profoundly shape all subsequent research on voluntary, philanthropic, and charitable activity.[38]

FOUNDATIONS AND THE "THIRD SECTOR"

The boundaries of this term, and whether there is even such a "sector," are hotly disputed, along with related words such as "nonprofit sector," "voluntary sector," "independent sector," and "civil society." Like the similarly imprecise term, *third world, third sector* continues to be used. Consequently, some discussion is necessary regarding its referents. "Tax-exempt organizations" and "non-governmental organizations" also are common in this discourse.

What is the third sector? The term usually identifies most organizations outside of business, government, and the family: churches, social welfare agencies, trade associations, sports and arts clubs, character-building groups such as the Boy Scouts and Girl Scouts, private schools and universities, cultural institutions, advocacy groups, political movements and parties, research institutes, charities, hospitals, unions, foundations, and others. One subset is particularly noteworthy: those organizations covered by Section 501 (c) (3) of the Internal Revenue Code. These are the "religious, charitable, scientific, or educational" organizations whose receipts are tax-exempt, and whose contributions are tax-deductible for the donors. They are generally the only organizations that receive foundation grants. In turn, they must restrict political advocacy and may not support partisan election campaigns. Another type of nonprofit, the 501 (c) (4) "social welfare" organization, is exempt from taxes on its receipts, but its donors cannot deduct contributions from their taxes, and foundations may not support them. These often are political groups, such as the Sierra Club, which can engage in lobbying and propaganda. Both kinds are prohibited from distributing profits to shareholders, although some conduct businesslike activities.

The term *nonprofit sector* often is used as a synonym for "third sector," and it refers only to nongovernmental organizations, although technically government also is "nonprofit." Note that some "nonprofit" organizations are not tax-exempt, some because they have not applied; many small grassroots groups without formal leadership or bylaws do not bother to apply or do not wish to abide by political restrictions. Others may not qualify, such as militias. Also, many nonprofits are not benevolent organizations (e.g., trade associations and country clubs).

Exemption from local property taxes often is more important to nonprofits than exemption from federal income tax, as many have no net income. Traditionally, state and local governments do not tax most religious property, although this exemption can be regarded as a subsidy to religion in violation of the "establishment" clause, and it is unclear what "public purpose" is being served. About half of all individual charitable donations goes to religious institutions, and mostly this is for the support of the clergy, buildings, and members' activities; charitable work represents a small part of expenditure.

More controversy has arisen over the taxation of hospitals. Most of the highly respected ones are nonprofits, although for-profit chains are gaining ground. Some local governments claim that hospitals, although founded as charities and originally supported by donations, volunteers, and pro bono work, do not now serve any charitable purpose, as they require cash, insurance, or Medicaid from all patients. They appear to be indistinguishable from businesses, except for the nondistribution of profits. This does not preclude astronomical salaries for executives and doctors, as is often the case with health maintenance organizations. Thus there are some current attempts to impose property taxes and, by scholars, to exclude such institutions from consideration in the "nonprofit sector."[39]

"Voluntary sector" alludes to the way many institutions originated, with individual charitable donations and volunteer labor. Today, funding (except for churches) from other sources is generally more significant. For example, most private colleges have modest endowments and alumni drives; they rely on tuition payments, government grants, and loans. Museums charge admission and gain income from sales (of paintings and trinkets) and support from corporate foundations, which are hardly "free will" donations based on benevolence.

Volunteers still serve in soup kitchens, community arts councils, and the numerous small nonbureaucratic nonprofits; many are senior citizens or others seeking connections, whether social, business, or spiritual. However, professional staff predominates in the largest third-sector institutions—hospitals, private schools, universities, foundations, social service agencies, museums, zoos, and aquaria. Even where volunteers were once common, they are in decline. The wealthy woman volunteer in arts or social service agencies often is resented by the professionally trained staff. The ladies bountiful, in turn, influenced by feminism, see that their own self-esteem could be enhanced by professional training and careers, and many are following that path. The "woman of leisure" has all but disappeared from the middle class (and never existed in the working class); she also is losing status in the upper class. The semi-voluntary labor once performed by nuns, and once essential to many school and hospital staffs, is disappearing as the vocation's lure diminishes.

Volunteers sometimes are resented in occupations where unions are strong; they are deemed to be depressing service workers' wages. Increasing government regulation and accounting requirements for tax-exempt organizations also have played a role in professionalizing the "third sector."[40] Few foundations use volunteers. However, some social change foundations, such as the Haymarket People's Fund, have volunteer boards of activists making funding decisions; in addition, most have full-time professional staff. Finally, the demands and values of modern technological society have led to the professionalization of many fields; interesting exceptions are politics and family based feeding and child rearing. Volunteerism remains important in the larger scheme of hegemony, but it is becoming less significant for staffing. Therefore, the term *voluntary sector* generally will be avoided.

"Independent Sector" (IS) is the name the cat gave to itself, but many scholars regard the term to be a misnomer, and they emphasize the interdependence of business, government, and nonprofits. The IS is the major trade association of the "third sector" and includes private foundations, corporate foundations, advocacy groups, churches, private schools and universities, and charities. "The Coca-Cola Company" is included with "Alliance for Children and Families," as in our schools and communities.[41] Nonprofit organizations are increasingly government regulated and subsidized, and they serve as contractors for the public sector. Now even churches can be so characterized.

Corporations are now engaged in their own philanthropic work; they were, of course, the original financing for almost all foundations. The assets of churches, charities, foundations, universities, and unions are invested in the stock market, rarely with a "screen." Corporations are even donors to many government programs, from local schools to the CIA's overthrow of Allende in Chile.

A further source of interdependence is the "revolving door" and less visible but nonetheless significant, simultaneous service as directors and/or executives in government, business, and the "third sector." Top government officials are selected not only from the business world but also from foundations, private universities, and charities. In some years, membership in "nonprofits" such as the Council on Foreign Relations or the Trilateral Commission was held by a majority of Cabinet members.

"Civil society," as first used by German philosopher G. W. F. Hegel, included both business and nonprofit organizations; it was contrasted to the "state," which he saw as the realm of universality rather than particularity. Today, it often is used in relation to Eastern Europe "transition" movements, which rejected the all-encompassing communist systems and tried to create a realm (both for welfare and economic activity) autonomous from state control. (This will be discussed further in chapter 9.)

In the United States, "civil society" has taken on a somewhat different meaning and is often cited in the discussion sparked by Robert Putnam's work on "social capital," *Bowling Alone*.[42] It generally means "third sector," exclusive of business, and it has strong connotations of local- and member-controlled organizations rather than bureaucratic corporations such as the Red Cross or the

American Enterprise Institute. For conservatives, civil society is associated with "Points of Light" and, sometimes, civility. Jon Van Til states: "'Civil society' is a hopelessly murky and polysemic (one term, many meanings) concept, which can be molded into almost any shape."[43] (This term will be discussed in chapter 3 in relation to ideology.)

"Nongovernmental organization" (NGO) almost always refers to a nonprofit rather than a business, and welfare and advocacy groups rather than schools, orchestras, and sports clubs. It is often used in international discourse, as NGOs have working arrangements and designated status at the UN and other international governmental organizations. Official UN conferences (on, e.g., women or the environment) often are shadowed by parallel NGO conferences (funded usually by foundations). In turn, protest organizations sometimes have their own presence, indicating "a plague on both your establishments."

STATISTICS

As of 1998, there were 1.6 million nonprofit organizations. Of these, 1.23 million are considered "independent sector organizations," consisting of 354,000 religious organizations (not required to register with the IRS), 734,000 charitable organizations (501 [c] 3), and 140,000 "social welfare" organizations (501 [c] 4).[44] Other types include social clubs, cooperatives, and fraternal organizations. The independent sector had revenues of $664.8 billion (in 1997) and had about 11 million paid employees.[45] Only about 20 percent of this funding came from donations; much more originated in fees and government support. This is not surprising, considering the cost of nonprofit health care, which uses more than half of the total revenue, and the college and university sectors. The top 1 percent of institutions, excluding foundations, owns two-fifths of nonprofit assets. The vast majority of nonprofits are poor and not required to report to the IRS. However, the larger institutions are very well organized; in addition to Independent Sector, each type has its own trade association (e.g., hospitals, colleges, and zoos).

Foundations, which are the planning and coordinating arms of this sector, have assets of about $450 billion. The 50,000 grant-making foundations spent about $27.6 billion in 2000.[46] About three-quarters of the funds (1999 figures) went to education (24%), health (17%), human services (15%), and arts and culture (15%).[47] Even large institutions, with other funding, can be influenced by these grants, as they often are for innovation rather than fixed expenses. Other grants are divided among public/society benefit (12%), including civil rights and social action, community improvement, philanthropy and voluntarism, and public affairs; environment and animals (6%); science and technology (4%); international affairs (3%); social science (3%); and religion (2%).

The largest private foundations include the Gates Foundation, with assets of $21 billion, the Lilly Endowment ($16 billion), and the Ford Foundation ($15

Leftie (radhos
Liberal (ord, Carnegie, Rockefeller, etc.
Vanguard, Liberty Hill

20   FOUNDATIONS AND PUBLIC POLICY

billion).[48] Corporate foundations are a rapidly growing source of philanthropy; the three largest are Fidelity (Massachusetts, with assets of $555 million), Alcoa (Pennsylvania, with $496 million), and Fannie Mae (D.C., with $407 million).[49] In 2000, all foundation giving was estimated at $27.6 billion.[50] Corporate foundations made one-third of their donations to universities, which yield both specific donor benefits such as public relations, research, and recruiting, and the general benefit of having a finger in the knowledge production pie.[51] Overseas corporate philanthropy also has rapidly expanded in the last decade.

A significant development is the joint project, which combines direct corporate donations with those of the private foundations (often with government grants as well). One reason private foundations were established was to create some distance between corporation and grantee. The sentimental veil is no longer needed; capitalism enjoys fine public relations in almost all quarters, including public and private colleges and universities. In addition, unlike the bohemians of the early 1900s, today's artists rarely experience conflicts about corporate money; a rare few may object to Philip Morris grants.

Although there is a convergence tendency among large foundations, not all are the same. The large, general-purpose private foundation is the major subject of this book. There are thousands of small foundations with no particular interest in public policy; nevertheless, they help maintain the system. They may provide jobs for unemployable family members, thereby keeping them out of trouble. Others may plant and maintain flowerbeds on Main Street, providing a service that the market will not. Some foundations exist for a single purpose, such as one to celebrate the life of Paul Robeson with, surprisingly, David Rockefeller as honorary vice chair. Many have a religious function, although they may not, as in the case of the Wycliffe Bible Translators, be all that innocent.[52]

Foundations with public policy objectives may be roughly classified as liberal, conservative, or "alternative." The latter also are known as "social change," "Left," or "Progressive," but I will avoid the latter term, as I maintain that "liberal" foundations are following the Progressive agenda. A few of those generally considered conservative are the Olin, Smith Richardson, Scaife, Murdock, and Bradley foundations; those considered liberal are the MacArthur, Ford, Rockefeller, Carnegie, and Century foundations. Social change foundations (often "public charities") include the Haymarket People's Fund, Liberty Hill Foundation, North Star Fund, Resist, and Vanguard Public Foundation. To these should be added a large national foundation, Jessie Smith Noyes, which provides important support to the environmental justice movement. This is a potential threat to the system, as it reveals the human and environmental costs of our military preparedness and economic prosperity.

One reason for the scarcity of left-wing foundations is that the very format conflicts with radical concepts of democracy. Foundations are an example of mortmain, the dead hand of past wealth controlling the future. Thus some radical foundations were designed to spend their assets and close up shop, such as the Garland Fund, and therefore they are no longer in the picture.

Liberal and social change foundations are most likely to fund grassroots organizing, while conservative foundations concentrate on promoting ideology via think tanks and publications, since bankers do not do or need grassroots organizing. Many liberal foundations will give to both sides of the equation, and both liberal and conservative ones give to the arts, hospitals, private colleges and universities, and other institutions. Individual foundations and their grantees will be discussed throughout this book.

FOUNDATION ORGANIZATION

The Council on Foundations is the major association. It sponsors the Foundation Center, providing statistics and numerous publications, which may be accessed on its Web site or at branch libraries in every state. The National Committee for Responsive Philanthropy originated among dissenters from the mainstream and it advocates for minority and low-income grantees, as does the National Network of Grantmakers. Regional social change foundations have united in the Funding Exchange. Right-wing foundations cooperate at the Philanthropy Roundtable and the National Commission on Philanthropy and Civic Renewal. There are many specialized organizations, such as the Midwest Center for Nonprofit Leadership, Hispanics in Philanthropy, the National Society for Fund-Raising Executives, the National Center for Nonprofit Boards, and ARNOVA, the Association for Research on Nonprofit Organizations and Voluntary Action. The Aspen Institute sponsors a Nonprofit Sector Research Fund, and centers for the study of philanthropy exist at about fifteen universities. There are two major research journals in the field, *Nonprofit and Voluntary Action Quarterly* and *Voluntas* (with an international focus), and many periodicals, such as the *Chronicle of Philanthropy, Foundation News,* and *Black Philanthropy.* The large foundations and most associations have newsletters and web sites; particularly useful is Guidestar, a large, nonprofit database, which includes posted tax forms.[53]

THE THIRD SECTOR AS A PROTECTIVE LAYER

A closer look at the "third sector" belies its frequent profession of neutral benevolence. Although all radical organizations are found within this sector, challengers to the system are rare and generally invisible. The third sector is largely devoted to activities that directly or indirectly protect and promote capitalism. The most visible institutions are religious organizations. Churches have fostered major reforms in American life, providing resources and inspiration for the antislavery, civil rights, and peace movements, and they continue to support and legitimate social justice advocates. On the other hand, most churches and syna-gogues are conservative in their intention and function, accept imperialism and war, and have their funds invested in corporations. The clergy of many denomi-nations has been inspired by liberation theology, yet middle-class congregations seem basically content with the status quo. The fundamentalist religious groups have received great attention as supporters of the extreme right wing, but the political implications of mainstream churches are less frequently analyzed. Pri-vate charitable contributions are the mainstay of religious organizations, which receive only 2 percent of foundation grant money.

Aside from religion, most philanthropy funds private schools, colleges, and universities, private hospitals, and cultural institutions. United Way agencies, the Boy Scouts and Girl Scouts, and other traditional charities and character-build-ing organizations also receive support. The small funds for "public interest activ-ities and political affairs" are, again, largely supportive of capitalism. This includes ideology and public policy planning, which may be produced directly by foundation programs, or through universities and supported think tanks (e.g., the Brookings Institution or the American Enterprise Institute).

Foundations are the funders and organizers of this "third sector" that largely functions as a protective layer for capitalism. How does it work?

First, nonprofits often pick up the slack caused by industrial decline, as hospi-tals and arts centers become significant to urban economies. Local economic devel-opment corporations (supported by philanthropy and government) help rescue des-perately poor areas, both urban and rural. Programs such as "microcredit" promoted by the Ford Foundation in U.S. communities and overseas (e.g., the Grameen Bank in Bangladesh) indicate that capitalism can work for the poorest and keep enter-prising and potentially disruptive activists busy with small enterprises.[54]

Second, the nonprofit sector provides goods and services that the market cannot—from homeless shelters to opera and British TV dramas. The latter are quite important, as the defection of intellectuals tends to be more dangerous to capitalism than starving peasants. Thus we feel good about living in a society where there are many ballet companies and grateful to foundations and Philip Morris for funding them. Similarly, we enjoy the new Hall of Biodiversity at the American Museum of Natural History, provided by the Monsanto Foundation.

Unprofitable but necessary activities could be carried out by government, and they are in many countries. For historic reasons, the United States leaves much to the private sector, and these institutions are quite celebrated, for exam-ple, volunteer fire departments. One counterexample, ironically the provenance of Andrew Carnegie, is the public library, which continues to flourish as a mul-timedia socialist institution. However, privatization, an essential ingredient of neoliberalism, is advancing here and elsewhere, often through the influence of nonprofit "think tanks." For example, the Brookings Institution, once considered a "New Deal" advocacy institute, now supports advocates of voucher systems that draw public resources away from public education.

The privatization of charity, culture, education, and reform has many advantages. The assets of nonprofit organizations are tax-exempt and invested in the corporate economy. Their grants or projects are not subject to political debate. Staff members, unlike civil servants, know that their jobs are dependent on philanthropy and its visible, hugging arms. In contrast, civil servants are a dangerous class, often forming the backbone of socialist parties abroad.

Foundation funding carries control over content. It is easier to shape programs begun in the private sector—family planning clinics or a Peace Corps type of foreign aid—even if they are later adopted by government. By then, the form and content are established, and public agencies generally limit themselves to minor tinkering. Today, implementation of many government programs is entrusted to private organizations, co-funded by foundation grants and other private sources. This gives the third sector the best of all possible worlds: its cash is freed to move elsewhere, and its projects continue, strongly insulated from popular control.

These unprofitable functions also might be performed by political parties, unions, or social movements, which here and abroad have sponsored youth groups, day care centers, children's camps, health clinics, and other charitable and educational activities. One might think it particularly appropriate in a democracy for political parties to supply political research and advocacy. Nevertheless, in the United States, this is largely performed by foundation-supported nonpartisan organizations.

Neoliberalism promises great prosperity to the Third World and the former communist countries, yet even by the World Bank's own reckoning, marketization has failed to provide adequate jobs, housing, health care, or even safe streets. Now hundreds of nonprofits, working with government and international agencies, are distributing surplus wealth overseas in the hopes of sponging up the distress. They are not just handing out relief packages but are creating countless small NGOs for development, civil society, empowerment, democratization, social safety net, the media, or whatever, staffed by locals. Salaries are low by NATO democracies' standards, but so high by local standards that a brain drain occurs from governments, political parties, and purely domestic-funded NGOs. Capable and ambitious people appreciate this world of good pay and frequent flights and conferences.

This brings us to the third protective technique of the nonprofit sector: co-optation. Foundations and NGOs in the United States provide jobs for the sons and daughters of the elite who might otherwise be unemployed and disaffected, along with people of any class who are dissident and potentially dangerous. They help resolve the great threat to capitalism, identified by Joseph Schumpeter:

> The capitalist process, . . . eventually decreases the importance of the function by which the capitalist class lives. We have also seen that it tends to wear away protective strata, to break down its own defenses, to

disperse the garrisons of its entrenchments. And we have finally seen that capitalism creates a critical frame of mind which, after having destroyed the moral authority of so many other institutions, in the end turns against its own; the bourgeois finds to his amazement that the rationalist attitude does not stop at the credentials of kings and popes but goes on to attack private property and the whole scheme of bourgeois values.[55]

Here is an arena where the angry poor can comfortably interact with T-shirted sons and daughters of millionaires who are environmental or human rights activists. On the local level also, community foundations mute criticism of the corporate world. Volunteers or staff do not want to jeopardize their grants, or those for their neighbor's charity.

Apart from the effects of mingling, the NGO world provides many jobs and benefits for radicals willing to become pragmatic. Foundations sustain thousands of grassroots organizations, as long as they have reasonable goals, and almost all organizations seek corporate and foundation funding. Small donations or dues are rarely adequate for any major project and take considerable energy to collect; the NAACP Legal Defense and Education Fund was dependent on foundation money for the litigation leading to *Brown v. Board of Education* in 1954.[56] Journalists and ambitious academics also see advantages in the nonprofit sector, which can serve as a "gateway" to positions of power and wealth; consequently, critical examinations of liberal foundations and their grantees are rare.

The MacArthur Fellows Program, known as "genius grants," provides a way to reward and integrate activists and other intellectuals who might not be interested in institutional advancement, such as membership in the Council on Foreign Relations. However diverse and creative their use of the unrestricted funds, it is unlikely that critical studies of philanthropy will emerge.

A fourth form of protection provided by the foundation and NGO system is its fertile soil for multiculturalism. Dissidence is fragmented through the creation of organizations for blacks, Hispanics, gays, lesbians, the disabled, Native Americans, and even poor people, who are considered just another minority in need of rights.[57] Foundations have created and funded litigation organizations (e.g., the Puerto Rican Legal Defense and Education Fund, the Women's Law Fund, and the Mexican-American Legal Defense and Education Fund). In the early 1970s, the Ford Foundation began to fund women's studies research centers and academic programs; similar efforts resulted in institutions for other disadvantaged groups. Social movement activists are thereby transformed into researchers, managers, and litigators; and movements are fragmented into "identity politics."

Fifth, the foundation network can promote political change when necessary to head off disruptive or revolutionary movements. Elected representatives may be unwilling to act; our legislatures are not required to solve pressing problems, which is one reason courts often assume this role. In any case, the hidden hand of foundations can control the course of social change and deflect anger to targets other than elite power. For example, in response to the civil rights ferment foundations created the National Urban Coalition in 1967, which channeled support and status to moderates and redefined "black power" as "black capitalism." In a similar effort, intense foundation activity accompanied the collapse of South African apartheid to ensure the continuity of corporate economic control; the African National Congress originally had been a socialist movement.[58]

To perform its hegemonic role, foundations must absorb rising social power and allow the attainment of real benefits, while diverting systemic challenges. This function is best performed by the major liberal foundations, as they act in the long-range interests of the corporate world. Their trustees and staff are typical members of the power elite, but they have added blacks, women, Hispanics, and others to broaden support and deflect criticism.

Conservative foundations are less effective. For ideological reasons, and perhaps personal distaste, they wish no truck with performance artists or critical legal theorists. They tend to avoid grassroots community organizers, feminists, and civil rights activists, and hence they do not get a piece of the action. Think tanks such as the Heritage Foundation and the financing of campus newspapers are more their style. That their policies have been adopted is no great sign of their power; how much skill is needed to persuade the representatives of the wealthy to adopt policies favorable to the wealthy? On the other hand, many conservative ideological initiatives that neglected the "protective" role and resisted new trends failed or have been reversed: the defunding of social service agencies, the abolition of farm subsidies, the elimination of environmental laws and abortion rights, and the dissolution of the National Endowment for the Arts.

This book, therefore, will focus mainly on the liberal foundations that have had many successes and are the most powerful. Those of the Left and Right are a significant part of the picture; one hopes that many others will join this project to produce a full-scale mural.

3

Ideology and Information

The foundations do not control, simply because, in the direct and simple sense of the word, there is no need for them to do so. They have only to indicate the immediate direction of their minds for the whole university world to discover that it always meant to gravitate swiftly to that angle of the intellectual compass.

—Harold Laski, "Foundations, Universities, and Research"

Much attention is given to the shaping of mass opinion. There have been far fewer studies of how elite opinion is formed—how do intellectuals get their ideas? The sociology of knowledge is not in fashion these days, nor is its general conclusion that knowledge is related to resources welcome in many quarters, including colleges and universities.[1]

Intellectuals' orientations may be partly derived from family and religious background. Another important influence is university education, where certain ideas become dominant in specific disciplines, and in academic and extracurricular programs, lecture series, events, commencement speeches, hosted conferences, publications, and the discourse in the "common room" (assuming that this still exists).

Foundations provide funds and ideas for these higher education programs (e.g., service learning, women's studies, clinical legal education, and area studies). In addition, they exert a direct influence on professors through research grants, internships, fellowships, conferences, and support for professional organizations. The books published with foundation support become the influential ones, especially relied upon by those in other disciplines or outside of academia; they create the "common wisdom." Many academic fields have close foundation connections. For example, biology and agronomy, central to today's international environmental and political controversies, developed largely under the auspices of Rockefeller philanthropies.

Scholarly journals, serious periodicals (e.g., *The American Prospect*), reference books, national newspapers, public radio and TV, and Internet databases all help fill the minds of "opinion leaders." In these media, also, there is considerable foundation input, through funding or collaboration.

Foundation-supported think tanks and policy institutes, such as the American Enterprise Institute, the Brookings Institution, the Council on Foreign Relations, and the Urban Institute, have great influence. They produce books and reports (some intended to be textbooks), conferences, syndicated columnists, op-eds, and periodicals. They also deliver information directly to elected and appointed government officials (these are intellectuals in Gramsci's book). Conferences and organizations such as the National League of Cities are arenas for "revolving door" selection, where promising local officials are asked to join the big leagues. Those who are ambitious will not challenge the prevailing doctrines. Conformity to hegemonic ideology is easily imposed on those who are uncomfortable with being labeled fools, dogmatic, obsolete, extremist, paranoid, utopian, or conspiracy theorists. However, the dogma of the liberal foundations is not regarded as such; it is simply common sense and the expression of universal values.

The ideas of intellectuals "trickle down" to the general population; nonprofit leaders educate the general membership, and the buzzwords of national figures will be adopted by small town people on the make.

IDEOLOGY

Liberal foundations provide hegemonic ideology not only for the United States but also for export. They prevent any counterhegemonic ideology, whether of the Left or the Right, from gaining a foothold. Later in this chapter, we will see to what extent right-wing foundations provide a variation; left-wing foundations are examined more extensively in chapter 8.

The prevailing ideology has roots in the Progressive movement, which absorbed (and transformed) populist and socialist protest of the late nineteenth and early twentieth centuries.[2] In the first two decades of the twentieth century, it was normal for intellectuals to be socialists and to regard capitalism as the problem. However, Progressives gradually transformed notions of class struggle and social classes into "social problems" and tasks for social scientists. "The elitist and technocratic dimensions of foundations—their imperious and imperial stance—inhere in their belief that social change can occur and social ills can be redressed by highly trained professionals (scientists and technicians) who produce knowledge and proffer solutions."[3] Foundations, social science, and "social engineering" evolved together; the Progressive movement was their political, public arm.

Before the First World War, the Sage Foundation financed the professionalization of charity and promoted the idea (through publications, conferences and the journal *Survey*) that poverty was an individual problem requiring the intervention of social workers.[4] At the same time, the National Municipal League and its affiliates, supported by the Rockefeller Foundation, were advocating reforms that tended to reduce popular participation: "The council-manager form of government was a general device to depoliticize city government. It was part of a mystique of efficiency and expertise that brands the average person as incompetent to make political judgements."[5] Nonpartisan local elections, based on the theory that "there is no Republican or Democratic way to pave a street," assumed that there could be democracy without politics.

During the interwar period, socialist theories gradually lost their hold in the academic world. Empirical social science, fostered by the foundation-created Social Science Research Council and the Rockefeller-founded University of Chicago, became the conventional wisdom. Capitalism had invented the field of public relations, and postwar philanthropies of Rockefeller (in public health) and Carnegie (in libraries and college teachers' pensions) were diminishing anti-capitalist criticism. This also was a time of experimentation with employee profit sharing, company recreation and education programs, and credit unions. These were intended to compensate for permanent employee status, not previously part of the American Dream.[6] At Henry Ford's plant, many workers were able to afford the cars that they were producing, and all were invited to his clean-living square dance parties.

The Twentieth Century Fund, a foundation derived from Filene wealth, was especially supportive of these new ways of acculturation into the workforce; it did not even oppose unions. Its efforts contributed to replacing the earlier ideals of the craftsperson or the proprietor with the ultimately more attainable status of the consumer. The Fund also developed an ideology stressing the benign nature of capitalism. It sponsored Adolph Berle's and Gardiner Means's *The Modern Corporation and Private Property*.[7] This work argued that corporations should no longer be regarded as private property; they had been transformed by "managerialism."

> While elements of the private property system remain, the institutions which now direct the use of capital wealth—our corporations, financial organizations and insurance and investment companies—are to a significant degree public or quasi-public institutions.[8]

With the corporation under control, other loose ends had to be gathered. The fruits of the new empirical social science were on display in the *Recent Social Trends (RST)* report to President Hoover; it had been financed by the Rockefeller Foundation and produced by associates of the Social Science Research Council. *RST* took Progressive advocacy of centralization, managerialism, and social engineering a few steps farther (more on this report in chapters 4 and 6). Democratic politics, characterized by political parties and mass participation, was sliding out of view, even as an aspiration.

The Ford Foundation's entrance onto the national scene in 1949 heralded an intense collaboration between foundations and social science in efforts to solve social problems as well as to forestall ideological challenges. The elite was nervous in 1949. It looked as though communism was "on the march" in the world, there was continued uncertainty about U.S. economic stability, and the unfinished business of the Civil War, among other problems, had now become urgent. Racial segregation and Southern "justice" threatened dissension at home and sullied the moral leadership of the "free world," which would soon include new black nations.

The Ford Foundation's 1949 *Report* was a useful summary of Progressivism's evolution. It was the work of a study committee chaired by Rowan Gaither (director of the RAND Corporation), charged with discovering which problems of mankind to solve, and how. The *Report* advised using the vast discretionary funds of the Foundation ". . . to assist democracy to meet [the] challenge." The only way to fight communism was to meet all needs: ". . . to help man achieve his entire well-being." The dignity of man, equal rights, and equal opportunity to develop capabilities were all of great importance.

The *Report* was critical of the American political system. There were defects in political institutions and a shortage of competent people in government. Redbaiting, with its trampling on civil liberties, was considered counterproductive. Certain flaws were particularly ominous: maladjusted individuals, lack of political participation, and ". . . intergroup hostilities weaken our democratic strength by dissipating important resources of energy in internal conflicts, and by swelling the ranks of malcontents who constitute the seedbed for undemocratic ideologies."[9] The Ford Foundation, which, it was claimed, represented no interests and was not partisan, should be the agent to bring about the democratic utopia and universal peace. To further the latter aim:

> Foundation success in this field may at times require activities in public education long in advance of official policy formulation. In fact, a foundation can make a most significant contribution by anticipating critical issues and by stimulating awareness and understanding of them in advance of governmental action.[10]

Democracy should be promoted and apathy defeated by employing social scientists and educators to stimulate and mobilize an interest in public affairs.

The Foundation conceived of democracy in terms of "results." This is the same defense made today for judicial activism, wherein judges undertake the role of social engineers. While the *Report* indicated a need to improve citizens and government, it did not fault corporations or question the system of power, privilege, and hegemony.

The Rockefeller Foundation had supported extensive programs in public health (worldwide), medical education, agronomy, and biological sciences generally. These fields could support social engineering strategies as well as overseas expansion. An exotic touch was the Rockefeller Foundation's bankrolling of the Kinsey studies on sexual behavior—perhaps on the theory that sexual satisfaction would dampen revolutionary ardor. This was a reasonable derivation from the foundation-supported doctrine that anyone who embraced communism or other "extremist ideologies" was mentally ill. Other prophylactic measures supplied by the Rockefeller Foundation were the technology and theory of population control, which were rooted in the assumption that overpopulation causes revolution.

> [John D.] Rockefeller [III] . . . formed the Population Council. The Council was funded by generous grants from the Rockefeller Foundation and later the Ford Foundation. It quickly assumed a leadership role in the development of national population control policy. . . . They view political stability and reduction in international and domestic violence as desirable by-products of reduced population growth. . . .
>
> Population policy-making in America also provides a classic example of the non-decision. By focusing on population growth as the obstacle to improving the quality of life of the world's population, the more threatening questions of inequalities in the distribution of wealth between rich and poor nations and peoples can be bypassed.[11]

Although Ford and other foundations had undertaken ameliorative measures, "malcontents" started to spring up everywhere in the United States during the 1960s. Foundation ideology attributed the radical protests to defects in pluralism. The pluralist ideology holds that any interest is free to organize and to obtain benefits from the system, through peaceful processes of compromise.

Disadvantaged groups, such as blacks, Chicanos, women, children, and the poor, needed help in obtaining their rights.[12] Grant money would enable them to participate in the interest group process on an equal basis with the more advantaged groups, and then they would no longer waste their energies in futile disruptive actions. Note that according to foundation ideology, the poor are just another minority group. Poverty, militarism, racism, and environmental degradation are not by-products of the economic system or related to each other. They are merely defects to be corrected through the pluralist political process.

POLITICAL SCIENCE

In the post–World War II period, the creation of ideology and of political science had become so intertwined that it will be useful at this point to focus on the foundations' role in shaping the discipline. Foundations had from the outset been involved in academic and disciplinary design in many subjects, political science specifically, through their support for selected scholars, professional associations, public administration initiatives, and the Social Science Research Council. However, this dominant role was not systematically challenged by political scientists until 1967, when the Caucus for New Political Science developed within the American Political Science Association. Earlier congressional hearings had questioned the foundation-political science connection, but from a conservative "obsolete" perspective, that was disregarded by most professionals.

The Caucus originated to oppose current trends in political science, especially its lack of concern with the Vietnam War and mass protest movements. Of the thousands of panel papers at the 1967 convention, which supposedly reflect current research, none addressed these matters. Major issues on the original Caucus agenda were the foundations' influence on research topic choices and foundations' connections to political science more generally. The CIA's use of foundations as "pass-throughs" for funding professional and student organizations also was revealed in 1967, and this created a temporary scandal. The Caucus broadened the research agenda, provided a support system for dissident political scientists, and influenced the American Political Science Association (APSA) in many ways. Nevertheless, the foundation matter faded from Caucus concerns. This book, based on research in progress since 1982, is an attempt to further the original mission.

Political scientists study power, but they rarely consider themselves objects of power. Campaign finance studies indicate the considerable influence of resources on outcomes; how resources fund ideas is not a salient issue in political science. However, scholars in other fields, especially in history, sociology, and education, have undertaken studies of how foundations influence our ideas, our academic disciplines, and our societies. According to Stanley Katz:

> We can specify what researchers have always known: that major trends in research are ordinarily the result of funding decisions; that these decisions might well have gone another way, with quite different intellectual consequences; that sets of funding decisions constitute intellectual policies. To understand the history of research, that is, we must analyze the systematic behavior of funding agencies, whether they be governments, universities, philanthropic organizations or corporations.[13]

Political scientists are selective in the nongovernmental organizations that they investigate. They study parties and interest groups, yet the latter's creation and funding are usually neglected. The interlocking directorates among interest groups, foundations, and corporations are generally ignored.[14] Professional associations, conferences of state officials, think tanks, and integrative organizations such as the Social Science Research Council and the American Council of Learned Societies are rarely examined in political science research. Thus indexes in American government textbooks sometimes list Ford, Betty, and omit the Ford Foundation.

Even the tiny group of Marxist scholars will study the "state" and the corporation, and the connections between them, but it usually skips over the "cartilage" provided by the so-called "nonprofit" sector. This occurs despite considerable genuflection to Gramsci's theory of hegemony. Perhaps it is because Gramsci did not specifically discuss foundations, for the overarching "NGO" of his time and place was the Catholic Church. Today, that has changed; U.S.-style foundations, along with elite-sponsored "grassroots" organizations, have sprung up almost everywhere on earth, while the Catholics often play a subversive role.

Among the few political scientists who do study the "nonprofit" sector, the best known are Thomas Dye and Harmon Zeigler.[15] However, they are favorably impressed with elite institutions, and they maintain that elites, unlike the masses, disdain violent solutions. Unfortunately, missing from their analysis is the origin and clientele of the CIA, or the environmental consequences of Overseas Development Council projects. For critical views, we must look at the work of journalists, historians, Naderites, social psychologist William Domhoff, and the sociologists and educational theorists contributing to Robert Arnove's anthology, *Philanthropy and Cultural Imperialism.*

In recent years, conservative foundations (e.g., the Heritage and Olin foundations) have aggressively promoted ideology.[16] They are fairly visible, and their activities provoke liberal critique. On the other hand, the mainstream foundations are widely regarded as objective, neutral, and concerned solely with promoting the purest scientific scholarship or, alternatively, fostering diversity: the hundred best flowers, regardless of their color.

Here we contend that these liberal foundations are not neutral, but that they have steered political science toward ideology and research supportive of foundations and their source of funds—millionaires and corporations. Their power lies not only in their ability to create attractive new programs (or entire disciplines, such as the study of philanthropy), or to fund researchers. Their buffer organizations (e.g., the Social Science Research Council and the American Council of Learned Societies) play a large role in the socialization of political scientists into the professional culture.

The steering already is underway at the dissertation stage. In the oral histories of leading political scientists, Gabriel Almond reports that he was ordered by his advisor, Charles Merriam, to remove material from his dissertation:

> What he was concerned about was that I had done some psyching of John D. Rockefeller, who was the founder of the University of Chicago and the source of its funding; and I had gathered material on Carnegie, and the Carnegie Corporation was becoming an important source of research funds.[17]

Almond's future projects were more in the spirit of behavioralism, including a study of the "inner culture" of communism based on interviews with psychiatrists whose patients were communists.[18]

Even a dissident dissertation advisor might feel morally obliged to encourage topics that could get funded (either at the doctoral stage or for the later postdoctoral spin-off market). It would be prudent for the advisor also: only a rare cultural hero could survive a reputation as one whose students fail to be funded. Wealthy students also are likely to be advised against a maverick course, for foundation grants bestow not only resources but also legitimacy, and they help ensure future employment and publication. Having succeeded by following the correct approach, it is likely that political scientists will continue to accept the "gatekeeper" function of the foundations along the path to success (i.e., publications, appointments, promotions, professional recognition). Political scientists seeking a nonacademic, practical career, in government service or as reformers, also will be enveloped in the network of foundation-created and foundation-funded institutions, such as the Council on Foreign Relations, the League of Cities, or the Urban Institute.

Foundations shape the political culture within which most political scientists, as well as other intellectuals and political leaders, operate. Their conferences, publications, grants, and subsidiaries create the "conventional intellectual tradition in political science."[19] They also fund professional organizations and their special programs, such as the American Political Science Association and the International Political Science Association:

> The modern American foundation and American social science . . . grew from similar philosophical roots, which makes it possible to argue that our social sciences, even more than either the natural sciences or the arts, were given their special character for much of this century by the common values they shared with those who created and managed the first foundations.[20]

In 1924, the Social Science Research Council (SSRC) was created by the Rockefeller and Carnegie foundations, with additional funds from the Julius Rosenwald and Russell Sage foundations. The SSRC was to be an intermediary organization, to put some distance between the foundations and the production of social science. The organizers of the new council, Charles Merriam and Beardsley Ruml, were leading figures in the Rockefeller world, the University of Chicago, and professional organizations of social science (Merriam was APSA president). One study reports:

> It is absolutely clear that the SSRC was the central cog of a Rockefeller policy that was aimed at integrating social science disciplines. Externally the SSRC linked interdisciplinary research councils that had been created in those universities which the Laura Spelman Rockefeller Memorial chose as "centres of excellence." The most important university council was the one at Chicago. . . . Other centres at Columbia, North

Carolina, Harvard, Yale, Virginia, Texas and Stanford were linked into this scheme. . . . The Problems and Policy Committee in conjunction with a few full-time officers effectively ran the SSRC. All policy decisions were made by this body. Every key decision was taken with the leadership of a Rockefeller officer.[21]

The SSRC aimed to create a scientific politics as a tool of reform, based on integrated social science. At first, universities were supported with block grants; later, this was considered ineffective, and specific projects were funded. Nevertheless, the academic results were meager, although the foundations' reform agenda was not totally unproductive. A notable product was the 1933 report, *Recent Social Trends in the United States*.

Close ties between foundations and political science in the 1920s and 1930s did not result in a science of politics, but it did plant seeds for the later behavioral flowering. "Ideology" was deemed "unscientific" and inappropriate in political science. On the other hand, the premises of capitalist democracy were common sense, and their proponents were not regarded as ideological but scientific and neutral. Political scientists increasingly saw their function as service to the powerful, rather than providing leadership to populist or socialist movements. "The construction of a new State apparatus, emboldened by new links to the world of big corporations, armed by a standing military force, and supplied with regulatory powers over the American economy, was aided and abetted by the growing discipline."[22]

In the postwar period, the Ford Foundation became a major influence in the transformation of political science in a behavioral direction. "Behavioralism" (not to be confused with psychological "behaviorist" theory) was the attempt to transform all fields of political science into the scientific study of behavior, which included expressed attitudes, voting, abstaining, lobbying, coalition building, and other observable activities. Behavioralists are naturally drawn to matters that are measurable and accessible, so we learn much about "the man on the street" and little, if anything, about the politics of corporate boardrooms.

From its beginning [Ford Foundation's] Behavioral Science Division focused on practical solutions to problems identified by the 1949 study: problems of low voter turnout and the questioning of the classical democratic image. . . . More troubling was the possibility that the electoral process might become discredited as a means for changing American society, leading subordinate class members to illegitimate and extra-institutional means for changing the system. Consequently most of the Foundation's efforts in political sociology during this time were directed toward pragmatic understanding of American political behavior and the construction of a revised democratic theory to replace the idealistic and seemingly outdated classical view.

To accomplish this dramatic transformation of the field, the Foundation concentrated on building an institutional structure that would insure victory for the behavioralists. This required involvement at a number of different levels: support for individual scholars and creation of academic "stars" within disciplines: grants to elite universities, research institutes [it created the Center for Advanced Study in the Behavioral Sciences and others], and new "think tanks"; shaping of professional journals *(American Political Science Review, American Sociological Review, Journal of Politics)* and even the creation of new journals *(Behavioral Science);* domination of intermediary research clearinghouses such as the Social Science Research Council; and promotion of behavioral science techniques, especially survey research.[23]

It was no wonder that in 1961 Robert A. Dahl argued that an important factor in the emergence of the behavioral study of politics was

the influence of those uniquely American institutions, the great philanthropic foundations—especially Carnegie, Rockefeller, and more recently Ford—which because of their enormous financial contributions to scholarly research, and the inevitable selection among competing proposals that these entail, exert a considerable effect on the scholarly community.[24]

Although behavioralists may not agree, it is apparent "that the currency of the term was attributable to the desire of the officers of the Ford Foundation rather than to the intellectual merit of the idea."[25]

Between 1951 and 1957, Ford's Behavioral Sciences Division spent $23,000,000. "Behavioralism" marginalized those political scientists with different understandings—whether traditional or Marxist; conservative social scientists denounced foundation support in a 1954 congressional hearing.[26] Those with established reputations could continue in their old ways; however, the pressure on younger people and graduate students to follow the latest trend was nearly irresistible.

Andrew Hacker gave several reasons for the rise of behavioralism:

[T]he wealthiest of the foundations opted to give money to support behavioural *[sic]* rather than traditional studies. The consequence of this most worth noting is that postgraduate students and young lecturers—in their formative years—are provided with additional incomes at times when they most need them. A prominent professor at a large university will be given, say, $50,000 for a behavioural project. He will hire a half-dozen postgraduate students as research assistants; and they, in turn, will be able to use the data from the project for writing their doctoral theses.

Through this channel hundreds of young men have been recruited in behaviouralism. . . . The typical American political scientist is a liberal in his politics, but timid in his personality. . . . As a result he has plunged into the behavioural stream because it is pristinely non-controversial.[27]

Looking back, leading practitioners of behavioralism today admit its diversionary implications. David Truman, in an oral history, discussed the reaction against it:

I also think the reaction has been perfectly understandable, because there has been a tendency to get so fascinated with the gadgetry—particularly as sophisticated, quantitative techniques and the computers and even, I must say, the sample survey, have become more readily available—with what Lasswell used to refer to as the systematic elaboration of the obvious, a minute dissection of things that don't make any difference.[28]

David Easton emphasized the safety benefits of behavioralism's irrelevancy:

I think a detailed study of the development of the discipline would demonstrate that McCarthyism had something of an impact. In the ranks of those numerous academics who'd had any association with left-wing or liberal causes there was a great deal of legitimate fear of disastrous political harassment. Political science was at that time just starting up in the behavioral movement. The emphasis upon the basic character of research, upon pure science and the need to deal with fundamentals rather than with policy issues, served political scientists well at a moment when liberal positions on policy issues might expose and reveal them, or invite unfavorable attention to them.[29]

He agreed that in the process, consideration of urgent social problems dropped out of the picture: "[W]e began then to refine and measure many trivial problems that really didn't need measurement and weren't worth the time and effort that was spent on them, except that they helped us to sharpen and refine our measurement tools."[30] Such views of behavioralism were also joined by Robert Dahl, who opined that "political scientists have almost completely ignored problems of government, business, and the economic order."[31] Despite the critique of the Caucus people and the regrets of the practitioners, not much has changed; the *American Political Science Review* contains mainly mathematical articles that few read, which has generated another early twenty-first century protest in the Association.

Oddly enough, the foundations have had little luck in getting political science to notice their political "behavior." "[T]he academic professions—heavily subsidized by the Rockefellers and Fords—have shown a singular lack of interest in [their] alliances, power configurations and interests."[32] They are generally ignored, or their claims to objectivity are accepted unquestioningly. To throw critics off guard, liberal foundations sometimes emphasize how they have been cited as "left wing" or "socialistic" in congressional investigations.

Apart from their traditional concern with political parties and interest groups, few political scientists take any notice of the "third sector," or study philanthropy as a system of power. The recent interest in "civil society" encroaches on this subject, and scholars now discuss *government* promotion and its funding of "voluntary" organizations.[33] Nevertheless, the foundations' role in the creation and maintenance of "civil society" eludes systematic study.

In addition to behavioralism as a general principle for political science, foundations seek to define "conventional wisdom" in every subdiscipline. Their work in public administration is discussed in chapter 4, in public law, chapter 7.

INTERNATIONAL RELATIONS AND COMPARATIVE GOVERNMENT

In the 1920s and 1930s, much of the academic and practical work in "internationalism" and international organizations was supported by the Rockefeller Foundation and the Carnegie Endowment for International Peace. This included institutes, journals, organizations, and the funding of university programs (especially at Columbia). Preeminent still are the Council on Foreign Relations and its influential journal, *Foreign Affairs*. Carnegie's journal, *Foreign Policy*, was meant to be accessible to local elites, such as League of Women Voters leaders and newspaper editors.

After World War II, a "policy oriented intellectual infrastructure" was needed.

This . . . was engineered . . . by the foundations, as is made clear in a U.S. Office of Education report on Language and Area Centers (the subdivisions of International Studies). After reviewing the immense sums spent on establishing the programs by the Rockefeller, Carnegie and other Foundations ($34 million between 1945 and 1948 alone), the report declares: "It must be noted that the significance of the money granted is out of all proportion to the amounts involved since most universities would have no center program had they not been subsidized. Our individual inventories indicate clearly the lack of enthusiasm as well as of cash on the part of most college administrations for such programs."

These new international policy disciplines and "area studies" (e.g., Asian Studies) were provided with an avalanche of facilities—buildings, libraries, computer technology. Staffs and faculties were assembled, granted unprecedented autonomy and exalted in one jump to a kind of penthouse status in the academic hierarchy. They were provided freedom and leverage by abundant outside financing. With all of this backing, they quickly became the most powerful influence on the old horse-and-buggy departments, whose disciplines and concepts of scholarship began to follow the winning model set before them.[34]

Political science became an active participant in the Cold War and the internationalization of the U.S. economy. The "Managerial Presidency" was now enhanced with international capacity by the 1947 creation of the National Security Council and the Central Intelligence Agency. The CIA was supported and remains closely linked to the leading "capitalist front" organization, the (Rockefeller- and Carnegie-created) Council on Foreign Relations (1921), which unites business (and a few labor) leaders, government officials, journalists, and foreign policy academics.[35]

The CIA employs political scientists directly, and it also maintains close contact with those studying international relations or comparative government through sponsored university institutes, such as the Russian Research Center at Harvard, the European Institute at Columbia, or the Center for International Studies at the Massachusetts Institute of Technology (MIT). These were created on the advice of foundations, which assumed that an academic location for intelligence work, rather than being in some hollowed-out mountain, would allay scholars' hesitation. They also could publish unclassified parts of their research. Another inducement was that academics who did not work with the CIA risked being investigated by the Federal Bureau of Investigation (FBI).[36]

These institutes departed from normal academic procedures by their operation outside of the university departments, by their broad, interdisciplinary approaches (including humanities), and by their frequent waiver of academic credentials. Students, professors, and staff were funded by foundations, and former government officials or emigrés without degrees often became senior fellows. A further shift in academic conventions was their close association with government agencies and their considerable participation in classified research. One observer noted that the independent and highly respected, but noncooperating, Institute of Hispanic-American and Luso-Brazilian Studies at Stanford was destroyed in order to obtain Ford Foundation money.[37] Because funding and contacts were so important in the international and foreign studies fields, it was difficult to be a scholar outside of the foundation orbit. Furthermore, the highest awards and honors in the political science profession were regularly bestowed on the affiliates of this network (e.g., Samuel Huntington, Jeane Kirkpatrick, and Gabriel Almond). As the political scientists' *Oral Histories* makes clear, in all fields, local to international, foundation connections provided not only opportunities but also credibility.

Cooperation also was obtained through the attractions of this work. During the 1950s, an MIT psychological warfare project enabled social scientists to experience the thrill and prestige of the Manhattan Project. At the same time, they could negate its horrendous product. They could be the good guys; mind control would convert the misguided Soviets and the Left-leaning "developing nations" to peaceful capitalism, obviating the need to nuke them. Even those who questioned the goals often were seduced by the process. There was a "club atmosphere." It also was an opportunity to do interdisciplinary, collaborative work and to break loose from traditional disciplinary—as well as moral—restraints.[38]

"Development studies" were similarly endowed and often overlapped with area studies programs. Their ideology reflected the financial interests of foundation trustees and portfolios. Mainstream political scientists worked to create a well-educated Third World elite dedicated to capitalism and economic growth.[39] Programs at U.S. universities enrolled many African, Asian, and Latin American students, supported by foundation fellowships. In addition, the foundations invested heavily in social science departments throughout the world, for example, the University of Ibadan, Nigeria, the East African Institute of Social Research in Uganda, and the School of Economics in the University of the Philippines.[40] In 1961, the Ford Foundation established a National School of Law and Administration in the Congo:

> Designed to train a cadre of public administrators, the national school concept grew logically from Ford's interest in training a limited number of administrators who would play central roles in their nations' affairs. The success of the National School in performing this function is suggested by [Walter] Ashley, who notes that "by 1968, the 400 odd graduates of the school made up an elite corps of civil servants who are now holding important administrative and judicial posts throughout the Congo."[41]

In the process, anti-capitalist theories have faded from academic and popular discourse. Third World poverty is now attributed to "culture" or "geography."[42] Ironically, the leading lights in development studies often knew little about the Third World.[43] Legitimate specialists were ignored or forced into exile, because they were unsympathetic to the U.S. policy of counterrevolution. In these operations, empiricism took second place to foreign policy objectives. Charles Beard complained that scholars concentrated on U.S. policy pronouncements but avoided discussing either the activities or effects of its foreign policies. This distortion was "deliberately subsidized in our institutions of learning by funds derived from foundations established for propaganda purposes."[44]

DISSEMINATION OF POLITICAL SCIENCE

Despite the biases and gaps in U.S. political science, foundations have worked to install it throughout the world. Between 1919 and 1940, Rockefeller funding (close to $5,000,000) provided "the mainstay of the support that social science received" in Britain.[45] General funding, the creation of institutes, and research grants promoted both empirical methodology and "the ideological perspective of American philanthropy."[46] The transformation was especially dramatic in the London School of Economics, as it originally had been created (through a bequest to the Fabian Society) to train the administrators of a future socialist society.

Similarly, the development of American-style political science was stimulated by grants to the Royal Institute of International Affairs (London), the Graduate Institute of International Studies (Geneva), the Centre d'Études Politiques Étrangères (Paris), the Notgemeinschaft der Deutschen Wissenschaft (Berlin), the Institute of Economics and History at Copenhagen, Stockholm University, the University of Oslo, the Dutch Economic Institute, and others.[47] By the 1950s, the "Americanization" of political science was well underway in most of the world. In Finland: "The reorientation of the 1950s facilitated the acceptance of the strategies of the American political scientists," and utopian orientations gave way to "value-free and empirical science."[48]

The transmission of American political science also occurred through exchanges of professors, students, government officials, and "potential leaders." Political science professors working covertly with the CIA helped identify and recruit potential allies among foreign students.[49] The Institute for International Education, founded by the Carnegie Endowment in 1919, serviced the massive post–World War II exchange programs of the Carnegie, Rockefeller, and Ford foundations. Outposts such as the Salzburg Seminar in American Studies also projected American political science abroad. In 1988, the International Research and Exchanges Board (a subsidiary of the SSRC, funded by foundations and government) reported that:

> Recent articles in the press have shown that many alumni of these [Eastern European] programs now occupy important positions in the institutions responsible for the economic and political reform that could take place in Eastern Europe should current leadership in the Soviet Union remain in power. Past IREX participants can now be found in the Central Committees of several countries in Eastern Europe, in ministerial posts, and also in the policy-making hierarchies of educational institutions and Academies of Sciences. The placement of former grantees in decision-making bodies is certain to have a positive impact on the exchange process.[50]

One such grantee is political scientist Nora Ananieva, who became deputy prime minister of Bulgaria in February 1990.

United States' political science jargon was rife in the Soviet Union during the Perestroika period, when a Soviet scholar opined that ". . . we are passing from a totalitarian regime to an authoritarian one, since the direct transition from a totalitarian regime to democracy is impossible."[51] This accords with Seymour Martin Lipset's report that many in the Soviet intelligentsia admired Jeane Kirkpatrick.[52] Can one imagine a contemporary American political scientist describing the United States in terms of *Soviet* terminology, that is, "an imperialist regime of alienated masses kept in line by monopoly capitalists and their henchmen"?

The International Political Science Association (IPSA) has been supported by foundations that fund conferences, publications, travel, and secretariat. Its organization, under United Nations Educational, Scientific, and Cultural Organization (UNESCO) auspices, relates it to the UN, which itself was fostered by philanthropy (especially Rockefeller and Carnegie). The IPSA meets officially in two languages, English and French, but the sessions are overwhelmingly in English and reflective of U.S. political science. Consortiums, integrating U.S. and European Union (EU) scholars, are numerous. Their meetings, as well as mainstream study groups of the IPSA, often are the locus of fine wining, dining, and sightseeing. This is another seduction to stay on the beaten track; critical study groups must internalize the "sugar daddy" role.

LIBERAL FOUNDATIONS
AND OTHER FUNDING SOURCES

Research can be funded in various ways: self-funding through university salaries or private resources; political parties or membership organizations; private philanthropy (e.g., angels or Engels); foundations; government; international organizations; corporations; and sale of research or other profitable ventures. The work produced likely will reflect its funding. Somit and Tanenhaus estimate that during the 1950s and 1960s:

> [T]he Ford complex provided 90 percent of the money channeled to political science by American philanthropic institutions. Under these circumstances, political scientists would have been less than human were they not tempted to manifest a deep interest in the kinds of research known to be favored by Ford Foundation staff and advisers.[53]

Behavioral research required ample funds. The foundations were the obvious source, for in addition to their munificence, their subsidiaries (e.g., the SSRC) organized the projects.

Foundations like to initiate new institutions, but after they have "imprinted" their shape, they are willing to share the funding obligations with others. This is true of research as well as anti-poverty programs. The National

Endowment for the Humanities, the National Science Foundation, and Fulbright fellowships were based on earlier, foundation-created models. Now those government "foundations," the United States Information Agency, and the United Nations fund the SSRC, along with the Ford, Rockefeller, Carnegie, Mellon, and MacArthur foundations, and others.[54] Today scholars rarely object to government patronage. The National Security Education Act of 1992 requires that fellowship recipients report to the national security apparatus. Although a few area studies associations refused to cooperate, most do, and the SSRC finds such requirements acceptable.[55]

Conservative foundations also fund academic research. The John M. Olin Foundation granted $55 million in 1988, mostly to

> help underwrite university programs "intended to strengthen the economic, political, and cultural institutions upon which . . . private enterprise is based." The list of Olin beneficiaries reads like a who's who of the academic right: Allan Bloom, the 1960s-hating author of the 1987 best seller *The Closing of the American Mind,* is getting $3.6 million to run the University of Chicago's John M. Olin Center for Inquiry into the Theory and Practice of Democracy. Harvard University professor of government Samuel Huntington, best known as a Vietnam War strategist, is getting $1.4 million to establish the Olin Institute for Strategic Studies on campus, along with $618,000 to support the Olin Program in National Security Affairs and $100,000 for his own Olin Research Fellowship—a total of $2.1 million.[56]

The few small left-wing foundations rarely sponsor research, although in the past there were such funders, for example, the Rabinowitz Foundation, which has spent its assets and closed up shop. Liberal foundations have supported radicals and socialists. The Rockefeller Foundation gave grants to R. H. Tawney and Harold Laski; Ford has funded Roberto Unger, Michael Harrington, Sam Bowles, and Herbert Gintis. However, these people were already eminences rosâtres in their fields and would be hard to ignore in general gift giving. On the other hand, C. Wright Mills was denied Ford Foundation funding after he had published *The Power Elite.*[57] Currently the Aspen Institute provides grants to critical researchers such as Daniel Faber and Mary Anna Colwell. However, its more prominent undertakings include creating links between anti-poverty workers and the national security elite.

An indication of conformity in political science can be deduced from an article by Gabriel Almond, written to denounce ideological conflict in the profession.[58] Of those described as "extremists" (especially on the Left), nearly all mentioned are either not from the United States and/or are not political scientists. Similarly, a major Soviet study of American political science can find a "Left" orientation only by citing a bunch of sociologists.[59]

MULTICULTURALISM

In addition to specific disciplines, foundations promote ideologies by their influence over universities, cultural institutions, and the intellectual climate. Multiculturalism, while a response to genuine oppression, also serves Cold War strategies of encouraging nationalism, religion, and particularism. The foundation-CIA sponsored area studies institutes furthered such goals, as did the same team's financing of organizations and publications overseas, such as the Eastern European Cultural Foundation. In some cases, foundations gained a foothold through cultural grants where overt political intervention would have been resisted. Thus the Ford Foundation's publication of Indian classics in India and preservation of Buddhist religious heritage in Burma and the Soros Foundation's preservation of medieval Jewish literature in communist Hungary were tolerated activities. However, their content was as important as the access that these programs afforded. They aimed to demolish the hegemonic ideology of communists, socialists, and liberation movements, advocating that "workers of the world (maybe peasants, too) should unite." The foundation projects counterpoised identities of blood and faith, following precisely the recommendation of Brzezinski in *Alternative to Partition*. The National Endowment for Democracy (NED), created by Congress in 1983, became another channel for this cultural and political work (see the discussion of the NED in chapter 9).

The same tactics were used in the domestic Cold War. Public interest law, publications, institutes, and university programs (e.g., Mexican-American Legal Defense and Education Fund and Native American Studies) helped create "identity politics." Fragmentation was regarded as urgent. The Black Berets, a militant Chicano group in New Mexico, had been meeting with the Black Panthers, the Young Lords, and the American Indian Movement and expressing solidarity with Cuba. Their mission statement of 1971 included the following:

> In order to combat injustices, racial discrimination and oppression we have set up a defense against the repressive agencies which carry out these established practices against the Chicano and all Third World peoples.[60]

Identity politics, based on deeply felt needs, also could be used as a tool by the "good cops," who did not protest the associated police repression.

Beginning in the early 1970s, Ford began to fund women's studies: research centers, journals such as *Signs*, national organizations, academic programs at elite universities, programs in foreign countries, and international networks and conferences. Beyond the splintering effect, these initiatives helped transform radical movements into professional-led scholarly or bureaucratic organizations.[61] Many academic leftists support multiculturalism and diversity, and right-wing authors and foundations decry them. Nevertheless, these trends serve the elite:

The campus left speaks of equality, and then forgets about justice by ignoring economic and class distinctions. This failure is so fundamental that multiculturalists should no longer be considered "leftists." As long as they claim this description, some of us—those who still feel that elites ought to be accountable—are beginning to feel more comfortable as "populists."[62]

Outside the campus, diversity also served a diversionary purpose. The Ford Foundation extolled these gains:

In the summer of 1994, the Marine Corps, which has only 4 percent women, the smallest of any of the military services, named its first female two-star general, Carol A. Mutter. The first aircraft carrier with female crew members and aviators, the *Eisenhower,* will steam out of Norfolk this fall. And last year, Air Force Secretary Sheila E. Widnall became the first woman to head a branch of the military.[63]

In addition, Ford found that the Persian Gulf War was a "milestone" for women in the military.

Public opinion swung in favor of opening more combat jobs to women following a war in which 41,000 female service members were deployed to the Gulf region in jobs ranging from medics and truck drivers to helicopter pilots and fuel specialists. The war's fast-paced nature blurred the line between combat and noncombat positions.[64]

The military has long welcomed minorities, and for many blacks, Native Americans, and poor whites it has provided opportunities for status and education not otherwise available. It is not surprising that identity politics has severed anti-militarism from progressive politics.

Among many cultural programs (see chapter 5), the Ford Foundation endows ethnic news media and makes its transformative agenda plain when it states:

Just as San Francisco gave birth to the alternative press of the 1960's, the Bay Area's ethnic publications have become the alternative media of the 1990's. . . . [Sandy] Close [director of the Pacific News Service] puts it another way. "What is the new California?" she asks. "It's the neighborhood, the intimate life of the city, but in constant interaction with the homeland."[65]

One critic who is sympathetic to foundation social engineering finds "diversity" to be a failure.

Indeed, the ideologically driven pursuit of "diversity" and "inclusiveness" is perhaps the one area in which today's foundations are influencing public policy with anything like the force of their powerful predecessors of the '50s and '60s. To say that foundations influence policy, however, is not to say that the pursuit of "diversity" and "inclusiveness" they advocate is succeeding in our poor, multiracial cities.

That poverty in America is caused by racism and can be eliminated through education is one of the fundamental assumptions of the liberal politics American foundations so effectively promoted in the '50s and '60s. It has become increasingly difficult, however, to see America as a prosperous country, a minority of whose citizens are denied the right to vote or to work on the basis of their race. We are, instead, a prosperous country in which a well-educated, relatively well-integrated, professional elite rules over a poor and angry majority whose anger has made itself felt from the slums of L.A. to the plains of Oklahoma.[66]

Were we to "deconstruct" "postmodernism" and its dissemination, we would reach the most solid of foundations, providing excellent support for the hegemonic superstructure.

CIVIC RENEWAL

Foundations and NGOs promoting democracy throughout the world are fully aware of the weak spots at home, indicated by a mere 50 percent participation in the *most* popular political activity, voting in presidential elections. "Civic renewal" is their response to increasing political inactivity, for which progressive reforms are to some extent responsible. As we shall see in the next chapter, the reforms diminished the political role of poor and working-class communities in favor of middle- and upper-class ones. Today, certain forms of participation have declined across the board, for example, local party activity and candidacies for school board and town offices. However, among the affluent, voting is vigorous, check writing for candidates thrives, and contacting representatives is frequent. These people even attend town meetings with regularity.

The participation problem is mostly about the dispossessed, and this invokes in the elite fear of a legitimation crisis. In contrast to the United States 100 years ago, and to other capitalist democracies, participation is primarily the domain of affluent, well-educated people. This even applies to voting, which seemingly requires few resources. The likelihood that people will vote increases if they belong to any type of organization; thus low-income black church members have unexpectedly high rates of political participation.[67] Because of this correlation, associational activity is deemed very important to democracy. Debate over its apparent demise has been fueled by Robert Putnam's work, *Bowling Alone,* in which Putnam deplored the loss of "social capital" in the United States, meaning a dense network of community associations and related expressions of social trust.[68] The title is derived from his observation that more people than ever are bowling, but that bowling leagues have declined (along with fraternal organizations, political groups, service clubs, etc.). Since even bowling league members are more likely to vote than unaffiliated bowlers, Putnam's work has sounded an alarm.

Some argue that memberships have simply changed in nature, and that today people belong to national public interest organizations such as the Sierra Club, AARP, NRA, and NOW. Locally, there are small neighborhood associations, self-help groups, and others which have never registered as nonprofits. Yet these critics of Putnam will admit that organizations with any political clout represent mostly the educated, middle-class, and upper-class citizen.[69] Organizations of the early twentieth century often were segregated by gender, race, and religion, but they were sometimes economically inclusive; today, we have made some progress in "diversity," but cross-class associations are more rare.[70]

One way to correct the class disparity in political participation would be to attempt reduction surgery on the feverish activities of the rich, with which ordinary people could never compete. Sources of social capital such as the Rockefeller Foundation might then be noticed as participants in the political process. However, attempts to curtail check writing have not succeeded. The U.S. Supreme Court ruled in *Buckley v. Valeo* (424 U.S.1: 1976) that money equals speech and, consequently, that financial limits on advocacy would violate the First Amendment.

Foundation-sponsored projects to revive democracy find a safer focus at the local level and on poor people's behavior. The dangerous "lack of political participation" identified in the the Ford Foundation 1949 *Report* was still a problem in the 1990s, hence, the currently promoted ideology of "civil society." The term was once associated with the nineteenth-century German philosopher G. W. F. Hegel. Hegel, an idealist, was describing institutions that also represented stages in ethical development; we will not deal with this aspect. However, his concept of civil society is useful. It included businesses, government institutions that protected private property, such as police and courts, and public and private social welfare agencies and associations. While this realm represented a more advanced ethical idea than that of the family (which he believed was based on emotional dependency), Hegel indicated that civil society was a sphere of inequality, where even differences of abilities and resources were exaggerated.[71] In addition, it was imperialistic:

[D]espite an excess of wealth civil society is not rich enough, i.e., its own resources are insufficient to check excessive poverty and the creation of a penurious rabble.

This inner dialectic of civil society thus drives it—or at any rate drives a specific civil society—to push beyond its own limits and seek markets, and so its necessary means of subsistence, in other lands which are either deficient in the goods it has overproduced, or else generally backward in industry, &c.[72]

The ideology of "civil society" promoted by foundations today excludes much of Hegel's concept. It usually denotes organizations that are neither business nor government, as in the name "independent sector" or "nonprofit sector." This, of course, implies that one can detach group members from their business or government sponsors, and that the designated entities constitute a "sector." While these associations, as suggested by Alexis de Tocqueville's observations in *Democracy in America,* are considered essential for democracy, the sector contains the Ku Klux Klan, militias, Black Panthers, pacifists, exclusive country clubs, city clubs, foreign relations think tanks, fundamentalist religions of many denominations, and a variety of others. These inconvenient denizens are rarely, if ever, discussed. The Boy Scouts and the Freemasons are important occupants of "civil society"; their oaths and sexist or other discriminatory membership qualifications often are not scrutinized. The U.S. Supreme Court decision in *Boy Scouts of America v. Dale* (2000) illuminated the potentially exclusionary basis of any association.

The Kettering and Pew foundations are especially active in democracy renewal activities. Pew funded a National Commission on Civic Renewal, chaired by William Bennett and Sam Nunn, which leaned heavily toward right-wing partners, including the Heritage Foundation, the American Enterprise Institute, the Bradley Foundation, and corporations.

> National politics is deemed too contentious, so the [Commission's] report urges foundations and nonprofits to think locally, "because civic renewal begins at home." This ignores the powerful influence of many conservative foundations on national politics, an irony that may or may not have been lost on the Commission's corporate representatives.[73]

Mass political parties, social movements, or unions are treated as "failures" not to be revived. In recent years, religious bodies have become more central in both conservative and liberal renewal projects. Desirable public participation—for the common folk—is local and nonideological.

The institutions of the new democracy are similar to those of market research and other business practices, as in "roundtables," "visioning," and "focus groups." For example, "community indicators" projects to establish benchmarks for community health bring selected "stakeholders" together in an atmosphere that discourages conflict; known "troublemakers" are rarely invited. (Try this experiment: bring the same group together in a corporate penthouse boardroom and on a bench behind the barricades and see what kind of resolutions emerge.) Diversity is pursued: women, minorities, other-abled, and very young people (even children) may be participants; anti-corporate activists are rarely welcome.[74]

The renewal network's positive citizenship ideal is people working to solve local problems in collaboration with NGOs, businesses, and government agencies. All contentious politics is suspect. These advocates also tend to rail against "bloated Federal bureaucracies," without mentioning that it is bloated mainly in the Pentagon; federal employment has been declining in relation to burgeoning state and local governments. Also ignored is the impressive citizen participation enabled by EPA grants and federal technical assistance to the environmental justice movement.

A model of good civil society process has been posted on the Civic Practices Network by a Kettering Foundation associate. Citizens in a healthy community do not selfishly contest unwanted development:

> The ethic in this community is to share information. When the business decides it needs to expand, it approaches the local government and the neighborhood association and requests a meeting. At the meeting, the business lays out the economic reasons why it believes it is time for a major expansion. The neighborhood and government leaders ask questions about the data and the assumptions for future growth. The business agrees to meet again to provide additional information. After making certain all affected parties are at the table, all agree to a series of meetings.

> At subsequent meetings, all involved parties are able to reach consensus on the real need (somewhat less than originally projected by the business) and agree on a plan satisfying the needs of the business while protecting the neighborhood. When the business holds a press conference to unveil the plan, neighborhood leaders are there to support the proposal. The plan goes through the governmental review process with only a few minor changes and little community upset.[75]

Kettering also has been promoting a new political institution throughout the country, the Public Issues Forum, convened by Kettering's public policy institute affiliates at colleges and universities, or by organizations such as the League of Women Voters, the Foreign Policy Association, the General Federation of Women's Clubs, the Points of Light Foundation, and the like. Their purpose is to promote citizen deliberation about some public concern. Kettering's assumption, reflecting the "ungovernability" thesis of the Trilateral Commission's *Crisis of Democracy*, is that our political process is fraying because of divisiveness; the forums are structured to promote consensus.

> Since 1982, in communities across America, these forums have brought citizens together to deliberate about a wide variety of issues and to begin making the hard choices involved in addressing them. . . . These organizations often use issue books prepared by the Kettering Foundation

and Public Agenda, both nonpartisan research institutions. The books cover subjects important to the nation in every locality—issues like crime, jobs, health care, the environment, education.[76]

Issues have been "framed" to provide three choices for problem solutions. For example, at one session the author attended, the problem was "teenagers in trouble." The assumptions provided for finding a solution were "parents are irresponsible," "parents need more help from government and society," and "the culture is morally ambiguous and must be repaired." The forums are conducted by a team from Kettering, including expert facilitators. The participants are self-selected community members, although in the weekend training and framing sessions observed, people of color from outside of New Hampshire had been added.

Deliberation is supposed to result in common ground. People are urged to make the best case for the solution they least prefer and to examine the weaknesses of their own preferred choice. The process does seem to result in calm, pragmatic conclusions, while filtering out unusual ideas or systemic critique. The deliberative approach encourages people to base decisions on their own experience, or that of the other participants. This may impoverish discussion on issues that are fairly remote from their experience (e.g., trade, militarism, and other foreign policy questions). Perhaps more significantly, it discourages exploring the connections between remote matters and local problems.

As participants are self-selected, those who show up are comfortable with a middle-class liberal "League of Women Voters" type of meeting, and they have the time to spare. Few general community members were at the forum that I attended; most people there were either Kettering associates or those (mainly academics) interested in learning about the process.

The preliminary "framing" work also is a consensus project, performed by Kettering staff and others interested in devoting a weekend to this task. Thus at every stage, democratic representation is lacking, and this imbalance is exacerbated by the process. Because Kettering assumes that selfish interests or too much partisanship are the causes of our political malaise, interest groups or political parties are not invited as participants. Partisan behavior in the forums is discouraged. This has the effect of silencing political minorities. If your view is unique, you are likely to self-censor to preserve the friendly, collaborative atmosphere. If you speak up anyway, your nonconforming contributions may be eliminated at a later point, as they will not fit into the three broad problem-solving frames. This effect was underscored by one forum that I attended where people who not only shared attitudes but who had some history of joint action happened to be present. In that case, strong views were expressed and sustained, and mutual support was provided by the group. It indicated that "taking politics out of politics," as also occurs in nonpartisan city councils, is another form of disenfranchisement.

The forums are intended to influence policy through local newspapers, TV, and radio coverage, a Web site, and a newsletter. The forum outcomes also are to be presented directly to city councils, school boards, and state legislatures.

The New Hampshire forums, including one on school financing, which I did not attend, seem to have had the most significant impact on participants who were elected or appointed government officials. One selectman subsequently convened a regional selectmen's forum on school funding and presented the conclusions to the New Hampshire State Senate. These people normally hear complaints from citizens and advocacy from lobbyists; they rarely see citizens engaged in group political discussion. Yet the forums are even less representative than town meetings, which may bring out 10 percent of eligibles. What the enterprise reveals is how far our political processes diverge from the democratic ideal.

The Civic Renewal Movement's encouragement of local, noncontentious politics was to construct an alternative to the 1960s' movement politics. According to political scientist Jean Bethke Elshtain:

> [M]ovement politics is inherently unstable, ephemeral, and geared toward publicity. . . . Building and sustaining democratic institutions is at the heart of the democratic matter. And movements don't do that—don't build those ties of trust, reciprocity, accountability, mutual self-help over time. No, but institutions, sturdy but resilient institutions of democratic civil society, do. These institutions are, by definition, based on both giving and receiving; on creating a structure of expectations and molding reasonable and decent ways to meet those expectations.[77]

Parallel to these civil society efforts is the transformation of movements into local nonprofits, discussed in chapter 8. A related foundation project is abetting suitable political participation by students. This, promoted especially by the Carnegie Corporation, is now defined as "service learning." Acceptable activities are tutoring, working in soup kitchens, or building houses, rather than political organizing. Foundations also have created a number of university institutes to spur decent participation (e.g., the Lincoln Filene Center at Tufts, the Walt Whitman Center for the Culture and Politics of Democracy at Rutgers, and the Center for Democracy and Citizenship at Minnesota). Not coincidentally, the service learning idea was proposed by foundations shortly after 1960s' students evinced a different model of participation.

THINK TANKS

Think tanks produce books and reports, often used as textbooks, supply commentators for radio, television, and newspapers, hold conferences and provide speakers for others' conferences, integrate the ambitious and talented, and more generally originate and legitimate policies. They often are categorized as liberal, conservative, or progressive, but many foundations will fund institutions of diverse leanings, and in many cases, the ideological differences are not significant. For example, the Brookings Institution is said to be liberal and the American Enterprise Institute conservative. Both are funded by Ford, and they collaborate on projects. The Heritage Foundation appeared startlingly right wing at its inception; its views have become mainstream.

Similarly, the Cato Institute is libertarian and theoretically noninterventionist in foreign policy. However, it supported the Bush war on Afghanistan and advised only against fighting terrorists who had never attacked U.S. targets (e.g., Basque or Tamil).[78] There is a pull toward the Center, affecting both Left and Right. In addition to general interest think tanks, some serve specialized policy areas such as race, urban affairs, agriculture, health, and local government.[79]

In foreign policy and its domestic requirements, the Council on Foreign Relations (CFR), formed in 1924 by the Carnegie and Rockefeller foundations and now also supported by Ford and others, remains preeminent. It represents the international side of progressivism, aiming to project U.S. power throughout the world and to persuade U.S. citizens that this was the only acceptable concept of "national interest."[80] Membership links hegemonic elites and those aspiring to join them; serious presidential candidates and cabinet members dealing with foreign affairs normally are members. Leading journalists, including those considered "left wing," academics, bankers, lawyers, CEOs of multinationals, and the foundation people form part of its large membership and meet in its study groups and events. The CFR has sibling organizations in other countries, such as the Royal Institute of International Affairs in the United Kingdom, and it also has created other institutions as needed.

One such offshoot is known as "Bilderberg," after the hotel in the Netherlands where the first meeting was held in 1954. This is not really a think tank but an informal discussion group that meets in secret, at a different high-security location each year, and it includes the most powerful persons in North America and Western Europe. The originators included David Rockefeller, Dean Rusk (then head of the Rockefeller Foundation), Joseph Johnson (head of the Carnegie Endowment), and John J. McCloy (chairman of the board of the Ford Foundation), along with European notables. Its early focus was devising strategies to fight the Cold War in Europe and the Third World.

> At their first meeting, Bilderbergers covered the following broad areas, which remained focal points of discussion for successive meetings: Communism and the Soviet Union; Dependent areas and peoples overseas; Economic policies and problems; and European integration and the European Defense Community.[81]

Bilderberg publishes nothing to influence public opinion; indeed, meetings are closed to the press, and participants are pledged to silence. However, diligent researchers and leakers allow us to learn about these meetings.

Decisions are implemented through the power of the participants, who include many heads of state, prime ministers, and international organization executives, along with top business and foundation people. It also is an arena where rookies are fielded for selection to the big leagues; Tony Blair, Bill Clinton, and Mary Robinson were at Bilderberg before their prominence.

At the conclusion of the 2000 meeting, the Bilderberg group issued a press release, no doubt to allay the continuous criticisms of its secrecy. It described itself as follows:

> The 48th Bilderberg meeting was held in Brussels, Belgium, 1–3 June 2000. Among other subjects the Conference discussed U.S. Elections, Globalisation, New Economy, the Balkans, EU Enlargement, the European Far Right. Approximately 100 participants from North America and Europe attended the discussions.
>
> Bilderberg is a small, flexible, informal and off-the-record international forum in which different viewpoints can be expressed and mutual understanding enhanced. . . . Bilderberg's only activity is its annual conference. At the meetings, no resolutions are proposed, no votes taken, and no policy statements issued.[82]

U.S. participants included John Deutch, former director of the CIA; Christopher Dodd, U.S. senator; Donald Graham, *Washington Post* publisher; Kay Bailey, U.S. senator; Vernon Jordan, director, Lazard Freres; Henry Kissinger; Jessica Mathews, president, Carnegie Endowment; Bill Richardson, U.S. secretary of energy; David Rockefeller; George Soros; James Wolfensohn, president of the World Bank; Paul Wolfowitz, dean of the School of Advanced International Studies, Johns Hopkins University; and top businesspeople.

The Aspen Institute has aims and operating principles similar to the CFR, but its membership and interests are broader in scope. It has four offices in the United States and partners in Europe and Asia. National security people and other government officials, foundation heads, multinational corporations, university presidents, journalists, and the usual notables participate in study groups, organized and led by a full-time staff. The stated purpose is "to assist leaders, both in the United States and in the international community, to deal more effectively with emerging challenges."[83]

Along with strategic defense and other international programs, Aspen covers many domestic issues. For example, it has an Economic Opportunities Program, which "identifies, investigates and promotes highly promising solutions to poverty and underemployment in the United States." Its director is Kirsten Moy, an expert in community development finance. Karl Marx's observation is applicable here:

[T]he circumstance that the Catholic Church in the Middle Ages formed its hierarchy with the best brains from among the people, without regard to estate, birth or wealth, was one of the principal means of consolidating priestly rule and the subordination of the laity. The more a ruling class is able to assimilate the most prominent men [sic] of the dominated classes the more stable and dangerous is its rule.[84]

The Trilateral Commission (TLC) is an international counterpart of the CFR. It was created in 1973 by David Rockefeller, Zbigniew Brzezinski, and McGeorge Bundy to develop constructive strategies among the leading capitalist nations in response to a new wave of political and monetary turmoil. The three "sides" were North America, Western Europe, and Japan.[85] The TLC's best known ideological statement is *The Crisis of Democracy*.[86] Its major theme was that an "excess of democracy" was destabilizing. Too much participation, in the form of citizen activism and demands, needed to be curtailed. One tack was to promote economic growth (even if it would require planning), along with other measures to eradicate poverty and soothe angry citizens with prosperity. Improved working conditions might be subsidized to forestall union demands for changes in the economic power structure. Political parties had to be invigorated; they would aggregate interests and work out compromises. Rash ideas about banning corporate financing of parties should be forgotten:

The danger that political parties will become unduly dependent upon and responsive to a few corporate interests can best be countered by (a) requiring full publicity for all political contributions and (b) insuring the availability of public monies as an alternative and balance to funds from the private sector.[87]

A stronger executive was suggested, and restraint was needed on the increasingly critical press:

Specifically, there is a need to insure to the press its right to print what it wants without prior restraint except in most unusual circumstances. But there is also the need to assure to the government the right and the ability to withhold information at the source. In addition, there is no reason for denying to public officials equal protection of the laws against libel, and the courts should consider moving promptly to reinstate the law of libel as a necessary and appropriate check upon the abuses of power by the press.[88]

Another hazard arises from the expansion of higher education:

The result of this expansion, however, can be the overproduction of people with university education in relation to the jobs available for them, the expenditure of substantial sums of scarce public monies and the imposition on the lower classes of taxes to pay for the free public education of the children of the middle and upper classes. The expansion of higher education can create frustrations and psychological hardships among university graduates who are unable to secure the types of jobs to which they believe their education entitles them, and it can also create frustrations and material hardships for nongraduates who are unable to secure jobs which were previously open to them.[89]

The TLC's role as a farm team for the big leagues came to the (attentive) public's attention when it was revealed that without any base in the Democratic Party

Jimmy Carter had been the one Democratic governor chosen among sixty North American members of the Trilateral Commission in 1973.... He proudly mentioned his Trilateral studies and trips whenever questions of his international experience popped up in the early presidential campaign.... The Trilateral Commission's executive director, Zbigniew Brzezinski, became quite literally Jimmy Carter's tutor, and now, of course, directs the White House foreign policy staff.[90]

Like its counterpart, the CFR, the TLC maintains a Web site where goals, projects, and directors' names are posted.

The increase in "globalization" and its challengers, both among Third World governments and activist citizens everywhere, called for a more integrative discussion group. Created by U.S. and foreign foundations and corporations, the World Economic Forum has evolved into a meeting of the global elite held annually at Davos, Switzerland (New York in 2002), with regional groups convening at other times. Its central theme is that globalization and economic growth will ensure wealth and happiness for all, eventually. Participants are divided among those who believe that the "free market" will fix all problems and those who suggest that some help is needed, such as government regulation of labor, environment, and income security.

The usual top corporate people (from 1,000 companies) are members, but here the starchy bankers of Bilderberg are outshone by the moguls of the new economy, such as Bill Gates. Information technology and biotechnology now receive special attention at Davos. Another star is George Soros, investment banker, philanthropist, and creator of many new institutions in former communist countries. Many presidents and prime ministers show up; in 2001, these included Pastrana of Colombia, Mori of Japan, Mbeki of South Africa, and Kostunica of Yugoslavia. The Persian Gulf states were well represented. No region of the world is omitted, although Castro has not shown his head in these mountains. There are the usual journalists, academics, and foundation heads, many of whom also are members of the CFR. However, hegemonic influence is furthered by inviting potentially disruptive elements: rising young leaders, writers and artists (Bono), and "thirty-six representatives of Non-Governmental Organizations," including Greenpeace, Amnesty International, and Vandana Shiva of Third World Network, a leading critic of globalization and biotechnology. Demonstrations and protests at these meetings, as well as those of the governmental summits (G-7, the World Trade Organization, the World Bank, etc.), have led to the domestication of the more reasonable activists; by bringing some inside, the opposition is divided. Although some sessions are closed, much information about the participants and the proceedings, and live Webcasts, can be found on the Web site.[91]

The Carnegie Endowment for International Peace has some characteristics of a think tank; it is a foundation that operates its own programs, and it is a prime supporter of the CFR and other organizations. Its materials reach a broader public than those of the CFR; its major organ, *Foreign Policy*, a magazine with advertising, promotes globalization. A typical article is one demonstrating quantitatively that countries more globalized in their economies have greater civil rights and liberties and less income inequality, thus suggesting that anti-globalization activists are enemies of progress and humanity.[92] Furthermore, globalization does not stifle local cultures; instead, it liberates people from oppressive nationalism: "Globalization extends radically to all citizens of this planet the possibility to construct their individual cultural identities through voluntary action, according to their preferences and intimate motivations."[93]

Carnegie's current activities are consistent with Horace Coon's view of the Endowment—that it does not have much to do with peace. Its self-description does not mention it: "Founded in 1910, the Carnegie Endowment is a private nonprofit organization dedicated to advancing cooperation among nations and promoting active international engagement by the United States."[94] Recent concerns have been "humanitarian intervention," "ousting foreign strongmen," and making sure that the United States "remains the leading military power."

Conservative and liberal institutes show the most differences in abortion rights, multiculturalism, affirmative action, and other social issues. Even the "far Right" policy groups such as the Free Congress Foundation or the John Birch Society are most vocal on cultural and social concerns. When it is a question of foreign policy, trade, and general economic regulation and intervention, differences are small. Nevertheless, this is a fertile field for scholarly investigation and comparison.

There are some think tanks considered left wing or Progressive. They do important work, especially in documenting the activities and consequences of corporate and government policies. Nevertheless, almost all are funded by the liberal foundations; their challenges to the system are muted. These include the Interhemispheric Resource Center, the Institute for Policy Studies, the Institute for Agriculture and Trade Policy, the Worldwatch Institute, Redefining Progress, the Paul Robeson Foundation, the Center for Responsive Politics, Cultural Survival, the North American Congress on Latin America, the National Priorities Project, the National Security Archives, the American Civil Liberties Union (ACLU), the NAACP, and many others. Some, like the Economic Policy Institute (see chapter 6), the Natural Resources Defense Council, and Human Rights Watch, were initiated with major foundation involvement.

Others began with the intention of providing radical alternatives. There are several possible explanations for the mellowing that has occurred, including foundation funding and, sometimes, foundation staff joining the boards of funded institutes. Of course, there has been a change in the general climate of opinion, greatly influenced by foundation activities. Another source of deradicalization is the proliferation of specialized, narrow think tanks, which become competitive with each other in the quest for grants. On the other hand, there may have been internal factors moving organizations in a moderate direction. Some theorists posit a life cycle of organizations, which leads to bureaucratization and greater conservatism, variants of Robert Michels's Iron Law of Oligarchy. Perhaps the researchers and staffs became older and more concerned about their children's college expenses and their own retirement annuities, or maybe they saw the folly of their earlier enthusiasm. There also is the possibility that the radicals were wrong to begin with, and that things were either getting better with current practices, and/or that the dire consequences that they predicted from unfettered economic growth, agricultural chemicals, nuclear power, or globalization were unfounded. Many case studies need to be collected before any definitive explanation can be proffered.

Some think tanks are concerned with philanthropy itself. Most, whether national organizations, such as the National Committee for Responsive Philanthropy, or institutes attached to universities, such as the Yale Program on Non-Profit Organizations, are promoters of philanthropy, funded and aligned with the liberal foundations, and they welcome criticism only in the details. An exception is the Capital Research Center (CRC), a libertarian-leaning watchdog, which is especially critical of liberal foundations. Its major theme is that foundations are disloyal to their founders:

> By financially supporting liberal groups that espouse a philosophy that contradicts market principles, the Mott family and the trustees of the Mott foundations ignore the source of their tremendous wealth. They turn a blind eye to the harm that many of their grantees inflict on the free society that enabled Charles Stewart Mott to succeed in the marketplace.[95]

The CRC deplores grants to environmental organizations such as the Sierra Club and the Tides Center, and to radical poverty organizations such as the Center for Community Change and the National Council of La Raza (see chapter 8). The Aspen Institute also is singled out as a "liberal organization," inappropriate for funding, although its honorary trustees include Henry Kissinger, Robert McNamara, Paul Volcker, Robert O. Anderson, Warren Rudman, and Cyrus Vance. On the other hand, the CRC gives Mott credit for some good grants, such as to the American Enterprise Institute and the Hudson Institute, which supports Wisconsin's welfare reform.

MEDIA

When the media is examined for bias and control, critics tend to focus on government and/or corporate influence; foundations are barely noticed. We cannot assume lack of bias without further examination. In addition, the collaboration between corporations and foundations in support of productions drags public broadcasting closer to commercial broadcasting; for example, PBS children's programs now sell toys, drugs, and junk food.[96]

In addition to supplying talking heads for TV and radio and writing heads for the press, the foundations and their network use the media in several other ways. They produce their own publications and sponsor books, videos, and TV shows produced by others. Certain publishers, such as Island Press, specializing in environmental texts, receive generous foundation funding. Many of the books that shape our intellectual culture have been supported by foundations: W. W. Rostow's *The Stages of Economic Growth*, Seymour Martin Lipset's *Political Man*, Daniel Bell's *End of Ideology*, Robert Putnam's *Bowling Alone*, and Erik Erikson's *Young Man Luther*.

Reference books also are a source for conventional wisdom; *The Encyclopedia of the Social Sciences* (1930–1935) was funded by the Carnegie, Rockefeller, and Russell Sage foundations, and its successor, *The International Encyclopedia of the Social Sciences*, was organized by the Ford Foundation and commercially produced. The connections between foundations and reference materials and the funding of scholarly and professional journals could use an avid researcher.

Magazines of opinion receive foundation grants (along with donations from readers) and acquire nonprofit status for this purpose; foundations may not fund for-profit businesses. Generally speaking, conservative foundations can devote more resources to media and think tanks because they do not send much money to grassroots activists. Right-wing foundations also finance conservative student newspapers and journals at colleges and universities. However, there is not a conflict of interest when corporate money goes to produce pro-corporate ideology. On the other hand, the dependence of the "Left" press on elite subsidies can result in mellowing and avoiding topics embarrassing to the funders. Nevertheless, left-wing journalists often complain that those on the Right are getting more money:

Based on a search through foundation grant reports and information gleaned from my colleagues in the alternative press, I found more than

$2.7 million in foundation grants between 1990 and 1992 going to four magazines on the right: *The American Spectator, The National Interest, The Public Interest,* and *The New Criterion.* During the same period, I can identify only $269,500 in combined grants from private foundations for the four leading progressive publications: *The Nation* (through its affiliate, the Nation Institute), *Mother Jones, The Progressive,* and *In These Times.* In other words, the four left publications got less than 10 percent of the total received by the four right-wing journals.[97]

The Progressive has advisory board members on the CFR and also receives grants from the Ford Foundation, including one for $100,000 in 2000; *The Nation*'s editor is a CFR member. We will not know how that affects editorial policy unless we look into the matter.

Through its "Civic Journalism" program, which aims to stimulate local political participation, the Pew Charitable Trusts subsidizes special features in newspapers and on radio and TV stations. This angers critics both Left and Right:

The next time you read a big front-page news feature or "special" project in the *[San Francisco] Chronicle* or *San Jose Mercury News,* or see an in-depth news report on KRON-TV, or hear a community forum on KQED radio, ask yourself a question: who paid for it?

The answer might surprise you. The *Chron, Mercury News,* and other wealthy private media outfits, along with public broadcasters like KQED, are increasingly hustling grants from private nonprofit foundations to underwrite their news coverage—and the foundations set strict guidelines on what types of stories the media outlets that receive the grants can do.[98]

The CRC's "Foundation Watch" reports that:

Federal law prohibits foundations from donating money to for-profit organizations, such as newspapers. That's why the Pew Charitable Trust makes its donations to the Tides Foundation, which in turn funds the Pew Center [for Civic Journalism in Washington, D.C.], which pays the newspapers.[99]

A Pew grant sometimes helps create the news that it pays newspapers to cover. For example, in 1995, Pew funded polling and focus groups in Derry, New Hampshire, which was then covered by the *Boston Globe*'s Pew-funded "People's Voice" series.

News services, especially "alternative" ones, are fondly funded by foundations. The Institute for Alternative Journalism (IAJ) was created in 1983 as a syndication service for alternative papers. In the 1990s, it moved from Washington, D.C., to San Francisco, and it

ubsumed by a much wider political agenda, one determined
the desires of foundation funders. . . . IAJ has been soliciting
ince at least 1991 from the Tides Foundation, which has
ᴗᴗ   the central clearinghouse and demonstration project for Presidio privatization. . . . IAJ used to hold its board meetings in the offices
of the Pew-created Energy Foundation, which helped fund Presidio privatization planning and later moved into Presidio offices.[100]

The IAJ also is closely affiliated with Pacifica radio, whose subservience to foundation and corporate funders led to a bitter revolt among KPFA staff and supporters.

Even the *New York Times* has questioned Pew's and others' grants to newspapers and broadcasters, with special concern for the increased funding of
National Public Radio News. "The fire wall seems to bend a little when donors
restrict their gifts, permitting the money to be spent only for coverage of specific
topics."[101] Public broadcasting originally was promoted by foundations (Ford and
Carnegie especially), and it continues to receive their support. However, it was
supposed to provide an alternative to commercial stations; now the increasing
corporate hand is driving the programming in that direction.

[O]ur public broadcasting system still has to grapple with how it can
fulfill its founding mission—to "provide a voice for groups in the community that may otherwise be unheard," serve as "a forum for controversy and debate," and broadcast programs that "help us see America
whole, in all its diversity"—that the Carnegie Commission articulated
so eloquently more than three decades ago.[102]

FAIR's analysis found that in documentary and public affairs programs, alternative perspectives were rare; most sources and guests were government, professional, and corporate. This was especially the case with economic news, where
corporate voices were overwhelming; the views of labor organizations, working
people, or consumer advocates rarely were heard.

All in all, public television's coverage of social security reform did not
give any hint about alternative reform plans, suggesting that the debate
is no broader than how or how much to privatize social security. And,
tellingly, there were no voices of labor or senior citizen groups, two of
the key stakeholders in the reform process.[103]

Another significant finding was that by 1998, coverage of international affairs
had dropped by more than 50 percent from 1992, and it represented only 5.4 percent of public affairs programming. Commercial TV coverage of international
news also had declined during this period. Since TV often is the sole source of
news for people, one might expect some compensatory programming here.

This neglect is consistent with one of the most infuriating aspects of public television. General Electric, which owns NBC, and cable channels, also has its electrodes all over public television. It sponsors *The McLaughlin Group*, which regards controversy as pitting a Brookings Institution type against an American Enterprise Institute type. Totally unrequested, it mails "Viewers' Guides" for the *McLaughlin* program to college professors. These might define "what issues are important" in a presidential election, and they are likely to inform this "guided" viewer (presumably one is to distribute this to students) that international affairs are not important to citizens.

Public broadcasting's entertainment programs also may sustain hegemonic ideologies. There is the well-noticed heavy scheduling of British upper-class drama, especially on *Masterpiece Theater*. Working-class stories appear on British TV, but they are rarely imported. Diversity is represented as "multiculturalism"; system-challenging art and literature is scarce. A very popular NPR program is *Prairie Home Companion*, a folksy show, and it well represents the spirit of public broadcasting. Garrison Keillor is certainly funny, and the program is expertly produced. However, it satirizes shy people, churchgoers, and health food "nuts"; the music features Girl Scout songs, gospel, country, and the rich multicultural contributions of Cajun and others. Only one thing is missing: the folk tradition of the twentieth century was political, and music was part of its project to change the world. One will find civil rights songs of all minorities on this program, but not the songs challenging multinational corporations or U.S. foreign policy.

In addition to foundation and corporate elites, the national security apparatus is well represented in public broadcasting. The president of NPR, Kevin Close, the vice president, Kenneth Stern, and the president of the Corporation for Public Broadcasting, Robert Coonrod, are veterans of Voice of America, Radio and TV Marti, Radio Free Europe, and Radio Liberty.[104]

Among NPR's underwriters is the government of Kuwait:

> Naturally, a foreign government funding a newscast raises questions about a news organization's ability to remain unbiased while covering that country. But it's been especially alarming to some that Kuwait, a country that is often in the news and has a vested interest in affecting the views of NPR's listeners, is sponsoring news programs. It's also alarming because the Kuwaiti government has a history of using public relations campaigns to influence American public opinion.[105]

We have hardly begun to study the political implications of the World Wide Web. Clearly, it enables very small "countercultural" organizations to publish their material at low cost, accessible to the whole world. However, it is not at no cost, and foundation money may be used to design and maintain attractive Web sites. Does this affect the message? There remains the problem of directing people to one's site. Links from related causes may be a good way to get attention, and browsers may lead people to formerly unknown organizations. In both cases, a prior interest in the general topic or a related issue is more likely to produce visitors.

Databases require the same analysis as reference books. Some provide excellent information (although foundation funded): the *Center for Responsive Politics* and *Project Vote Smart* (both for campaign funding and other information about representatives); the *National Security Archives* (selected declassified CIA documents), and others. Government information is copious and increasingly user-friendly: *Thomas* (U.S. Congress), the General Accounting Office, and the Environmental Protection Agency are fine examples.

If one seeks diverse information from foreign countries (especially when one does not know the language), problems arise. The U.S. Department of Commerce has a comprehensive database of translated news and documents, the *World News Connection*, but it is extremely expensive for the average browser or liberal arts college library. On the other hand, free and accessible newspapers are published in English in many countries; these usually are oriented to international business interests and rarely provide a spectrum of opinion. Another copious source are the many databases owned or affiliated with the multiplex George Soros foundations. For example, *Transitions on Line* includes news, opinion, book reviews, and features covering Central and Eastern Europe, the Balkans, and the former Soviet Union. It aims to integrate all media, nonprofit organizations, and journalists in these areas. In addition to Soros's Open Society Institutes, its sponsors include the Westminster Foundation for Democracy (the British counterpart to the National Endowment for Democracy) and corporations. The Radio Free Europe archives, purchased by Soros, are contained in this database. Partnered projects include similar databases for Central Asia and other areas.[106] The news provided by this "independent" Soros-funded press is almost entirely pro-market and anti-socialist or social democratic. Judging by election results, public opinion is rather more nuanced in those countries. An on-line "alternative" news service, the *OneWorld Network*, has the Ford and Rockefeller foundations as funders and enjoys an alliance with the World Bank, among other institutions.

Does that cover all bases? Many information sources important to policy, influenced by foundations, have not been discussed, especially those concerning environmental and health issues. On the other hand, plenty of political information exists that is largely free of foundation support or connections: newspapers, popular magazines, and commercial TV and radio. Sometimes their obvious corporate sponsorship sends people scurrying to the "neutral" elite information sources. Some independent writers, teachers, college professors, and clergy as well as popular political lore exist. "Extremists" of the right or left often unearth obscure information, some of it quite accurate. Public interest media organizations, such as *Fairness & Accuracy in Reporting* (FAIR), *Alternet*, or the *Institute for Public Accuracy*, and groups such as the American Friends Service Committee, the Southwest Organizing Project, or the Highlander Research and

Education Center have preserved considerable independence. A big gap is the absence of comprehensive research centers affiliated with either major or minor parties. Left-wing foundations also neglect research; they are reasonably deterred by fear of the "Iron Law of Oligarchy."

Alternative information often is hard to find; however, that is not the greatest problem. For young, ambitious intellectuals (in the broad Gramsci sense), adherence to the overarching ideology is simply the most pragmatic course. Those who find this distasteful sometimes decamp to some rural area, producing rye muffins or bentwood furniture, and their political voices become faint. Even here, should they decide open a bakery/craft workshop for disabled or delinquent rural youth, the Points of Light Foundation will get them.

4

Reforming Government

> Prior to the reforms of the Progressive Era, city government con-
> sisted primarily of confederations of local wards, each of which was
> represented on the city's legislative body. Each ward frequently had
> its own elementary schools and ward-elected school boards which
> administered them. . . . The ward system of government especially
> gave representation in city affairs to lower- and middle-class
> groups. Most elected ward officials were from these groups, and
> they, in turn, constituted the major opposition to reforms in munic-
> ipal government.
>
> —Samuel Hays, "The Politics of Reform in
> Municipal Government in the Progressive Era"

LOCAL GOVERNMENT

The major liberal foundations, Rockefeller, Sage, and Carnegie, were created
during the heyday of Progressivism and became prime movers of the municipal
reform movement. Existing organizations, such as the National Municipal
League (1894), were increasingly supported and guided by foundations. Carnegie
and Rockefeller financed the Bureau of Municipal Research of New York City,
founded in 1907. This was a project of the Progressives, at a time when that
movement was still influenced by populists and socialists in its midst and had not
yet become the exclusive property of elitist "social engineers."

> Its concept of efficient citizenship posited that urban citizens owned
> their government and as owners had a duty to get involved in city
> affairs and instruct politicians and public administrators in "share-
> holder" demands.[1]

The Bureau would open up the political process to the average citizen by publishing information from public records in usable form, and by urging the city to keep better records. Most citizens at the time obtained information from sensationalist accounts in newspapers. Furthermore, the Bureau promoted the idea that citizens themselves should engage in municipal research. For example, co-director Henry Bruere

> [told] people how to test police efficiency. They should prepare a precinct map, list the regulations the police are supposed to enforce in the precinct, and note patent violations. They should examine police records to see what the agency has done about such violations, record any arrests made, and trace 200–500 cases through the courts.[2]

Even children were to be active citizens by monitoring their schools, housing, and sanitation, and by learning how to read and understand government reports. Unions were invited to take part in governmental oversight.

This radical approach to citizenship threatened elite control, and the Bureau's principal funder, John D. Rockefeller Sr., insisted in 1914 that it change its policies. He forced a reorganization to stop the promotion of active citizenship, especially in the schools.[3] Because of this imposition, one of the co-directors, Dr. William H. Allen, resigned. Allen later testified to the Walsh Commission investigating foundations (see chapter 2) and emphasized that JDR "tried in this instance to determine not only where their own funds went and how they were to be expended, but how funds contributed by other donors were to be disbursed."[4]

Foundation funding gradually transformed populist Progressive initiatives into elite-controlled institutions. In addition, the academic field of public administration largely was created during the 1920s and 1930s by the Rockefeller Foundation and its affiliates (the Laura Spelman Rockefeller Memorial, 1918–1928, and the Spelman Fund, 1928–1949). Foundation directors were engaged in long-range policy planning for the social sciences, and with their ample resources, they were able to carry out their objectives. They funded research institutes, such as Brookings and the National Bureau of Economic Research, and "peak" organizations (which combined the functions of pressure groups and research), such as the American Municipal Association, the American Public Welfare Association, the National Association of Housing Officials, the Council of State Governments, and the Municipal Finance Officers Association. For training government personnel, the Rockefeller Foundation created departments of public administration at

> Universities of California, Chicago, Cincinnati, Harvard, Minnesota, Virginia, and the American University. The grant to Harvard helped to organize the activity in public service training on a graduate level, and

the work was the forerunner of the A[merican] S[ociety] for P[ublic] A[dministration]. . . . Foundation assistance also went to the National Institute of Public Affairs, which directed in Washington the recruitment of college graduates as interns in practical career-service training in various federal departments and agencies.[5]

To consolidate this new field, the Spelman Fund developed and financed the Public Administration Clearing House in Chicago "under the guidance of Charles E. Merriam, Beardsley Ruml, and Guy Moffett . . . and associated with the University [of Chicago]."[6] The University of Chicago had close ties to Rockefeller interests. It was transformed from an obscure institution into a major university in the 1890s by John D. Rockefeller's philanthropy.

The Social Science Research Council (created in 1924 by the Rockefeller and Carnegie foundations, funded also by the Julius Rosenwald and Russell Sage foundations) had an advisory committee on public administration. Typical of interlocking directorates in these endeavors, the director of the Clearing House and the chairman of the SSRC's Committee on Public Administration were the same person, Louis Brownlow. Fund subsidies also aided the staffing, publications, and conferences of the American Society for Public Administration, founded in 1939.

Because Rockefeller initiatives still were regarded with suspicion in the 1920s and 1930s, the Spelman Fund claimed that public administration was strictly nonpolitical, and that it was only providing methods and techniques for carrying out established programs that were no longer controversial.

> The politics-administration dichotomy—an already well-known idea that suggested a certain sphere of governmental work could be considered "nonpolitical"—was a rhetorical device that allowed the philanthropies to defend their support of "governmental research."[7]

By the late 1930s, the associations were ready to see their theories put into practice, and they drifted away from the nonpolitical stance. A consulting service affiliated with the Clearing House, the Public Administration Service, began "installing model practices and methods in state and local government."[8]

As the foundations had the plans, organizations, and finances, they put their stamp on this new field. Even if we assume (and there is no evidence for this) that all major ideas were supplied by the individual political scientists and administrators who acted as advisors to the foundations, the choice of which trends to fund, and which to consign to oblivion, was made by the funders. The ideology of public administration that has evolved accords with the general foundation view that social disorder must be "treated" by experts: the "social engineering" perspective. Furthermore, the causes of disorder might be psychological, sociological, or political (i.e., lack of good institutions or adequately trained civil servants), but they are not to be found in the unequal distribution of wealth and power. It is highly unlikely that anyone who even hints at such causes will be funded, will head institutes, or will achieve status in the profession.

As local governments adopted "technical" reforms, the Progressive movement itself was transformed. Before World War I, Progressivism and socialism sometimes were allied, and local governments headed by socialist mayors generally provided "reformed" administration: adequate municipal services without corruption.[9] While "social engineering" concepts were general throughout Progressivism, during its early phase some believed that expertise alone would not solve the major problems created by the regime of robber barons, and that a radical redistribution of wealth and effective political power was needed.

In contrast, reformers of the 1920s and 1930s focused on the "quality" of municipal governance. Reforms such as nonpartisan elections, at-large elections, independent school boards, and autonomous commissions (e.g., planning) systematically promoted business and upper-middle-class interests in local government. At the same time, they doomed the representation of the working class, minorities, and socialists (whose support was primarily from low-income wards). Of course, there were many reasons for the decline of socialism after World War I, but the "gentrification" of local politics is part of the story. Progressive measures have been largely promoted as furthering "democratization." That has hardly been their effect; they have aided in the depoliticization of the working class.

Among the institutional innovations of this era, the "council-manager" form of local government is noteworthy. The "city manager" reflects the idea that local government should be run like a business; a manager hired by the city council would presumably carry out its instructions and manage the staff, insulating city workers from council politics. The concept was endorsed by the National Municipal League as its "Model City Charter" beginning in 1915 and received rave reviews in a 1940 Social Science Research Council report on its progress. Today the manager form is promoted by the International City Management Association, which receives major support from the Rockefeller Foundation. "[I]t became the orthodox ideal of the municipal reformers."[10] The notion of a hired chief executive for a municipality is rarely challenged in public administration textbooks or by those who have been "socialized" into the field of public administration. The leading role of "expertise" and the benefits of "depoliticization" appear to be "common sense." In practice, there is little effective policy making or oversight exercised by city councils, especially since this system frequently is combined with nonpartisan elections.[11] Amateur, part-time, atomized councilors revert to the role of ombudsmen; they are no match for the organized bureaucracy of the manager.

Local government policy and administration continue to be heavily influenced by foundations, which support the many NGOs that are associations of mayors, governors, city managers, state attorney generals, planners, welfare commissioners, and other officials. These are both pressure groups and think tanks to which most public executives belong, although they are not required to do so. They are arenas for the dissemination of innovation and also for the selection of likely state officials for national government and nonprofit leadership. Thus they play an important role in incorporating local talent into national and international hegemonic institutions. For example, Stephen B. Heintz, now president of the Rockefeller Brothers Fund (RBF), served as Connecticut's welfare commissioner. He stated in an interview:

> Eventually, I became active at the national level. I was selected by my peers—the other forty-nine state welfare commissioners—to lead a national welfare reform project in the late 1980s, which culminated in [the] passage of what I consider to be the first really significant welfare reform since the passage of welfare in 1935, legislation called the Family Support Act of 1988.[12]

Before his appointment at RBF, Heintz directed the Prague office of the Institute for EastWest Studies and then went on to found Demos, "a nonprofit network dedicated to promoting democracy and shared economic prosperity in the United States."

Foundations also influence local government policy through "good government awards" and direct grants. The latter may be small in comparison to total budgets, but their existence at all as a source of public finance might raise some eyebrows. Furthermore, these grants are almost always for innovation, so their effect cannot be measured in strictly quantitative terms.

Criticism of such grants (as of judicial review) almost always comes from those objecting to the substance of a program. Thus parents in Kentucky protested against a public school requirement for genital examinations.

> Who authorized the intrusive program? Not the state legislature. The program, imposed by state bureaucrats, was bankrolled by a private foundation, the Annie E. Casey Foundation.
>
> U.S. charitable foundations dole out about $100 million each year to state and local governments. Today virtually every state accepts social agenda grants from private foundations.
>
> "They bribe government to take on projects they would not otherwise do," says Kim Dennis, until recently executive director of the Philanthropy Roundtable, an Indianapolis-based trade association for grantmakers.
>
> Bribe may not be too strong a word. "The government's for sale," says attorney Kent Masterson Brown, who is suing on behalf of Kentucky citizens to void the state's $299,500 contract with the Robert Wood Johnson Foundation. The 1994 contract provided that the foundation would fund the design of a comprehensive health care program for the state.[13]

On rare occasions, liberal critics question the process by which foundations have become gatekeepers to almost all local innovation. Rob Gurwitt reports:

> In the late fall of 1996, a select subcommittee of the Pennsylvania House of Representatives made a startling accusation: Private foundations had been using their grant money to buy public policy. In particular, the legislators declared, the Robert Wood Johnson Foundation, the influential New Jersey health care giant, had been spreading dollars around in an effort to reshape the state's health care system, pursuing its own agenda without regard for legislative niceties.
>
> The subcommittee's report was blunt. "It appears that the Robert Wood Johnson Foundation, the Pew Charitable Trusts, and other foundations are providing grants as 'seed money' to state, county, and local governmental bodies to develop new or to expand existing government programs, all without the informed consent of the General Assembly," it said. Calling these foundations "purchasers of public policy," it went on in outraged tones: "It is one thing to seek change, it is quite another when changes in public policy are influenced by the offering of private money to state governmental institutions."[14]

Gurwitt adds that foundations fund every state government, and that in addition to the longtime supporters, such as Ford and Carnegie, many new ones are now involved, such as the Enterprise, Edna McConnell Clark, Annie E. Casey, Kellogg, McKnight, and Annenberg foundations.

EDUCATION

The activities of foundations in public education (including colleges and universities) have been extensive.[15] Nineteenth-century philanthropies, the Peabody and Slater Funds, which prefigured modern foundations, and the Phelps-Stokes Fund (1911) were concerned with Southern education, which hardly existed for any poor children, and with the education of blacks more generally. Even before the Rockefeller Foundation, JDR established the General Education Board (1903–1960). Henry S. Pritchett, president in 1906 of the Carnegie Foundation for the Advancement of Teaching, put ". . . pressures on public officials in Washington and congressmen to lay off of intervention in areas like national educational policy and science where he felt private philanthropy more appropriate."[16]

It is hardly an exaggeration to say that foundations have been the source of almost all innovations in education (private as well as public), using their normal methods of influence: ideology, grants, litigation, policy networks and think tanks, and the revolving door. For example, John W. Gardner, president of Carnegie Corporation, became the secretary of health, education, and welfare in the Johnson administration; during his tenure, first Francis Keppel, a Ford Foundation associate, and then Harold Howe, a Ford vice president, were commissioners of education.

The course credit system and centrally administered college entrance examinations came about as a requirement for the college teachers' pension program (now TIAA-CREF), started by the Carnegie Corporation for the Advancement of Teaching. These had a major effect on standardizing high school education throughout the United States, as college admission increasingly dictated curricula. Carnegie later initiated "new math," "Sesame Street," and "service learning." The work of a Gardner-chaired task force became the Elementary and Secondary Education Act of 1965. This was designed like a foundation grant program and incorporated some features of the earlier Ford "Great Cities" project.

The Ford Foundation created a separate division for education, the Fund for the Advancement of Education (FAE) (1951–1967), which at first served as a think tank to complement the school integration campaign being pursued by litigation (see chapter 7). The FAE then concerned itself with promoting excellence, a goal sparked by the "Sputnik" competition.[17] Some FAE experiments were early college admissions and the national merit scholarship program. Turning attention to improving failing schools, schools were persuaded to institute team teaching, to use teacher aides, and to employ technology, such as television. Ford and Carnegie were the major promoters of educational television and developers of the Corporation for Public Broadcasting. Headstart, Upward Bound, and alternative schools also were attempts to reverse dismal outcomes.

Ford decided that community influences might be more important than technology to educational outcomes and persuaded New York City to undertake the controversial decentralization experiment, creating local community school boards.

[I]n 1967, Mayor John Lindsay of New York appointed [McGeorge] Bundy [president of the Ford Foundation] to head a panel of private citizens to prepare recommendations. Its purpose was to decentralize the school system of New York. Later that year the panel submitted a report to the mayor entitled *Reconnection for Learning: A Community School System for New York City*. The report contained detailed recommendations for decentralization as well as a draft of a bill to be submitted to the Albany legislature for that purpose. In 1969 the state legislature voted to decentralize the schools.[18]

Finally, Ford supported the opposite strategy, encouraging more centralization in an effort to provide more equitable resources for schools. District patterns of school financing were challenged on the grounds that vastly unequal resources violated equal protection of the laws required by the Fourteenth Amendment. Although the U.S. Supreme Court denied this claim, many state courts declared

their school funding practices to be in violation of the national and/or state constitution. (Ford's financing of this litigation is discussed in chapter 7.) Compensatory financing or an entirely new school taxation method has been ordered in
many states. It is perhaps too soon to tell whether this will fix the broken schools.
Ford (along with other foundations) continues to develop new programs, such as
dropout prevention, partnerships with workplaces for high school student internships, and standardized testing for both students and teachers.

Public-private boundaries also are fading in education. Some school systems are hiring private corporations to run their schools, independent "charter"
schools are financed by school boards, and "voucher" systems give a public subsidy for students attending private schools, including, in some districts,
parochial schools. The Brookings Institution has published studies favoring the
voucher approach, thus blurring the boundaries between "liberal" and "conservative" think tanks.[19] Many schools use commercial advertising and junk food
vending machines as fund-raisers; even textbooks and curricula are linked to
corporate marketing strategies.

Corporate foundations are particularly interested in such goals as increasing
"the number of students in the math, science and information technology
pipeline." Buzz Bartlett, Director of Corporate Affairs for Lockheed Martin, testified before the U.S. House Committee on Science, stating that Lockheed gives
$800,000 a year for K–12 education. This is not merely a grant program; Buzz
and others participate actively in the education reform network, which includes
the Business Roundtable's Education Working Group. In addition to the Lockheed national headquarters' efforts, "[m]ost if not all of our over fifty operating
companies are involved in programs in their [sic] schools."[20]

NATIONAL GOVERNMENT

National government reform also was on the foundation network's agenda. The
Institute for Government Research (IGR) was created in 1916, led by a busi-
nessman and trustee of the Carnegie Endowment for International Peace,
Robert Brookings. "The presence of Rockefeller Foundation men and money in
the young IGR led to suspicions that it was a Rockefeller front-group."[21] The
IGR proposed and Congress adopted in 1921 the Budget and Accounting Act,
which turned budget initiation over to the president and a newly created Bureau
of the Budget (BOB). Although this appeared to be merely a move toward efficiency, it altered the power relations between legislature and executive. The
"executive budget" eventually was adopted by state and local governments. Previously, Congress controlled the entire budget process; the president's role was
to submit estimates for the White House and his advisors. Now all branches and
agencies submitted their requests first to the BOB, which presented a consoli-
dated budget to Congress. The IGR eventually became the Brookings Institu-

tion, which provides planning and advice on all aspects of policy and continues to be supported by foundations, now including Ford.

The Depression increased the urgency for reform. A multiyear study by social scientists, *Recent Social Trends in the United States*, was published in 1933.[22] It had been initiated by President Hoover, organized by the SSRC, and funded by the Rockefeller Foundation. Its program of social reform (discussed in chapter 6) required radical institutional changes in U.S. government. Metropolitan government and regional planning were promoted to replace obsolete local government structures. The report advocated centralization from state to national government institutions, the creation of a stronger national executive, and the initiation of new governance institutions, such as quasigovernmental and mixed public-private corporations. It proposed a National Advisory Council, which would undertake planning for science, education, government reform, industry, agriculture, and labor.

The report reflected international trends toward "managerialism," such as the Five Year Plans of the Soviet Union and the corporatism of Fascist Italy. To the business world, these innovations made sense; they would not run their corporations without planning or executive control. The proposals were justified by "efficiency," as local progressive reforms had been portrayed. The report also warned that if change were not directed by social scientists, a violent revolution could result.[23]

A number of the new institutions did appear in the ad hoc New Deal programs. Business and agriculture recovery programs were designed and monitored by public-private collaboration. The Tennessee Valley Authority (and its counterparts), both multistate and multifunctional, was an example of regional planning and a quasigovernmental corporation, which insulated it from congressional control. The flocking of businessmen and academics to Washington to serve as advisors or temporary employees was a departure from the "civil service" model of government administration and blurred public-private boundaries for the sake of "expertise." The report itself exemplified the desired process:

> A privately financed effort which utilised [sic] the support of government staff and agencies as well as staffs from public and private research institutions, it remains a unique model of the kind of co-operative public-private effort of which the founders of the major foundations had dreamed.[24]

The reformers hoped to make permanent some of the ad hoc arrangements and to institute a "Managerial Presidency." Congress ratified this departure by creating the Executive Office of the President in 1939.

> The programme [sic] which led to the establishment of the Executive Office of the President had been prepared by a group supported in part by the Rockefeller Foundation, indirectly, to be sure, through the Social Science Research Council, but supported by it nonetheless.[25]

A key part of this new office was the National Resource Planning Board, which was intended to utilize social scientists for indicative economic planning, as proposed in *Recent Social Trends*. Charles Merriam and other foundation protegés served on this board, but it was abolished in 1943, as it was too discordant with market ideology. However, during World War II, planning was widely considered necessary and desirable. Public-private partnerships were used extensively; the Manhattan Project to create the atomic bomb was typical in its use of subcontractors for weapons production. Ultimately, even military planning and operations sometimes were contracted to private corporations.[26]

The participation of businesspeople, lawyers, and academics in federal government agencies and task forces was intense and seemingly required by patriotism. For the professors, there also was a new sense of importance; not only was their status enhanced, but at last their talents were serving some practical purpose. With a singular goal, winning the war, boundaries among academic, business, and government people tended to dissolve. The role of intellectual as critic seemed irrelevant to the task at hand, and social scientists increasingly became a brain trust in the service of elites.[27]

During the war, an elite committee within the Council on Foreign Relations, the War-Peace Studies group, had been meeting to plan the postwar world, with special funding from the Rockefeller Foundation. It decided that the economic terrain required by the U.S. economy

> which came to be known as the "Grand Area," included Latin America, Europe, the colonies of the British Empire, and all of Southeast Asia. Southeast Asia was necessary as a source of raw materials for Great Britain and Japan and as a consumer of Japanese products. The American national interest was then defined in terms of the integration and defense of the Grand Area, which led to plans for the United Nations, the International Monetary Fund, and the World Bank and eventually to the decision to defend Vietnam from a communist takeover at all costs.[28]

The new international monetary institutions, created in 1944 at Bretton Woods, New Hampshire, were not to be jeopardized by U.S. economic instability. Consequently, after World War II, the "Managerial Presidency" was enlarged to include a Council of Economic Advisers (CEA). The CEA's role was to institutionalize Keynesian economic planning for economic stability and to implement the Employment Act of 1946. Brookings Institution staff frequently were members of the CEA, but it did not live up to its ambitious design or perform the role anticipated in *Recent Social Trends*. International institutions were to become more significant and, ultimately, "globalization" of the economy would render many Keynesian techniques problematic. However, authority over trade regulation, advocated by the Council on Foreign Relations, increasingly passed to the president.[29]

A significant enhancement of presidential power occurred in 1947, when the National Security Council (NSC) was created and located in the Executive Office of the President. Now the President was equipped as manager of the "free world." Presidential initiative in foreign policy had long been growing at the expense of Congress; the NSC institutionalized this change. The U.S. Constitution does not specify which branch of government is to formulate foreign policy (other than foreign commerce, clearly a congressional function); perhaps there was not supposed to be much of it.

One wartime collaboration between government and social scientists had been somewhat ominous. The Office of Strategic Services (OSS) had happily employed left-wing intellectuals, along with upper-class Ivy Leaguers, to wage psychological warfare against the Fascist enemy. The CIA, also created by the 1947 National Security Act, was to emerge from the OSS with a continued role for scholars in psychological warfare, espionage, and "dirty tricks," such as subversion, infiltration, and assassination.[30] Now the enemy was not so clear-cut; targeted were nationalists and neutralists, as well as communists and socialists, while fascists and crooks often were the "good guys." This covert effort, which continues to this day, enlists not only individuals but creates "public-private partnerships" with universities, foundations, and other organizations of the "third sector," including religious ones.

The CIA was intended to centralize intelligence for presidential consumption; its director was a member of the NSC. The CIA, as intended, crosses many boundaries. Its budget is hidden from congressional scrutiny, which violates a basic principle of democracy, legislative control of policy via budget authorization. While ostensibly a "staff agency" limited to advisory roles, it engages in operations. Many of these violate international law as well as U.S. law. Remarkably, it undertakes these operations even in the face of specific congressional prohibition. Furthermore, the UN Charter (largely devised by the same network that created the CIA) makes war illegal.

Supposedly a major reason for the Declaration of Independence and the precautions in our Constitution was to prevent citizens' lives, liberties, and property from being dragged into the King's private wars. Yet the CIA came into existence without much public debate. Critics were muted by fear of disloyalty charges, which had severe consequences. Others may have been co-opted by the thrill of "dirty tricks," or the hope that "psychological warfare" would prove the usefulness of social science. Glory had rained on the physical scientists of the Manhattan Project; now the social scientists could have their "Project Camelot" and also help save the world for democratic capitalism.

The Council on Foreign Relations and its foundation sponsors favored the Agency. For the influential but private Council, composed of several hundred of the country's top political, military, business, and academic leaders, has long been the CIA's principal "constituency" in the

American public. When the agency has needed prominent citizens to front for its proprietary companies or for other special assistance, it has often turned to Council members.[31]

The "third sector" is likewise a cooperative channel; CIA operations utilized secret funding for the National Student Association, the National Education Association, and the Boston Symphony Orchestra.[32] Every so often, there is public outrage at some shocking practice of the CIA, but it remains.

New institutions also have been devised to fight the Cold War at home by quelling urban disorder. One is the community development corporation, embodying the public-private partnership advocated in *Recent Social Trends* (discussed in chapter 6). Another model is the military. The RAND (Research and Development) Corporation, created after World War II with a grant from the Ford Foundation, at first did weapons system research for the U.S. Air Force. Gradually,

> RAND not only spawned a host of imitators, but its alumni began drifting into key positions in academia. . . . In time, all the military "think tanks" broadened their scope, and began to apply their approaches and methodologies to problems in the civil sector, for example, in the management of urban services and of various social service delivery systems.[33]

The activist national administrations of the 1960s and 1970s, which pursued the "War on Poverty," civil rights legislation, and environmental and consumer regulation, prompted a backlash. The more conservative wing of the business elite—those with short-term perspectives—challenged some of the "social engineering" approaches of the liberal foundations. There was not much conflict over foreign policy, although some conservatives complained that the CIA was doing the job of the military. The use of mercenaries, either foreigners or U.S. military retirees (honorably discharged or otherwise), seemed to satisfy all factions; besides, this was a prime example of public-private partnerships for efficient government.

On the domestic scene, the "Reagan Revolution" was heralded by new think tanks, most notably the Heritage Foundation, a rejuvenated American Enterprise Institute, and a rightward move by the Brookings Institution. Heritage, an operating rather than a granting foundation, was supported by other foundations and direct corporate funding, led by Adolph Coors. Although this movement sloganized "get government off our backs," government was welcome at its fronts. The social welfare and regulatory roles of government were deplored, not aid to business.

Heritage produced a 1,000-page analysis of the federal government, *Mandate for Leadership*, which it distributed in 1980 to leading executive branch officials and to all members of Congress. Reforms were suggested for every government department, mostly along the lines of "deregulation," "privatization," and elimination of entitlement programs.

The Heritage agenda had considerable success, although its practical effect was diminished somewhat because existing regulatory law had been meagerly enforced. The backlash put social welfare measures on the defensive (e.g., federal housing programs). While many housing projects had been badly designed, and the program was rife with graft, affordable housing was nevertheless desperately needed, and it was not forthcoming from the market. The backlash prevented well-designed, monitored programs from getting a fair hearing. Furthermore, deplorable housing conditions were the cause of many other social problems, including automobile pollution engendered by workers' long commutes. On the other hand, subsidized housing is a highly effective economic stimulus, producing avid consumers and labor-intensive employment.

A major consequence of the Heritage–Reaganite ideological offensive was to create a public opinion that government's domestic activities were either incompetent or downright malicious. A related development in academia was the popularity of rational choice theory, which suggested that collective provision was a deprivation of liberty. Not only did such ideas put a damper on progressive reform, they threatened the fortunes of the Democratic Party, which tended to be associated with an activist government.

One response was a new trend popularly called "Reinventing Government," after the title of a book by David Osborne and Ted Gaebler.[34] This countermovement was supported by the liberal foundations through grants, the creation of think tanks, awards programs, and networks such as National League of Cities, the National Governors Association, and the International City Management Association.

> The Alliance for Redesigning Government is in fact an example of foundations getting involved in public policy: the Ford Foundation, the Rockefeller Foundation, the Carnegie Corporation, the Annie E. Casey Foundation, the Lilly Endowment, and the Pew Charitable Trusts. The foundations decided that the movement in this country to redesign government and move it toward more citizen engagement and accountability for performance warranted their support.[35]

The strategy was to accept that government was frequently incompetent, wasteful, and overbearing, but to insist that it could be improved. The basic ideas of "reinventing government" were "buzzwords" and included many measures that already were being adopted by federal, state, and local governments (e.g., productivity incentives and participatory workplaces). Here is one summary of the principles:

Government should be 1. A catalyst . . . 2. Community-owned . . . 3. Competitive . . . 4. Mission-driven . . . 5. Results oriented . . . 6. Customer-driven . . . 7. Enterprising . . . 8. Anticipatory . . . 9. Decentralized . . . 10. Market oriented.[36]

Repeated themes associated with reinventing government are citizens as customers, government as entrepreneur, public-private partnerships, and contracting out government services. This is a reincarnation of the pro-corporate Progressives' century-old agenda to make government more like business.

That these ideas were strongly endorsed by the Clinton Democratic administration indicates the convergence among conservative and liberal ideologies and politicians of all stripes. An excerpt from "The Blair House Papers" follows:

> In 1993, with Executive Order 12862, the President [Clinton] called for a revolution in government's customer service to deliver services equal to the best in business. In response, agencies throughout the government are making changes that customers have noticed. Here are some examples of the successes. . . .
>
> Regulated businesses know how to make regulatory agencies more effective; businesses with good track records of compliance can be valuable partners and advisors. Medical device manufacturers in the Southwest said that [the] FDA could be more effective by taking a new approach with companies that have good records. They suggested [that the] FDA give advance warning of inspections so companies could have the paperwork ready without a scramble.[37]

One problem with the concept of citizens as customers is that it ignores the role of government in improving the quality of life generally and preserving the environment for the future. Furthermore, not all customers are concerned about the status of those who produce their goods and services. Consequently, "contracting out" government services to firms with low-paid, non-benefited workers, an increasing practice, will seem like a "bargain." Another shortcoming is that

> when agencies view middle-class citizens as customers, no reason exists to think these clients will care whether the city delivers equal services to rich and poor. This is why a key difference in the owner and customer models relates to the role of private-sector alternatives. The reinventing government paradigm assumes that it is proper for people who are unhappy with public services to seek education or security on the private market. . . . Only when citizens are viewed as owners, is the assumption made that they will try to fix the business rather than abandon it.[38]

The latest twist in public-private partnerships crosses yet another boundary. For several years now, those foundations concerned with urban ills, as well as the proponents of "civil renewal" (see chapter 3), have been issuing grants and undertaking studies suggesting that religion might be incorporated into local government service delivery. Perhaps a *deus ex machina* would fix things. For example, in 1997, the Ford Foundation gave an Innovations in American Government Award, worth $100,000, to the Boston Ten-Point Coalition, a group of forty religious leaders. It had created an alliance with the police, and the violent crime rate had dropped significantly.

> Now, through grants totaling $1.2 million, the Foundation is supporting similar faith-based initiatives to curb youth violence, boost literacy, and improve access to jobs in six other cities (Denver, Detroit, New York, Philadelphia, Pittsburgh, and San Francisco). Public/Private Ventures (P/PV), a Philadelphia nonprofit that works on employment and youth development issues, is coordinating and evaluating the project.
>
> The Foundation's support for this work reflects a growing belief that churches and other religious institutions can play a key role in tackling social problems.
>
> "There's a sense that secular institutions have failed, so people are turning more and more to faith-based organizations," says Bernadine Watson, a P/PV vice president. "Conservatives like the Boston model because it's tough on crime; liberals like it because it invests in young people."[39]

This approach may work, although it treads on the church-state separation that earlier foundation programs generally had respected. Now Rockefeller and other liberal foundations are exploring the admixture of religion and government. Reliance on deities seems retrogressive in the twenty-first century, and they rarely were featured in the pictures presented in *Recent Social Trends* or in the Ford Foundation's 1949 *Report*. Both of these documents expressed faith primarily in social science and implied that "cultural lag" and irrationality were the problems. Nevertheless, religion now has been rediscovered as being useful for social control (and for fighting the Cold War against Godless communism). This is not a policy of "conservatives" but of hegemons, underscored by the Ten Point Coalition's lead minister, Reverend Eugene Rivers:

> "This is not your grandma's Baptist church," says Rivers, now 49. "It's closer to a Catholic mission or a co-ed religious order. In some ways, we're the black church's version of Latin American liberation theology, in our case with intellectuals and activists working to emancipate poor, inner-city youth from violence and mayhem."[40]

Here is a fine example of "emergent trends" being incorporated into hegemonic ideology; the main point of liberation theology, its critique of capitalism and imperialism, has been excised.

Progressive reforms, which include making government more like a business, and more collaborative with business and other private-sector institutions, undoubtedly have promoted efficiency. On the other hand, although strongly endorsed by political scientists and "opinion leaders," they modify democracy in significant ways and, on balance, have a "depoliticizing" effect. Ordinary citizens likely will be astounded when told that they are the "owners" of our political system. Even congressional representatives are denied the basic information needed to make policy; they are victims of CIA disinformation, just like the rest of us.

5

Market Supplement

Arts and Culture

The mind has its needs as well as the body. Those of the latter are the
basis for government, which is readily accepted because of the former. Government and laws provide security and well-being to the
multitude. Science, literature, and the arts spread flowery garlands
over the iron chains of law, inducing consent without obvious coer-
cion. Thus all memory of their natural birthright liberty is stifled;
they come to love their enslavement, and they are transformed into a
law abiding populace. Need created the powers that be; the arts and
sciences fortified them. Great nations, love talents and reward those
who cultivate them!
                —Jean-Jacques Rousseau, *Discourse on the Arts and Sciences*

The nonprofit sector provides goods and services that the market cannot (or
will not)—from homeless shelters to opera and British TV dramas. The latter
are quite important, as the defection of intellectuals tends to be more dangerous to capitalism than starving peasants. Thus we feel good about living in a
society where there are many ballet companies and grateful to foundations and
Philip Morris for funding them. Similarly, we enjoy the new Hall of Biodiversity at the American Museum of Natural History, provided by the Monsanto Foundation.

That shaky invisible hand drops the ball so much that spontaneous charitable activity alone cannot do the system-sustaining work, contrary to the assertions of Herbert Spencer's followers. Inadequacies lie in three broad areas
(although they are not mutually exclusive): culture, social welfare, and the economy. There also are many arenas where it is not so much a case of shortfall as
massive dysfunction and destruction, as in the environment and war.

Although today elites seem to prefer that compensatory activities be undertaken by the nonprofit sector, at times governments are called upon to organize, supplement, and fund them. Often, government must be prodded and helped. This is where foundations, as general societal planners and as "managers" of the "third sector," play a role. Perhaps, as indicated in *Recent Social Trends,* their preference was for an official government planning agency. Given that it did not happen, the large liberal foundations were quite willing to assume that function.[1]

One way that government helps fund private cultural endeavors is by giving favorable tax treatment to the nonprofit world. Foundations' assets are subject to only a small excise tax, 501 (c) (3) nonprofits are not taxed, and donors receive tax deductions for charitable contributions. It is not only the market but altruism that needs help.

The world of culture and the arts is important; both producers and audiences are types that become easily disaffected. Perhaps the experience of the Works Progress Administration (WPA) during the 1930s persuaded some hegemons that artists need not only employment or income; they also may need steering in regard to content. The down-and-out culture workers of the Depression era were mostly leftists, so WPA funding produced some incendiary murals, dissenting folk concerts, and Marxist children's plays such as *The Revolt of the Beavers.*

Pop culture, including rock music, Gothic novels, sitcoms, adventure films, Disney products, and pornography, is sustained by the market. If that were all that there were, intellectuals would be very unhappy. "High" culture—opera, symphonies, ballet, art museums, and literature—is maintained by paying customers, wealthy donors, private foundations, corporate foundations, and small amounts of government funding. This still leaves out the "multiculturalism" that has been so energetically promoted, the emerging trends that hegemonic institutions must incorporate, local arts projects, and experimental and beginning artists, who are numerous in a "postindustrial" society that places a high value on self-expression.

This is where, because other donors shy away, foundation sponsorship becomes most significant. Funding these cultural endeavors can prevent disaffection of vulnerable minorities, can provide self-esteem and employment and, furthermore, can be a source of economic revitalization for depressed communities and the economy as a whole. In the process, some steering can be done so that artistic representations do not consistently attack the system or its dominant institutions.

The Rockefeller philanthropies provided early funding and sponsorship of emerging art forms: modern art, film as art, primitive and Asian art, and even jazz (on WRVR, the radio station of Riverside Church). While the personal taste of Abby and Nelson Rockefeller may have inspired patronage, it also was a useful control, as avant-garde enthusiasts often harbored anti-capitalist notions. Perhaps because much of modern art was nonrepresentational, it could be regarded as politically innocuous. Modernists certainly laughed off the wall the socialist realism of nineteenth-century Britain, exemplified by Walter Crane. Regardless, freedom generally reigned at the Museum of Modern Art, and the incendiary mural "Guernica," by the communist artist Picasso, was not hidden in the shadows. However, there was one spectacular case of censorship a few blocks away. Diego Rivera's mural, commissioned for Rockefeller Center, had to be blasted off, because he refused to remove images of degenerate capitalists and a heroic Lenin.

Today, arts funders themselves are collectivized and have their own peak organization within the Council on Foundations, Grantmakers in the Arts, and a think tank in Washington, D.C., Center for Arts and Culture. In addition, government foundations have been created at the urging of the foundations, modeled on them, and work collaboratively with them: the National Endowment for the Arts (NEA), the National Endowment for the Humanities, the Institute for Museum and Library Services, the Corporation for Public Broadcasting, and the National Trust for Historic Preservation. Therefore, general planning for the arts has become feasible. "Cultural funders, both public and private, seem to be reconsidering the axiom of 'art for art's sake' as a guiding principle and are showing increased interest in the social and/or civic uses of the arts as well as in the public purposes of the arts."[2]

Modern funders are careful to avoid the crude manipulation of the "Industrial Drama Movement" of the earlier times. For example, in 1920, Western Electric Company's Hawthorne Works put on a company show:

> The show, entitled *Hawthorne Follies*, ran for a full week in downtown Chicago. The *Follies* opened with the Hawthorne Minstrels, a cast of sixty-five white employees in blackface with Liberty in the center of their minstrel half circle. This was followed by a comic skit depicting a day in the company medical clinic during the height of the then-recent influenza epidemic. The *Follies* included numerous songs and dances, ranging from pseudo-ragtime to patriotic numbers.[3]

We also have come a long way from Henry Ford's square dancing and hammered dulcimer concerts that he deemed suitable workers' recreation and entertainment.

Today, arts planners find the market so unreliable that it is not merely a question of adjusting supply to demand. Both supply and demand must be reengineered. Foundations are now engaged in "audience development."[4] It seems that the rock music generation, upon turning forty, did not join its parents in the family circle at the opera and symphony. It was more likely joining its children at the Monsanto exhibit, or at an art museum (now heavily supported by corporate foundations), if not at a commercial Disneyworld or other theme park.[5]

The Ford Foundation once was the leading funder of the arts; it has been surpassed by both the NEA and by foundations such as Lila Wallace-Reader's

, Mellon, Pew, and McArthur.[6] However, Ford remains a major sup-
ternative, local, and vernacular arts. It works to increase the supply
ˢⁱᶜ⁻, ling to Ruth Mayleas, Ford's arts director in 1991:

In the area of multiculturalism, . . . there is an urgent need for enlarging
the pool of trained people, both artists and administrators. This is an
enormous challenge that is not being addressed in any major way. It's
certainly something this Foundation could do.[7]

Ford's generous grants reach deeply troubled neighborhoods and do not avoid
potentially subversive subject matter. Thus a program entitled "Meet the Com-
poser" funds three-year residencies with local institutions:

Joseph Julian Gonzalez wrote a mass for Orqesta de Baja call "Misa
Azteca," inspired by his work with cultural organizations along the San
Diego-Tijuana border. . . . Donald Harrison is writing a jazz opera about
a poor polluted area in New Orleans known as "Cancer Alley."[8]

Along with the NEA, other foundations, and local businesses, Ford supports the
Guadalupe Cultural Arts Center in the barrio of San Antonio, Texas, which,
despite energetic community development activities, remains a severely depressed
area. Half the students drop out of school before finishing the ninth grade.[9] Nevertheless, the center has renewed respect and identity for Mexican-American culture, not just for the local residents; it is a beacon for Latinos nationwide. Ford
also provides substantial support for the arts in Appalachia, another perpetually
depressed area; one of its grantees is Appalshop, a consortium of arts companies
centered in Whitesburg, Kentucky.[10]

Ford has supported a project to preserve and restore the black tradition in
modern dance. Dances from an earlier era are performed, videotaped, and anno-
tated (using a system devised for this purpose).

One of the first dances to be reconstructed through the ADF project
was [Donald] McKayle's *Rainbow 'Round my Shoulder*. . . . The dance,
which premiered in 1959, vividly illustrates the labor and longing that
fill the lives of prisoners on a Southern chain gang.[11]

Does this suggest parallels with our prison-industrial complex and the current
revival of chain gangs?
Foundations provide visibility and access for old and new arts, and in some cases,
they literally prevent artifacts from crumbling. For example, the Rockefeller philanthropies were the major source of film preservation, which enabled not only scholars
and artists but also kids (who in the old days might "hang out" at the Museum of
Modern Art) to see, at a very low cost, the great masterpieces of film art.

In 1998, the Ford Foundation gave a $100,000 grant to the Paul Robeson Foundation "for an exhibition of archival holdings and to acquire audio-visual materials to represent the actor's lifetime body of work."[12] Undoubtedly, his political work will figure in the exhibit. Although it would be safe now, even considered "misguided naïveté" in today's ideological climate, who could bite the hand that fosters such exhibits?

Foundation funding for the arts was always, to some extent, part of the "Cold War," for one goal of the elite is to prevent negative thoughts about our political system and serious consideration of alternatives. Not only are artists and audiences susceptible members of the defectable classes, but there are wise guys, neither producing nor consuming art, who might nevertheless complain: "What kind of a system is this where commercial pop-porn and the like are all that is produced?" In the early 1950s, when the total-mobilization Cold War was getting underway, they might have made comparisons with other countries, which were much poorer. Europe had long subsidized the arts, with governments assuming feudal traditions of patronage. "High culture" was affordable and patronized by working-class people in most European countries, with the possible exception of Britain, where cultural class divisions were fairly rigid. Worse, communist nations lavishly funded the arts: classical, early modern, folk, vernacular, and even children's theater. Ordinary people apparently were happily attending performances. Our coldest Cold Warriors may have argued that people went only because there was no heat in their flats, but still there was cause for nervousness.

The cultural Cold War initiated concerted action by foundations and the CIA; a major objective was to persuade European intellectuals that the United States was not only a "free" society but also a worthy, culturally rich one that did not repress its artists as did the proponents of "socialist realism." Foundations were used as "pass-throughs" for government money; they also funded government-approved projects themselves.

> The architects of the [Ford] foundation's cultural policy in the aftermath of the Second World War were perfectly attuned to the political imperatives which supported America's looming presence on the world stage. At times, it seemed as if the Ford Foundation was simply an extension of government in the area of international cultural propaganda. The foundation had a record of close involvement in covert actions in Europe, working closely with Marshall Plan and CIA officials on specific projects.[13]

Ford, the Kaplan Foundation, and others became "pass-throughs" for the CIA project, Congress for Cultural Freedom (CCF).[14] In addition, starting in 1957, Ford provided funds for the CCF.[15] This entanglement of public and private funds is even more Byzantine today, especially in Eastern Europe. The CCF sponsored writers and journals, including the notorious *Encounter*, throughout Europe. American jazz was highly regarded, especially among the targeted European "communist sympathizers," but U.S. symphonic composition and performance were barely known, so the Boston Symphony Orchestra was sent on tour to fight the Cold War.

One of the strangest episodes was the CCF's traveling exhibit of abstract expressionist art, including works by Jackson Pollock and Mark Rothko. The idea was to show the European intellectuals that not only was the United States rich in avant-garde culture, but that it was honored and rewarded. In contrast, artists in communist countries were stifled by puritanical, socialist realist strictures. Years later, the defenders of CIA covert operations used this example to argue that covert operations generally were necessary, because projects like these could never be mounted by the U.S. State Department. Congressional leaders holding the purse strings would not provide for such works; they admired the "capitalist realism" of Norman Rockwell.

Ford, through its Intercultural Publications Program, produced the *Perspectives* journal, appearing in four languages to "lure . . . leftist intellectuals" and to showcase United States' cultural achievements.[16] The foundation also supported the Institute of Contemporary Arts in Washington for international appearances by Aaron Copland, Robert Lowell, and Martha Graham.[17]

Foundation cultural initiatives abroad were not limited to Europe. They had long been active in the "Third World"; CIA programs often were modeled on these earlier private activities. A very old story was the sending of missionaries, who acted as a bridge for economic development interests. One such case was the Wycliffe Bible Translators, a Rockefeller-funded organization. Agents would go into aboriginal territory, such as the Amazon basin, and make connections with the more outward-looking tribesmen. These in turn would help them translate the Bible into native languages. In the process, the tribal linguists often were co-opted as middlemen in resource extraction enterprises.[18]

In the 1950s' Cold War effort, religion was used in a slightly different way. The Ford Foundation undertook a "Books for India" program to counter the influence of inexpensive communist publications. Ford's program not only translated Western works to show the merits of "free world" culture but also produced books intended to revitalize traditional Indian religions, on the theory that any religion would help the anti-communist cause.[19] Similarly, Ford officials visiting Burma in 1952 were nervous about communist insurgents; they helped the country host the Sixth World Buddhist Synod in Rangoon:

> Approved in 1953, Ford's $250,000 grant provided assistance for construction of the conference meeting hall, which was to serve as an Institute for the Advanced Study of Pali (the language of ancient Buddhist scriptures) after the Synod ended.[20]

Despite its potential as a Cold War weapon, religion may not constitutionally be promoted by official U.S. government programs, hence the convenience of private foundations tending to this department. Cultural and religious revitalization and the stirring up of "identity" politics have served as an anti-communist tactic; the major programs of the Ford and Soros foundations and others seem to have had the intended effects in Eastern Europe, albeit with some volatile side effects. (This will be further illustrated in chapter 9.)

International funders continue to steer the content of foreign cultural projects. Here is an example among thousands. The Ford Foundation now funds the Philippine Educational Theater Association (PETA), a professional group formed in the 1960s that was influenced by Bertolt Brecht. This political theater was created to educate, and during the 1970s and 1980s, it produced plays such as *Baby Ruth* that "explored the United States's exploitation of the Philippines."[21] "Since the fall of Marcos, PETA has passed from what it terms 'the theater of confrontation' to 'the theater of empowerment,' which is how PETA's Women's Theater Program evolved."[22] The women noted that although many of them were actors, few were directors; in addition, they thought that the performances rarely addressed women's concerns. Now they tour the country with plays about domestic violence and reproductive health. Topics that most women rarely discuss—violent husbands, prostitutes with AIDS, abortion, sterilization, and the like—are brought into the open with the group's audience participation techniques. In Ford's report on this group and a related children's political street theater, there is no mention of such themes as women's agricultural and assembly-line employment in multinational corporation (MNC) enterprises, or U.S. military base contribution to prostitution and AIDS problems. Of course, the report might not be telling the whole story, especially since audience participation cannot be easily controlled.

Arts philanthropy continues not only as a means of mollifying dissident artists or dissatisfied consumers but also, where necessary, to transform content from structural critique to multicultural identity themes. The demise of communism has meant that cultural institutions, and often universities and the mass media, are now heavily dependent on Western subventions. Cultural aid can slip in where more direct intervention might be suspect. Furthermore, the arts everywhere have an increasing role in economic stability; tourism, recreation, and culture are major industries where manufacturing has declined, and farms have been wiped out by agribusiness. The arts can provide exports and "supply the raw materials for advertising."

6

Market Supplement

Social Welfare and the Economy

The idea of a national minimum standard—in health, in education, in
culture as well as in income—below which citizens should not be
allowed to fall is applicable to localities as well as to individuals.
—Wesley Mitchell, in *Recent Social Trends in the United States*

Recent Social Trends, a massive study commissioned by President Hoover and
financed by the Rockefeller Foundation, was produced by a team of social scientists. Published in 1933, it identified major problems from soil erosion to "excessive breeding by degenerates." Among the most serious was the Depression,
which was attributed to both cyclical and technological unemployment.[1] The
remedy proposed was government planning. World War I had shown that it
would work; now it should be used for social welfare. Directing social change
from above was an alternative to class conflict: "It is . . . to be anticipated that the
initiative in a wide variety of emerging problems will be assumed by research centers, groups, bureaus, institutes, and foundations."[2]

The foundation-created and foundation-funded Social Science Research
Council was considered the appropriate instrumentality for social planning; most
of the authors were SSRC members. The idea of central planning never appealed
to Congress, yet important aspects of the *RST* program have been enacted,
almost always with heavy involvement of the foundation policy-planning people
and organizations. The "New Deal" was largely created with such help, although
". . . Roosevelt preferred to conceal the fact that so many of his major advisers on
policy and some of his major programmes *[sic]* in social reform were the result of
support by one or more of the private foundations."[3]

The Social Security program was proposed by the American Association for Labor Legislation, a group funded by industrialists and by the Carnegie, Milbank, and Sage foundations.[4] One original motive was to phase out older workers gently; the Depression gave the project more urgency.

> The main work on the program was done by experts from a private organization called Industrial Relations Counselors, Inc., which had been founded in 1921 by John D. Rockefeller, Jr., to search for ways to deal with labor unrest and avoid unionization. The organization was closely linked to both the family's main oil companies . . . and charitable foundations. These Rockefeller experts worked with other experts and some business leaders through committees of the Social Science Research Council. . . .
> Many of these committee members, including three employees from Industrial Relations Counselors, Inc., were appointed to President Roosevelt's Social Security task force.[5]

After Social Security was enacted, there was still the problem of administering this bold new program. The Social Science Research Council's Committee on Social Security (also supported by the Twentieth Century Fund) was awarded $430,000 (between 1935 and 1940) by the Rockefeller Foundation and

> it was the RF's intent that the CSS should coordinate the whole field of social security on behalf of Rockefeller philanthropy. The CSS was created as an adjunct to the federal social security legislation and fulfilled the role of research planner and organizer for the S[ocial] S[ecurity] B[ureau].[6]

The Social Security Bureau (SSB) was grateful for the extensive assistance of the Committee on Social Security (CSS), which helped select personnel and gave technical advice to federal and state officials.

The Depression was an obvious case of "market failure." There are also—during good times—the stubborn problems of persistent poverty, insufficient demand, insufficient investment, regional stagnation, and externalities that threaten future prosperity, to say nothing of life on the planet. We might add that measures undertaken to deal with these problems, such as creating a military-industrial complex and accelerating foreign trade and investment, carry with them risks of total nuclear war, in addition to the disruption and exploitation of the people who are invested upon.

Our propaganda portrays the "free market" as a heavenly bower; nevertheless, educated people in the United States are aware of its dysfunctions, and certainly those in the foundations are. Yet there is nothing in our Constitution, adopted in 1789, that compels the political system to notice or correct any flaws. Congress was given considerable power to regulate commerce in Art. I, Sec. 8, and the states may do so by their inherent "police powers," but no one is required to take action. Our "unwritten" political system of parties and interest groups plays to the middle and to wealthy interests, not necessarily protecting the "system in general" or being attentive to weak spots, however severe. Even if we had a majoritarian system, with no political action committees (PACs) or malapportionment, and all citizens informed and voting, we might not do much better.

The theory of democracy, on which our institutions are based, comes to us from Ancient Athens, where the majority was poor, the case in all countries until the twentieth century. Thus a democratic system was expected to operate on behalf of the poor majority and to provide some ameliorative policies. That is why checks and limitations on majority rule were written into our Constitution by its elite drafters. However, today the majority in the United States (and generally in the "developed" world) enjoys at least an adequate material standard of living. Neither a poor people's political party nor an interest group could achieve much political power, even in the fairest system.

Currently there are advocates of a "progressive" majority who believe that power could be attained if all who felt oppressed because of poverty, race, religion, sexual orientation, or disability joined in a "Rainbow Coalition" with those concerned about environmental degradation, imperialism, and war. There is not yet evidence that such a coalition could be created and sustained.

Lacking majorities for change, foundation social engineering has promoted ameliorative measures. It has not been alone; popular movements, especially of labor, have exerted substantial pressure for reform. However, while popular activism is well documented, the foundation role is shadowy. Furthermore, it is likely that given the majority's general affluence (notwithstanding overwork and insecurity), further progress will be even more dependent on elite intervention.

Elites have not always succeeded in getting their programs adopted, or in producing the results they sought. For example, Social Security, according to the SSRC and Industrial Relations Counselors (IRC) planners, was to have been much more comprehensive and was to include national health insurance. As enacted and evolved, it has fulfilled its mission of providing basic security for retired workers. It also has functioned in a Keynesian manner, creating demand for new and old products and services. On the other hand, some see negative implications in the "ghettoization" of the elderly and the "liberation" from three-generation households.

The Twentieth Century Fund, created by Edward Filene in 1919, was dedicated to increasing market demand. Understandably, from a department store perspective, it wanted to create a mass consumption society and develop appropriate institutions and ideology. In the early twentieth century, credit for consumer durables generally was not available to working-class people.

. . . Filene saw an incipient working-class consumption and the pursuit of higher standards of living as the core of American democracy. He and the organizations he supported thought of credit as fundamentally an economic problem. A prolific thinker about mass consumption, Filene maintained that mass production required a more equitable distribution of national income and affordable access to credit. He believed that only an empowered "consuming public" operating through self-supporting democratic institutions such as credit unions could effectively restructure the nation's political economy.[7]

Twentieth Century Fund philanthropy supported the Credit Union National Extension Bureau: "By 1930, there were over one thousand credit unions, with assets of $45 million and annual loans of $60 million."[8] Perhaps it is hard to believe today, but the very idea of buying consumer goods on credit required much persuasion and promotion. It was not a respectable notion, especially in Filene's domain—the heart of Puritan New England. The Fund, aided by many nonprofit institutions—including the Boy Scouts, which required a speech on "installment buying" for its economics badge—adopted this cause, ultimately with great success. Today the Ford Foundation provides millions in grants and loans to support the Credit Union movement.

Filene also advocated the redistribution of income to the working classes; profit sharing was introduced in his own stores. In addition, "[t]he Fund would play a key role in drafting the National Labor Relations Act (1935), which would enable workers to enhance their purchasing power through collective bargaining."[9]

Agriculture might be considered the land that the invisible hand never knew. By the twentieth century, noncapitalist forms such as subsistence farming or slave plantations had been swept away; collective farms, although often successful, were unlikely to receive government and popular promotion. On the other hand, the "free market" system, eventually producing lavish supplies of cheap food, was a disaster from many other perspectives, including the self-exploitation of farmers and their families, feudalistic subjection to agribusiness, semi-slave conditions for migrant labor, huge resource consumption, environmental degradation, hormone- and pesticide-ridden food and, frequently, poverty for even the hardest working farmers.

Elites were well aware of these conditions. President Theodore Roosevelt had, in the spirit of Progressivism, established a Commission on Country Life. Its 1909 report, based on evidence taken during a rare "prosperous" time for farmers, painted a dreary picture; the Commission feared for the survival of rural life.[10] Among its concerns were the power imbalance between individual farmers and the corporations squeezing them on both the supply and marketing sides, soil depletion, the poverty of social and cultural life (even successful farmers often had no books in their houses), and the "burdens and narrow life of farm women." Policies enacted to improve matters, such as the Extension Service, more "scientific" agricultural training, and the encouragement of cooperation often accelerated the demise of the family farm and the domination of agribusiness. The

Depression revealed the persistent poverty and insecurity of farm life, and the dust storms illustrated what the agricultural "system" had done to the land. *Recent Social Trends* and the Agricultural Committee of the SSRC attested to these pervasive problems.

According to Domhoff, the concept for the farm subsidy program came from the Rockefeller Foundation.

> The idea was analyzed and amended by agricultural economists serving on the Agricultural Committee of the Social Sciences Research Council. . . . Archival records show that the agricultural economist most responsible for writing up the program and demonstrating its feasibility was in regular correspondence with the Rockefeller employee who introduced him to the idea.[11]

The farm subsidy program gave temporary relief to many middle-class farmers, but its continuation and expansion produced further dysfunction. Subsidies were partially abolished by Congress in 1996. The ensuing disasters led to a quiet restoration to the highest level ever. A different panacea for farmers offered by elites was the creation of a world market, first as a wartime by-product, then through trade and aid, and currently by biotechnology (e.g., genetically engineered miracle grains). Continued troubles suggest that agriculture may not be fixable within the boundaries of capitalist social engineering. For the farmer (as for the working mother), equipment can be applied to the job, but there still remains the eighty-hour workweek, which is no longer acceptable. Furthermore, in a democracy, the employment of peasants in home or field creates dissonance.

The New Deal reforms were especially helpful to the white working class, to the farmers, and to the elderly; Social Security at first did not cover nonindustrial occupations. The later incorporation of Keynesian-inspired fiscal and monetary techniques into national policies was facilitated by foundation-supported think tanks, such as the Brookings Institution and closely linked government agencies, such as the Council of Economic Advisers. Postwar planning by the War-Peace Studies group (Rockefeller-financed) of the Council on Foreign Relations focused on expanding trade and diplomatically and militarily protecting a "Grand Area." (See chapter 4 for further discussion.)

Despite wartime and postwar economic stimulation, including the military-industrial complex, by the 1950s it was apparent that there were still areas of intractable poverty and social decay. These included Native American lands, inner-city black and Hispanic ghettos, and white Appalachia. The Ford Foundation adopted this problem as a major public policy interest and provided leadership to the nonprofit world's remedial work.

Ford, since its emergence on the national scene in 1949, had been working closely with government foreign policy institutions. Our bipartisan Cold War policies protected the Foundation from accusations of undue political influence, associated in popular and congressional thought with "partisan" activities. Although Ford had been active in local education and litigation activities (see chapter 7), its direct relationship with the federal legislative and executive branches began slowly.

During the 1950s, the Foundation supported pilot studies concerning juvenile delinquency. This kind of problem was ripe for foundation social engineering; neither victims nor perpetrators were suitable candidates for interest group organizing, and conventional crime control approaches seemed ineffective. The Kennedy administration gave Ford the opportunity to provide both a theory and a model for a national attack on juvenile delinquency.

Ford's perspective rejected the prevailing individual pathology explanations for juvenile crime and instead indicted community disorganization.

> Revised and expanded by sociologists Richard Cloward and Lloyd Ohlin in the early 1960s, these ideas became the basis of the "opportunity theory" of delinquency which traced its causes to a broader systemic failure—of schools, social welfare agencies, political institutions, indeed, of society itself—to provide legitimate avenues of success for youth in poor neighborhoods.[12]

Kennedy's Committee on Juvenile Delinquency became an outpost of the Ford Foundation and funded the large-scale replication of its models, which was the beginning of Ford's dominant influence on the "War on Poverty." The Foundation's cure for juvenile delinquency, community renewal, would require a major reorganization of local government. Ford already was experimenting in its "Gray Areas" projects, so called because they were the areas between central business districts and suburbs, where poor black, white, and Hispanic migrants were settling. Public opinion was becoming receptive to the idea that "community action" was a legitimate federal government involvement. Ford's policy people were convinced that most local governments were excessively compartmentalized, too narrow geographically, and structurally obsolete. The Foundation's pilot programs, soon to be adopted by Congress, challenged usual local government structures and processes. They were nevertheless politically acceptable in Democratic-controlled cities that hoped for some federal largess from a Democratic administration.

In 1963, poverty became a major national concern; Michael Harrington's book, *The Other America*, and similar reports "discovered" the problem. The Democrats regarded poverty as a potential campaign issue; it provided a way to support the emerging civil rights movement that might placate poor whites.[13] Ford's integrated community action strategy was a central feature of the 1964 Economic Opportunity Act, a presidential initiative that Congress was persuaded to accept. The Gray Areas experiments "became a working model of the Federal Government's Great Society program."[14]

By 1967, the civil rights movement was becoming more militant, and the "black power" slogan, first used by the Student Non-Violent Coordinating Committee, made elites nervous. The Ford and Rockefeller foundations responded by creating the National Urban Coalition (NUC), to transform "black power" (whatever it might signify) into "black capitalism." The NUC was a significant departure in philanthropy; corporate foundations now joined with the private foundations to carry out system-sustaining projects, in addition to their normal business- or community-related benevolence. Ford was able to link its anti-poverty strategies to the civil rights movement through grants to moderate organizations. The Congress of Racial Equality (CORE) advocated "Black control of Black communities" in a way that could allow the penetration of the "black capitalism" concept. Roy Innis of CORE was named a Ford Foundation fellow, and he became a board member of the NUC.

Ford gave a $175,000 grant to the Cleveland CORE in 1967, primarily for voter education and registration. These activities helped elect Carl Stokes, the first black mayor of a major Northern city.[15] Stokes, an advocate of black capitalism, interpreted black power as job training programs for dropouts and the encouragement of black-owned local businesses.

The NUC and CORE endorsed federal legislation providing for community development corporations (CDCs), financed by government, corporations, and foundations, which were to establish small businesses and industries in depressed areas. The CDCs, often combining education, job training, legal services, housing, health services, and community organizing, were said by a Ford official to be "a proxy for local government."[16] These new entities erased the boundaries between traditional local government departments, public and private sectors, and local, state, and national governments. Local tax money was still part of the mix; other funding includes federal government and foundation grants, business donations and investments, and any returns on the investment. Boards are rarely elected; usually they are composed of appointed "stakeholders," with elites playing a major role. Consequently, democratic control is nearly impossible to maintain; today this format is used not only in impoverished communities but also by "economic development corporations" throughout the United States. Nevertheless, the Ford Foundation denied that the CDCs reduced accountability to citizens: "They represent a critical mass of development and programming potential more available and accountable to community people than the traditional public or private sectors."[17]

Another boundary that the CDCs erased was that between community organizing and service delivery:

> Built atop the wreckage of the Bedford-Stuyvesant race riots of 1964, the Bedford-Stuyvesant Restoration Corporation (BSRC) eschewed the radicalism of M[obilization] F[or] Y[outh] and rejected the poor people's democracy envisioned in the community action movement.

BSRC focused more on job development and environmental restoration of the dilapidated ghetto. Therefore, one of today's dominant forms of urban social welfare governance—the community development corporation—was born out of Ford's reaction against community action.[18]

The BSRC was the "flagship" of the CDCs, and its director, Franklin Thomas, subsequently became the first black president of the Ford Foundation. A New York City activist describes one CDC as follows:

> . . . [F]unding and administrative demands became the driving force of the organization I directed. . . . Many "organizers" no longer work for social change. Organizations that grew out of activist grassroots efforts are no longer the vehicles by which any "community" agenda is to be realized. Missions once framed around confronting and challenging the prevailing system of economic control in low income neighborhoods are now geared simply to accommodating the status quo and domesticating potentially troublesome local residents.[19]

Every year, corporations and foundations invest millions in CDCs; in 2000, one corporation alone, the Structured Employment Economic Development Corporation of New York, received a $5,000,000 grant from Ford. There are more than 2,000 CDCs, serving every type of poor enclave, for example, the

> Bedford-Stuyvesant Restoration Corporation (Brooklyn), Watts Labor Community Action Corporation (Los Angeles), The Woodlawn Organization (Chicago), Southeast Alabama Self-Help Association (Tuskegee), Mississippi Action for Community Education (Greenville), Zion Non-Profit Charitable Trust (Philadelphia), and Southern Development Foundation (Lafayette, La.) [black communities]; Spanish Speaking Unity Council (Oakland.), Mexican American Unity Council (San Antonio), Chicanos Por La Causa (Phoenix), and Home Education Livelihood Program (New Mexico) [Hispanic]; and Southeast Development, Inc. (Baltimore), and Kentucky Highlands Investment Corporation (London) [white].

Whether the industries thus financed will ever break even is uncertain. The evidence so far is not hopeful. "The vast majority of CDCs indicated that less than 5 percent of their budgets were comprised of profits or returns on investments."[20] Evaluations indicate that they can effectively provide subsidized housing and social services, but that they are not "taking off" and developing industries independent of subsidies.[21] A recent study finds that outcomes assessments, using the most "sophisticated evaluation techniques available," have been uniformly negative for philanthropy funded programs in welfare and employment training.[22] The provision of sufficient jobs "with a future" has been generally disappointing; in any case, each job produced has required a very large investment.

One of the more successful CDCs, according to Ford—also the largest as of 1995—is the New Community in Newark. It was Newark's largest private employer and New Jersey's largest nonprofit housing developer.[23] Welfare recipients and the hard to employ have been trained to work in child care, nursing homes, food service, and building maintenance. Many of the jobs are in the CDCs' own industries and therefore doubly subsidized. These occupations supposedly are the labor market's growing points; one wonders why the "market" does not hire and train these workers. It is not as though they were seeking work as philosophers or calligraphers.

The Rockefeller Foundation, which recently has declared that henceforth poverty is to be its main concern, has now endorsed "social purpose enterprise," or "philanthropic venture capitalism." Subsidized businesses are justified, as they provide a "social return," including savings in public service costs. They also are deemed necessary as a temporary or permanent source of employment for some individuals who, even in boom times, cannot find conventional employment.[24]

The CDCs, while not fostering much participation, have contributed to ghetto pacification and the development of moderate leadership. They probably are a wise investment when they provide subsidized jobs to potential troublemakers. However, these institutions challenge both democratic and capitalist theories. They dilute the force of the U.S. "marketization" message that is imposed on the rest of the world. Most problematic is their failure—even in boom times—to make much of a dent in persistent poverty.[25]

Ford has been a leader in many other poverty programs. It supports nonprofit housing development and gives transportation planning grants to help the urban unemployed commute to suburban jobs. It pioneered a 70 percent worker-owned home health care agency, Cooperative Home Care Associates, which provides training, benefits, and above-average wages.

"Microenterprise," modeled on the Grameen Bank in Bangladesh (for which Ford provided seed money in 1976), began in the United States in 1991 as a joint project of the Ms. Foundation for Women, Ford, and other foundations.[26] Its particular mission was to help low-income women start small businesses. Enterprises aided include catering, chauffeuring, dry cleaning, a beauty shop, and a computer consultancy. The program operates with peer support groups, entrepreneurship training, and loans that would not be available from "market" institutions.

Microenterprise is not limited to cities and women. Ford's Working Capital Program helps restauranteurs and craftspeople in Center Ossipee, a depressed area of New Hampshire, entrepreneurs on the Pine Ridge Reservation in South Dakota and in the Upper Peninsula of Michigan, and many other communities that the rising tide has not lifted. Accion International operates in a similar way throughout both Latin America and Latino communities in the United States, where the standard interest rate is 16 percent annually. In contrast:

The interest rates for Accion's Latin American clients are generally between 3 percent and 6 percent a month. These figures sound high when compared with those in the United States, but they are generally considered fair given the interest rates that banks in the region charge their commercial customers, which range from 15 percent to 45 percent a year.[27]

This helps explain why Latin American economic development is so dependent upon foreign aid and multilateral lending institutions, and the consequent power that the lenders have over those societies.

More generous than low-cost loans is the somewhat startling idea (although it has been recommended by conservative economists) of simply giving money to the poor. Low-income people have been selected to participate in an "asset-building" program: individual development accounts. For every dollar saved, public and private funders contribute from three to nine dollars.

> The goal of the six-year program is to test the extent to which low-income people will save when provided with the right incentives. Major donors like the Ford, Joyce, and Charles Stewart Mott foundations are giving $8 million, while local partners, including churches, corporations, and banks, are adding $4 million.[28]

The participants may use their assets for education, housing, or businesses. The program is justified as a successor to the Homestead Act of 1862, the GI Bill, IRAs, and mortgage-interest deduction, subsidies that enabled many to build assets and ascend the economic ladder. The Corporation for Enterprise Development and its foundation backers have received congressional funding for the IDA program, the Assets for Independence Act of 1998.[29] Such legislative measures also are part of the anti-poverty initiative.

Since 1986, foundations have supported a think tank, the Economic Policy Institute (EPI), to provide public policy advocacy for low- and middle-income workers. In the past, a few radical foundations (mostly expired), such as the Garland Fund, had ties to the labor movement. The EPI represents a new collaboration between mainstream foundations and organized labor on domestic issues.[30] In foreign policy, there has been a tight connection since the early Cold War days, which is said to have helped Lane Kirkland, an advisor to foundations, become the head of the AFL-CIO.[31]

During the North American Free Trade Agreement (NAFTA) debate, the EPI (funded by Ford and others) made technical objections to the models supporting the trade agreement. At the same time, a much greater effect was produced by Ford funding to the other side, which included grants to the Institute for International Economics, a think tank that emphasizes the benefits of NAFTA. In addition, the Ford Foundation also awarded grants to environmental groups and the Southwest Voters Research Institute to convene forums on NAFTA. These resulted in an alliance of 100 Latino organizations and elected officials, called the Latino Consensus on NAFTA, which provided conditional support for the agreement.[32]

Yet another workers' organization supported by foundations is Working Today, which is concerned about the jobs without benefits now held by one-third of the workforce. It is both a policy-advocacy group seeking changes in the tax laws and a mutual aid society that provides group rates for health insurance.[33]

In addition to many programs addressing economic revitalization with grant money, the nonprofit sector itself is economically significant. It employs one-tenth of the workforce directly and provides partial support for many others. Furthermore, nonprofits play an important role in the concentration and distribution of capital for the profit-making sector.[34] For example, nonprofit hospitals' boards of trustees include businesspeople, bankers, real estate developers, and insurance executives. Expansion plans of health centers, arts centers, universities, and the like stimulate regional economies and yield substantial contracts for the trustees' private corporations. "Deindustrialization" means that educational, health care, recreational, and cultural institutions must become the major employers, investors, and purchasers in our ghettos and Rust Belt.

7

Foundations and the Legal System

> The Court's power is a natural outcome of the necessity for maintaining capitalist dominance under democratic forms; . . . judicial review has proved to be a very convenient channel through which the driving forces of American economic life have found expression and achieved victory.
> —Max Lerner, "The Divine Right of Judges"

The literature of "power elite" theory is surprisingly silent on the role of the judiciary. This is strange, as the judiciary was designed to be the elite institution in the federal system, and evidence indicates that it has functioned as planned. The backgrounds of judges have been much investigated, and they explain concordance with elite interests and values. However, foundations have been largely neglected in current research on how the U.S. Supreme Court receives and processes elite demands. There are probably more critical studies of foundation garments than of the massive institutions overpinning our society. In earlier times, judicial activism was linked to foundations:

> Justice Holmes and Brandeis are credited with having broadened the field of judicial decision by interpreting legislation in the light of historic and social conditions, but one asks oneself, whence did these great judges derive their humane and enlightened point of view? Were they in their growing years given to reading the multitudinous studies in social science, so-called, patronized directly or indirectly by the great foundations?[1]

Progressives of the early twentieth century did not emphasize litigation strategies, as courts were considered the most reactionary of governmental institutions. Liberal foundations' interest in the legal system increased enormously after the Second World War; courts became more sympathetic to "social engineering." They have several other advantages. Litigation is a safe, conservative outlet for activists; it does not entail mass mobilization; and it does not jeopardize a foundation's tax-exempt status. Furthermore, even failed litigation can absorb energies of hotbloods.

The major early foundation effort directed specifically at the legal system was support (by the Rockefeller Foundation and Carnegie Corporation) of the American Law Institute for its restatement of the law. This was begun in the 1920s to promote uniformity of all states' laws, aiding in the rationalization and centralization of our political system.

In the 1950s, courts seemed amenable to the promotion of social reform. The successful litigation in *Brown v. Board of Education*, supported by foundations, indicated that the Supreme Court might play a progressive role. Subsequently, the Ford Foundation created programs and institutes to reform nearly every aspect of the legal system; other foundations participated in specific policy areas.

These efforts served the general foundation goal of both promoting and controlling social change. A major aim was to reduce racial tensions, which could produce domestic disruption. Furthermore, segregation was a diplomatic liability. It belied the pretensions of the United States as a "model" for the Third World, and it weakened our Cold War armory.

A second need was to combat domestic communist sympathies without destroying the civil liberties of innocent (i.e., noncommunist) U.S. citizens. This was the major purpose of the Ford Foundation spin-off, the Fund for the Republic. Nevertheless, at the suggestion of the Ford Foundation, the CIA collaborated with the New York City and other police departments in intelligence operations.[2] Another objective was to remedy the criminal "justice" system, which hardly existed in certain areas, especially for minorities. The Communist Party had been "capitalizing" on the mistreatment of blacks, as in its intervention in the "Scottsboro Boys" case.

By focusing their efforts on "rights," the foundations bolstered their prevailing ideology, which argued that our major social problems exist because disadvantaged groups are underrepresented in normal political processes. Blacks, women, Chicanos, gays, environmentalists, consumers, and the poor are all examples of the disadvantaged. They are different and do not carry weight in the system. There is nothing wrong with the system that representation cannot cure, and there is no link between various disadvantaged minorities. Poverty is merely another peculiar circumstance in which some people happen to find themselves. In sum, the Foundation-supported efforts at legal reform aimed to remove glaring inequalities, but ". . . will not disturb the basic political and economic organization of modern American society."[3]

Foundations influenced the climate of elite opinion through conferences, publications, grants, and the co-optation of ambitious intellectuals. More specific channels of legal influence included social science research; the creation or major support of research institutes, think tanks, and public interest organizations; new programs in legal education, especially the clinical education movement; law reviews; legal aid; and public interest law firms.

Also there was considerable direct contact between judges and foundations. Judges were board members and/or their freight was paid to foundation conferences. Justice William Douglas was a frequent conferee as well as a director of the Fund for the Republic, Justice Robert Jackson was a trustee of the Twentieth Century Fund, and Justice Warren Burger conferred at the Aspen Institute in 1976.

Public interest law has been a route to a Supreme Court appointment; Justice Louis Brandeis was an early example. Justice Thurgood Marshall was integrated into the national elite because of his leadership on the National Association for the Advancement of Colored People-Legal Defense and Educational Fund (NAACP-LDEF) team for *Brown v. Board of Education*. Similarly, Justice Ruth Bader Ginsburg had headed the litigation strategy of the Women's Rights Project. Their ties and sympathies with the principles animating public interest law, and with its foundation sponsors, do not disappear after they mount the bench. Supreme Court justices retain considerable freedom to interact with foundations; similar entanglements with partisan politics or corporations would be regarded as improper.

SOCIAL SCIENCE RESEARCH

Modern social science research has been almost entirely funded by foundations (see chapter 3). Two examples are especially relevant for litigation strategies. Gunnar Myrdal's *An American Dilemma* was sponsored by the Carnegie Corporation. Like most works of social science, it is both empirical and normative. The message of Myrdal's book is that not only does justice demand an end to segregation, but both national and international security will be threatened by the continued suppression of blacks. The plaintiffs' briefs in *Brown v. Board of Education* and the Court's opinion cite this work; it has been regarded as a powerful argument for the decision. In another area, the Twentieth Century Fund sponsored a major study of legislative reapportionment. It was intended to influence the Court to adopt the principle of one-man, one-vote, and to prepare public opinion for the acceptance of such a decision.

Foundations (especially the Fund for the Republic, the Twentieth Century Fund, and the Ford and Sage foundations) also have sponsored research in civil rights and liberties, criminal justice, corporations, unions, public opinion, and religion—every aspect of our economy, politics, and society. Most of the "classic" studies that have shaped the post–1945 mind have been aided and abetted by the funds. It might be instructive to compile a bibliography of nonfoundation-supported research and journals.

RESEARCH INSTITUTES

Research that provides ammunition for social change through litigation or otherwise is generally funded through foundation-created institutes. In the 1927 case of *Buck v. Bell,* the U.S. Supreme Court upheld the sterilization of an allegedly feeble-minded woman, relying on studies produced at the Cold Spring Eugenics Record Office, a Carnegie Institute of Washington think tank. The Sage Foundation financed the "Brandeis briefs" prepared by the National Consumers League, advocating federal regulation of women's hours of labor. The American Law Institute, mentioned previously, promoted centralization and uniformity in state laws, which facilitated the Supreme Court's pronouncements on state legislation, as in the abortion and criminal justice cases. Institutes sometimes initiated or joined in the litigation through amicus briefs.

> In a study of briefs and opinions in over 200 United States Supreme Court cases decided from 1954–1974, it was found that over 40% of the citations to social science works in the briefs were in amicus briefs, as opposed to the parties' briefs, and that the Court was as likely to cite the works mentioned in amicus briefs as those in the parties' briefs.[4]

The boundaries between research institutes and public interest advocacy organizations are fluid, but these distinctions are not important for this work. All of these organizations seek to influence public policy, and all are supported by foundations.[5] Examples of the channel to Supreme Court decision making include the Metropolitan Applied Research Center, headed by Kenneth Clark, which provided busing and school integration studies to litigants, and the National Municipal League, which produced extensive studies on reapportionment. Ford- and Rockefeller-supported Planned Parenthood organizations were involved as litigants in abortion cases. The Education Law Center (Ford) and the Education Finance Reform Project (Carnegie) produced data in support of equal school financing litigation, which lost in the Supreme Court but won significant victories in state courts. The Fund for the Republic dominated the liberal side of the civil liberties debate in the 1950s and 1960s and even contributed funds to support Senator Hennings's Subcommittee on Constitutional Rights. Foundations give grants to government when they want a specific job done; this is not a prohibited activity.

In the criminal justice field, the Vera Institute and the Police Foundation are two among many Ford-sponsored research arms. They promote procedural due process, along with greater centralization and coordination among police forces, the FBI, and the CIA. The Police Foundation was the model for the federal Law Enforcement Assistance Administration. Research directly sponsored by the Ford Foundation and funds granted through the American Bar Foundation in the mid-1950s led to five volumes on detection, arrest, prosecution, conviction, and sentencing. This was the first comprehensive study of the criminal justice system since the Wickersham Commission (1931), which had been cited in *Miranda v. Arizona.*

LEGAL EDUCATION

Erwin Griswold attributed nearly all innovations in legal education since the Second World War to the foundations.[6] The most significant development has been that of clinical legal education, with its network of institutes and policy-oriented law reviews. In 1957, the Ford Foundation began funding

> . . . a national series of experiments exposing law students to "social practice" through internships with welfare agencies, police departments, prosecutors' offices, lower courts, and civil rights groups. The program was institutionalized in 1959 in the National Council on Legal Clinics, assisted with Ford grants totaling $1,750,000.[7]

This later became the Council on Legal Education for Professional Responsibility, for which Ford had granted $10.9 million by 1979.

> By the 1970–1971 school year, 100 law schools were administering 204 clinical programs in fourteen different fields of law. In the next five years the clinical movement swelled so that by 1975–1976, CLEPR could conservatively estimate that slightly more than 90% of the American Bar Association-approved law schools provided some form of credit-granting clinical education.[8]

Law school institutes taught and researched advocacy and law reform in civil rights and liberties; poverty, environmental, women's rights, consumer, and school finance law; and criminal justice. Some examples are the Center on Social Welfare Policy and Law at Columbia Law School, the Institute for Criminal Law and Procedure at Georgetown, and the Center for Studies in Criminal Justice at the University of Chicago. Among the law reviews founded and funded were *Law and Society* at Northwestern (grant from Sage Foundation), Vanderbilt's *Race Relations Law Reporter* (Ford), the *Columbia Journal of Environmental Law* (Ford), and the *Harvard Civil Rights Civil Liberties Law Review* (several foundations).

Foundation money created these institutes and journals; their maintenance was sometimes later absorbed into the regular budget of the host institution. This gives the foundations even more power: they are then free to use their assets to innovate elsewhere. Obviously law students and professors wanted these new programs; they were in the "spirit of the times." But that "spirit" was in many ways shaped by the networks directed and financed by foundations.

Clinical legal education affects Supreme Court decision making in several ways. Judges in the Warren Court era were mostly too old to have experienced it directly but became aware of it through law reviews and contacts with law professors. Law review articles, including students' work, are cited in Court opinions. Scholars have found many influences outside of case materials that are not cited.[9] The law clerks at the Supreme Court, said by Rehnquist to be mostly "leftists," are really just full of the latest thing. ". . . [T]he clerks . . . are a conduit from the law schools to the Court. They bring with them . . . the intellectual atmosphere from which they are newly come."[10]

The latest thing in the law schools (from the 1950s to the 1970s) was to find some new right to be achieved by constitutional litigation. For example, Joel Klein, Justice Powell's new clerk in 1974, had been at Stanford's Center for Advanced Study in the Behavioral Sciences and at the ACLU's Mental Health Law Project.[11] He presumably would be familiar with the concept that mental patients should be subjects of special rights (e.g., to treatment) under the equal protection clause of the Fourteenth Amendment.

The Court was receptive to many of these assertions: the right to equal legislative representation, the right to integrated education, the right to privacy, and the right to counsel at pre-trial proceedings, although it rejected others (e.g., the right to equally funded education and the right to welfare). Nevertheless, all of these claims could appear as reasonable subjects for litigation; the public, especially elite opinion, had been prepared. Furthermore, the Court expanded the concept of standing and thus encouraged these suits. At another time, none of these claims might have been given a day in court. The "backgrounds" of the justices do not explain why they entertained an expanded notion of what the Constitution demands. It can, however, be accounted for by the "climate of the times," created by the foundation network of think thanks, research institutes, and legal education and practice innovations.

A major link between legal education and Supreme Court decision making was the accelerated development of public interest law. Legal clinics and law school institutes acted as "feeders" to public interest law firms. Students also were directly involved in litigation; the in-school institutes and public interest firms often were interconnected. Furthermore, such organizations as the Law Students Civil Rights Research Council of Washington, D.C. (supported by the Rockefeller Brothers Fund, among others) provided student assistants for lawyers in the civil rights movement.

PUBLIC INTEREST LAW

Public interest law, which is almost entirely a creation of the foundations, helped shape the agenda of the Supreme Court. Its goals, according to the Ford Foundation, are:

[t]o advance necessary social change constructively. It seeks to demonstrate that representation of the underrepresented in legal actions affecting class or general public interests is both feasible and socially useful, that public interest advocacy will improve the performance of administrative agencies, and that public confidence in the process of law will be strengthened by opening up traditional procedures to deal with new, legitimate grievances."[12]

Public interest law (PIL) is premised on the policy-making role of the courts: "Public Interest Law has been a response to the problem that policy formulation in our society is too often a one-sided affair—a process in which only the voices of the economically or politically powerful are heard."[13] Enter the foundations, and it becomes a one-and-a-half-sided affair: elitism masquerading as pluralism.

PIL was modeled after the NAACP-LDEF. That organization and the ACLU now receive crucial support from foundations, although they still have dues-paying members.[14] The following organizations were either created or vitally sustained by the Ford Foundation between 1967 and 1975:

> Center for National Policy Review; Lawyers Committee for Civil Rights under Law; Legal Action Center; Mexican-American Legal Defense and Education Fund; NAACP-LDEF; National Committee against Discrimination in Housing; Native American Rights Fund; Puerto Rican LDEF; Women's Law Fund; Women's Rights Project; Natural Resources Defense Council; Center for Law and Social Policy; Center for Law in the Public Interest; Citizen's Communications Center; Education Law Center; Environmental Defense Fund; Institute for Public Interest Representation; International Project; League of Women Voters Education Fund; Legal Action Center; Public Advocates; Sierra Club Legal Defense Fund; Research Center for the Defense of Public Interests (Bogota, Colombia)

Foundations such as Carnegie, the Rockefeller Brothers Fund, and Clark also contributed, but Ford's share was preponderant. Naturally, control also was exerted: ". . . each firm's board of trustees stays in close touch with the foundation's declared policies on public interest law."[15] A foundation-created holding agency, the Council for Public Interest Law, reported that some firms lose funding if their activities threaten the interests of the foundations: "For example, an environmental law center is convinced that it failed to secure the renewal of a grant from a major foundation because of a suit it filed to prevent clearcutting in a national forest."[16]

The firms intervene in administrative proceedings as well as litigate and enter cases as amici. In certain cases, legal fees are awarded to successful plaintiffs; nevertheless, the foundations provide the essential support. Ralph Nader and his public interest groups have collaborated and coordinated efforts with the foundation-supported public interest law organizations, and foundations have increasingly supported Nader's work.[17]

The motives of the foundations in backing legal reform stem from their long-range goals. Disorder and disruption in the 1960s and early 1970s—New Left, civil rights, anti-war and anti-nuke demonstrations, and urban riots—had to be channeled into safe reformist activities: "Foundation officials believed that the long-run stability of the representative policymaking system would be assured only if legitimate organizational channels could be provided for the frustration and anger being expressed in protests and outbreaks of political violence during this period."[18]

The "cold war" is not merely an international crusade; it has its domestic counterpart. Public interest law was an ideal channel for these radical energies: "Claims of legal rights envision a process of peaceful, orderly adjustment that can be confidently left in the hands of professionals."[19]

The clients who receive representation in this manner are passive onlookers; neither popular control nor political activity is fostered.[20] Elite interests are not threatened, as the outcome of even successful cases often is merely "symbolic reassurance." For example, the ACLU and other firms' litigation often aims at dramatic "breakthroughs" and neglects enforcement.[21] This approach supports foundation ideology by using courts to acquire rights for neglected "minorities"; it avoids looking at structural problems not amenable to these processes. PIL firms also are excellent arenas for the integration of activists and mainstream elites. The Lawyers' Committee for Civil Rights under Law (LCCRUL) has a black woman executive director, Barbara Arnwine. Its supporters include the Cravath, Swaine, and Moore law firm, the Colgate-Palmolive Company, and Time Warner. Among the lifetime trustees are Lloyd Cutler and Cyrus Vance.[22]

This model of assigning the definition of the public interest to law firms is currently being exported. For example, the Public Interest Law Initiative (PILI) in Transitional Societies, a program of the Ford and Soros foundations and Columbia Law School, is trying to create PIL in Central and Eastern Europe, Russia, and Central Asia. Its mission is to strengthen "the use of law as an instrument for addressing social issues in the name of the public interest."[23]

LEGAL AID

Legal aid is related to PIL, in that it seeks to provide representation for the underrepresented. Activist lawyers often move from representation of the poor in individual cases to class action suits challenging laws themselves. Normally, legal aid is merely supposed to help the poor get a fairer shake from the adversary system (whether in criminal or civil proceedings) and not attempt to change the laws; there are stipulations in government legal aid funding that attempt to prevent such expansion. In one area especially, legal aid promotes change in the rules: those relating to the circumstances under which defendants must be provided counsel.

The Ford and Rockefeller funds were poured into legal aid during the 1950s, well before the Supreme Court's "right to counsel" decree in 1963 (*Gideon v. Wainwright*, 372 U.S. 335). Between 1953 and 1972, the Ford Foundation alone gave $7.4 million to the National Legal Aid and Defender Association. The existence of legal aid and public defenders can induce courts to expand the rights to counsel, just as court-ordered expansion will create the need for legal aid. The accused get lawyers, and the lawyers get paid. This keeps everyone out of trouble.

SPECIFIC POLICY AREAS

Foundation ideology sustained and reinforced the trend on the postwar Supreme Court toward social engineering, derived from the Progressive movement as well as the sociological jurisprudence of Pound, Brandeis, and Cardozo.[24] The stream became a river, headed the way the foundation network sought. In at least three general ways, "landmark" court decisions furthered foundation aims: (1) The result-orientation of court decisions was a method of directing social change from above, (2) The centralizing tendencies of court decisions were a reflection of American Law Institute models for uniform state laws, and the ideology of foundation-supported public administration and planning organizations (National Municipal League, Regional Plan Association, American Society for Public Administration, International City Managers Association, National Planning Association), (3) The distinction between public and private was increasingly blurred.[25]

CIVIL LIBERTIES

In 1952, the Ford Foundation established the Fund for the Republic

> ... to assist the promotion of a national security based on freedom and justice. The fund would take into account: (a) The persistent Communist effort to penetrate and disrupt free nations; (b) The effects in international tensions on national security in the forms of hatred and suspicion; (c) The effects of shortsighted or irresponsible efforts to combat domestic Communism; (d) The need to better understand the spiritual and political significance of freedom and justice in the United States; (e) The need to rededicate ourselves to the vision of a free, just and unafraid America.[26]

The Fund was active until 1957, and in 1959 it was succeeded by the Center for the Study of Democratic Institutions. Its mission was the intelligent waging of the Cold War, without the McCarthyite excesses. Its methods included direct sponsorship of studies, for example, Samuel Stouffer's *Communism, Conformism, and Civil Liberties* (1955); Clinton Rossiter's series on communism in America; and John Cogley's report on blacklisting. It also made grants to a wide variety of organizations, from the New York City Bar Association for a study of loyalty-security programs, to the American Friends Service Committee for radio programs, to Senator Hennings's Subcommittee on Constitutional Rights. Awards were given to those "defending individual freedom" (e.g., $5,000 to Plymouth Quaker Meeting for retaining their librarian, Mary Knowles, who had refused to sign a loyalty oath). The Fund supplied pamphlets and books for study groups in schools, colleges, libraries, churches, and civic organizations. It supported legal defense through bar associations and the American Friends Service Committee. Altogether, $11 million was spent by the Fund for the Republic on civil rights as well as civil liberties issues.

The Fund dominated the liberal side of the civil liberties discussion. It promoted Stouffer's thesis that civil liberties were especially endangered by those who felt threatened by the "urban power structure."[27] McCarthy was said to represent the low-status, insecure, and uneducated people; while elites were the natural defenders of civil liberties.[28] The Fund maintained that people should not be *unjustly* accused of being communists; it had no interest in defending actual communists, or in serious discussion of communism—or capitalism.

The Supreme Court civil liberties decisions during the 1950s and 1960s closely followed the Fund for the Republic line. One of the Court's leading civil libertarians, Justice William Douglas, was a director of the Fund during this period. The worst excesses of congressional investigations were curtailed, and the Smith Act became unenforceable, although not found to be in conflict with the First Amendment (*Yates v. U.S.* 354 U.S. 298:1957). Procedural due process rather than freedom of speech was vindicated: "In *Watkins* (354 U.S. 178:1957), despite the stirring rhetoric of Chief Justice Warren's opinion, the actual decision was keyed to the technical requirement that the pertinency of the Committee's questions must be made clear to a witness if he is to be legally compelled to answer."[29]

Even these victories were symbolic in an important sense:

> ... By 1954 most voices of dissent had long been shackled. The Communist Party and the Progressive Party were in ruins, radical strength in the labor movement had been almost completely destroyed, opposition to American cold war foreign policies was practically unheard of, and suggestions of radical alternatives to the existing political and economic structure in America were almost equally rare.[30]

CIVIL RIGHTS

The foundations and their forerunners, the "industrial philanthropies," had long been interested in race issues. The Peabody Educational Fund (1867) and the Slater Fund (1881) attempted to shape Southern black education: "The General Education Board, established in 1902 by John D. Rockefeller, served as a clearinghouse for industrial philanthropy and disbursed grants to educational institutions and state departments of education."[31] The General Education Board (GEB) absorbed old and new foundations: the Peabody and Slater funds, the Jeanes Foundation, Phelps-Stokes, Julius Rosenwald, the Carnegie Corporation, and the Laura Spelman Rockefeller Memorial Fund. "The industrial philanthropists were more concerned with black education as a means to economic efficiency and political stability than with equal rights for southern blacks."[32] The NAACP (founded in 1909) represented a conservative, elite-led approach to racial integration and was aided during its formative years by the Rosenwald and Peabody funds. Its original anti-imperialist tendencies were gradually transformed as pragmatic gains seemed possible.[33] The early donors were joined by J. D. Rockefeller Jr., Edsel Ford, and the Garland Fund, among others. "By 1928, on the eve of the Depression, the NAACP had amassed a sufficient surplus of funds to invest part of its income in an impressive array of stocks and bonds."[34]

In the late 1930s, the racism of the white elite (e.g., the eugenic movement) was modified by a recognition of the need for racial integration. The Carnegie Corporation financed the massive study by Gunnar Myrdal, *An American Dilemma* (1944); Kenneth Clark, Otto Klineberg, Howard Odum, and many other researchers participated in the project. This work was a prime shaper of the postwar civil rights debate, as well as an authority cited in briefs, amici briefs, and opinion in *Brown v. Board of Education*. Justice Felix Frankfurter had been a member of the NAACP as well as the ACLU until he joined the Court; this may have mitigated his resistance to judicial policy making. Ford Foundation funding was critical: "Without the help Ford gave through the NAACP, the litigation which led to the United States Supreme Court's 1954 schools decision could not have been pursued."[35]

The Fund for the Republic originally had included race relations in its domain; Harry Ashmore's report, *The Negro and the Schools,* appeared on May 16, 1954, one day before the Brown decision. The urban disorders of the 1960s prompted the Ford Foundation to begin massively funding civil rights activism in 1967, when McGeorge Bundy became its president. Millions were given to a variety of civil rights organizations: the National Urban League ($17.8 million between 1966 and 1977); the Southern Regional Council ($8.6 million between 1953 and 1977); and open housing organizations ($11.3 million between 1961 and 1977). Grants for civil rights litigation amounted to $18 million, mostly for the NAACP and the NAACP-LDEF. The Ford-funded

Metropolitan Applied Research Center, headed by Kenneth Clark, produced equal educational opportunity research and provided ammunition for school integration and busing litigation.

Foundation-financed organizations have been active in all civil rights areas. The NAACP and the NAACP-LDEF "contributed to the landmark decision in *Griggs v. Duke Power Co.* (401 U.S. 424: 1971)," which found that irrelevant tests were a mask for employment discrimination.[36] Voting rights litigation was undertaken by Common Cause, with grants from the Stern Fund, and by the Lawyers' Committee for Civil Rights under Law, which also pursued affirmative action cases. The whole array of Mexican-American LDEF and cognate firms was supported by the Ford Foundation (see list *supra*). Ford was a pioneer in supporting women's rights litigation through the Women's Law Fund, NOW/LDEF, and other organizations. Gay and lesbian public interest law firms, along with traditional civil rights interveners, including the NAACP and the Mexican-American LDEF, filed amicus curiae briefs supporting Dale, the gay Boy Scout leader whose firing was upheld by the U.S. Supreme Court (120 S.CT. 2446: 2000).

CRIMINAL JUSTICE

After the Second World War (fought for freedom and democracy), it was apparent that "standards" of criminal "justice" in a number of states compared unfavorably with those in "backward" countries. In addition, the United Nations Universal Declaration of Human Rights (1948), enthusiastically supported by the U.S. delegation, imposed a moral obligation. Change was necessary to validate the U.S. claim that it was not only a civilized nation, but indeed the leader of civilization. Another problem was the persistent entrance of the U.S. Communist Party into ordinary criminal cases (especially those with black defendants, as in the Scottsboro case), illuminating prevailing inequities.

There was no major political party interest or effective pressure group for criminal justice. Furthermore, the restrictions of federalism meant that the situation could persist indefinitely. Although pluralist theory asserts that any interest can organize, poor minority criminal defendants, or those convicted without due process, did not have the resources, skills, or even mailing lists of each other. Here is where "social engineering" fills the bill. The Supreme Court was receptive to the reformers' initiatives, which resulted in unprecedented control by the federal government over state criminal justice procedures. In theory, the "due process" clause of the Fourteenth Amendment provides adequate justification for federal control over state criminal procedures and gives Congress the job of implementation. Nevertheless, the decisions announced in *Mapp v. Ohio* (367 U.S. 643: 1961)—exclusion of illegally seized evidence; *Gideon v. Wainwright* (372 U.S. 335: 1963)—right to counsel; and *Miranda v. Arizona* (384 U.S. 436: 1966)—right to remain silent—represented an enormous shift in the locus of power over state police processes.

It is to the credit of the Supreme Court that it recognized that the nation was in the midst of a social revolution before this became apparent to most of the elected representatives of the people, and that it sought to eliminate the basic defects in our system for the administration of criminal justice within our present structure. The result of this perceptive approach has been to immunize the Court from much of the alienation expressed against other institutions of our society, not only by the disadvantaged, but also by large numbers of our youth, upon whom the future of the nation depends.[37]

The American Law Institute's model codes made it easier for the Court to require standardized practices in the states. By the late 1960s, millions had been granted by Ford and other foundations for criminal justice studies. Support for legal aid ensured a good supply of criminal justice cases to the Supreme Court. The Police Foundation, the Vera Institute, the American Bar Foundation, and criminal justice institutes at many major law schools refined concepts of due process. Ford monies also were employed to improve the efficiency of police and criminal justice processes, through better equipment, computerization, and coordination of local and national police (e.g., encouraging CIA-NYC Police cooperation).[38] Another element shaping Supreme Court attitudes was the development of clinical legal education in criminal justice. The energies of brighter students were enlisted in this formerly disdained specialty when it developed a challenging constitutional dimension.

REAPPORTIONMENT

The reapportionment decisions also lacked a mass constituency, although politicians (generally Democratic) who felt underrepresented because of the usually rural "rotten boroughs" supported the litigation. Existing districting for legislatures (state and Congress) was criticized on two grounds. One, applied to state lower houses and the U.S. House of Representatives, found rural areas overrepresented. The legislatures produced by these obsolete allocations (as the rural population had greatly declined in the first half of the twentieth century) would not reapportion themselves out of their seats. A different problem was the basis for seats in the upper houses of state legislatures. Some states gave one or two seats to each town, county, or city, regardless of population, on the model of the U.S. Senate. The groundwork for challenging both of these deviations from "one-person, one-vote" was prepared by the National Municipal League (Ford- and Rockefeller-funded) and the Twentieth Century Fund. *New York Times* reporter Anthony Lewis, while a fellow of the Nieman Foundation at Harvard Law School, wrote an influential article for the *Harvard Law Review,* in which he argued that unequally drawn districts for legislatures violated the Fourteenth

Amendment guarantee of equal protection of the law.[39] Lewis subsequently was cited in the Supreme Court opinion, *Baker v. Carr* (369 U.S. 186: 1962), which asserted the Court's jurisdiction over malapportionment. The National Municipal League then received "emergency funds" from the Ford Foundation to work for a "one-man [sic], one-vote" ruling from the Supreme Court. The *Baker* case had triggered reapportionment litigation in state courts also, and the NML circulated the favorable rulings to create a persuasive body of legal opinion.

> The National Municipal League obtained, reproduced, and published opinions on all [state] cases and distributed them rapidly to litigants and defendants alike. The League learned of new cases through contacts it had in each state—universities, citizen groups, and lawyers. It wrote to court clerks in all states in which decisions were pending. Each opinion had to be duplicated on a special machine, since only an exact reproduction could be used as court evidence. As soon as there were enough cases, the League bound and published them. For a while, during the feverish period of 1962–65, the League each month brought out a 100- to 200-page volume, *Court Decisions on Legislative Apportionment*. Its availability was announced to a mailing list of 1,000, which included Federal judges, state attorneys general and legislators, interested lawyers, the U.S. Department of Justice, state research bureaus, and civic organizations such as the League of Women Voters. Today, there are thirty-two volumes totalling 6,122 pages.[40]

Other studies, such as the Twentieth Century Fund's *Reapportionment*, promoted the interpretation that the Constitution required "one-man, one-vote" in legislative districting.[41] It is puzzling why Chief Justice Warren believed that the reapportionment decisions were the most important of his tenure. Certainly they were an enormous generator of litigation, which still goes on. Politicians have been kept busy, and political scientists have been employed by the various foundation supported research-in-reapportionment institutes. Oddly, the rationale for the Court's decision in *Reynolds v. Sims* (377 U.S. 533:1964), "Legislators represent people, not trees or acres. Legislators are elected by voters, not farms or cities or economic interests," bore little relation to the mainstream pluralist ideology, which asserted that ordinary citizens are represented in the political process through group affiliations—not geographical constituency.

ABORTION

Organizations studying sex and birth control have all been offsprings of the foundations. In the 1950s, Rockefeller and Ford funded the Population Council, which conducted research into contraception and undertook a policy planning role. In addition, ". . . efforts were begun to restructure public opinion regarding population control through the use of the mass media."[42] In 1959, the American Law Institute published a draft model state abortion law which ". . . focused public opinion on the need for change, dramatized the issue, and aggregated support for new policies."[43] Throughout the 1960s and early 1970s, foundation money, sometimes specifically designated for abortion studies, was injected into Planned Parenthood local chapters. Litigation for the right to abortion was conducted by Planned Parenthood, the American Civil Liberties Union, and women's rights organizations, as well as a number of bodies oddly called the "James Madison Constitutional Law Institute." This fine name was borne by abortion litigation firms throughout the country; shy foundations could discreetly make their grants. An entry in the *Foundation Grants Index* of 1973 indicates that in 1972 the Rockefeller Foundation gave $50,000 to the James Madison Constitutional Law Institute of New York City for "population law."

Studies of Justice Blackmun's opinion in *Roe v. Wade* (410 U.S. 113: 1973) have indicated that judicial notice was liberally employed, and that "The Court based its opinion on only one school of thought."[44] The "school of thought" was that of the foundation-funded population policy-planning network.

POVERTY LAW

Poverty became a "problem" after Michael Harrington published *The Other America* in 1962.[45]

> Harrington, a socialist, while working on projects at the Center for the Study of Democratic Institutions, had become acutely aware of the submerged nation of the poor. Harrington wrote a book based on his findings—entitled *The Other America* at Cogley's suggestion—which caught the attention of President Kennedy and led to the planning of the "war on poverty," which was waged by Lyndon Johnson after Kennedy's assassination. Thus the Center study convinced these presidents that the nation's economic policies were not bringing benefits to millions of Americans.[46]

Poor people, in the foundation view of the world, were simply another disadvantaged group that needed more adequate representation. Accordingly, in 1963, Ford funded a community law office in New Haven, which later became the model for the Office of Economic Opportunity legal centers. In 1965, Ford money helped establish the Center on Social Welfare Law and Policy at Columbia Law School, which sought a landmark Supreme Court decision declaring welfare a right.[47] This did not happen, but the Center's efforts yielded some successes: the invalidation of "man in the house" laws (*King v. Smith*, 392 U.S. 309:

1968); the outlawing of residency requirements (*Shapiro v. Thompson*, 394 U.S. 618: 1969); and the requirement of due process before benefits were terminated (*Goldberg v. Kelly*, 397 U.S. 254: 1970).

SCHOOL FINANCE

Here is another instance in which foundation efforts did not result in the desired Supreme Court decision: that state toleration of unequally funded school districts violated equal protection of the laws. Nevertheless, state court victories achieved some of the objectives. The Carnegie Corporation and the Ford Foundation have spent many millions to litigate equal funding for school districts. Grants have been channeled through the Lawyers Committee for Civil Rights under Law, the National Urban Coalition, the League of Women Voters, the Massachusetts Advocacy Center, the National Conference of State Legislatures, Stanford University Law School, the University of California Law School at Berkeley, and other groups. Public Advocates, Inc., a California public interest law firm supported by Ford, ". . . became chief counsel in *Serrano v. Priest* after OEO funding ran out."[48] *Serrano* was a California Supreme Court decision holding that unequal school funding violated state constitutional requirements for equality (5 Cal3d 584: 1971). The decision influenced similar findings by courts in other states.

In 1974, the Ford Foundation established the Education Law Center to specialize in this type of litigation and the Foundation claimed that ". . . litigators partially supported with our funds have helped to win perhaps ten significant state school finance cases on state constitutional grounds."[49]

As with the reapportionment decisions, the school finance cases gave rise to a minor industry of lawyers, school finance experts, and other specialists. The "positive" results in the state cases also have had a centralizing and depoliticizing effect:

> Ford efforts to make school finance and the delivery of educational services more equitable have produced unanticipated outcomes. The emerging role of state educational bureaucracies in monitoring these reforms has increased their authority relative to that of local school districts. Consequently, it has become more difficult for parents and citizens to have a voice in school governance and policymaking on the local level.[50]

Thus we see that foundations have provided much of the substance of Supreme Court activism by their support for ideology promoting social engineering, law school innovations, social science data, and public interest law firms. Judicial activism can thus be regarded as a channel for elite demands developed through a "policy-formation" process.

There is a vast literature on the controversial issue of judicial activism; the following is but a footnote. We can ask: (1) Have the goals of the foundations been achieved? (2) What have been the costs of reform through litigation? Major changes were instituted when they coincided with elite interests (e.g., civil rights and abortion rights). Some scholars suggest that these might have come about without Court or foundation intervention. Reapportionment of legislatures has occurred, with little impact on policy.[51] There may have been some loss of identity for towns previously represented in upper houses of state legislatures. In the US Congress, rural communities have lost power, while the "farm bloc," after a temporary setback in 1996, prevails, regardless of numbers. Civil liberties have been defended by the Supreme Court at the same time that anti-communism has become normalized. Now the dominant ideology proclaims that in the United States and throughout the world, there are no communists, just disadvantaged people pragmatically seeking rights. Repression takes other forms, for example, military surveillance of protesters (upheld by the Supreme Court in *Laird v. Tatum* 408 U.S. 1:1972) or employer and social intolerance of dissent. Criminal justice reform has been substantial, yet just when we have devised the perfectly fair trial, plea bargaining has become the norm. Furthermore, high rates of incarceration, prison conditions, and the death penalty have again raised questions about whether the United States is a model leader of the "free world."

In some significant matters there have been no litigation efforts by the liberal foundations, including illegal wars overt and covert, and CIA-prohibited domestic activities. Perhaps a step in this direction has been made by the Ford Foundation, which provides support for the National Security Archives, a database of selected, declassified CIA documents.

Where the resolution of social ills presented a basic challenge to the system there were no landmark decisions (e.g., concerning the environment, consumers, or poverty). Environmentalists, consumers, and the poor are not simply disadvantaged minorities. They are not demanding integration into the system but a different allocation of resources.

Court victories have been won; the results often have been symbolic only. Organizations and lawyers have strong incentives to achieve dramatic declarations of rights. However, they receive few rewards from monitoring enforcement, which could practically affect the lives of ordinary people. "Symbolic reassurance" might well be an aim of the foundations, which seek to reduce ". . . the ranks of malcontents who constitute the seedbed for undemocratic ideologies."[52]

One foundation objective, to channel discontent into harmless waters, seems to have worked. The energies of protesters and radical leaders have been expended in litigation campaigns for rights. An eminent legal scholar, Arthur S. Miller, claims that this is precisely the function of judicial activism: "By helping to siphon off discontent and channel it into innocuous forms, the Court enables that [ruling] class to remain on top while giving up only the barest minimum necessary to quell disastrous social disorder."[53]

What have been the costs of reform through litigation? First, there has been an increase in centralization and depoliticization—government has been removed even farther from the people. Ironically, even reapportionment, which was supposed to strengthen state government, has had this effect, by shifting political power from legislatures and parties to bureaucrats, judges, and academic researchers who were henceforth engaged in drawing boundary lines determining the extent of "natural" communities, and so forth.[54] Studies of the impact of reapportionment have shown little effect on policy, even in those states where the most shocking malapportionment had existed.[55]

Litigation leaves little role for nonprofessionals, popular control of organizations, or political activity. Citizens may play a role by writing checks, but the decisions about what is important to challenge are made in law firms and think tanks supervised by hegemons. According to elite ideology, this is a good thing, as the masses are prone to authoritarianism.

CONSERVATIVE LITIGATION

Right-wing foundations have adopted the strategies of the liberals, but so far without much success in redefining the dominant ideologies. The Pacific Legal Foundation, created by the California Chamber of Commerce in 1973, inspired Coors, oil companies, and others to found "public" interest law firms, such as the Washington Legal Foundation, the National Legal Center for the Public Interest, and the Mountain States Legal Foundation.[56] These were closely allied with the Heritage Foundation and propelled James Watt, Ann Burford, and their allies into public office.

Their agendas include opposition to affirmative action and equal rights legislation. However, most efforts are expended to counter economic and environmental regulation; they are the legal arm of the "wise use" movement. A favored tactic has been to seek new court interpretations of the Fifth Amendment clause: "Nor shall private property be taken for public use, without just compensation." These law firms have tried to establish that any regulation (as it is likely to impose costs) is a "taking" and hence invalid unless there is full compensation. The courts have not supported this interpretation and have upheld the right to regulate. In practice, regulation often is lax, and penalties for violations are small, long-standing tendencies not attributable to this new "right wing."

Another conservative approach has been to seek court decisions that would establish local county control over federal lands. Yet "[t]he courts have dealt a serious blow to county supremacy groups by striking down ordinances that would have given counties the right to determine how public lands within their boundaries would be used."[57]

The conservative legal foundations also have tried to invalidate all rule-making authority of federal regulatory agencies. A recent case thwarted this attempt.

The American Trucking Association, supported by the Institute for Justice, the Cato Institute, and conservative philanthropies, had prevailed in the Court of Appeals against the EPA, claiming that its authority to set air quality standards was an unconstitutional delegation of legislative power by Congress. The Supreme Court reversed the decision, thereby upholding the general right of regulation, which would have become a practical impossibility if Congress had to specify every rule or standard.[58]

Conservative foundations, including Mellon, Bradley, Olin, and Smith Richardson, directly finance law school programs embodying the "Law and Economics" philosophy, which aims to make the "free market" the basis for all law and legal interpretation.[59] They also have picked up the tab for judges' attendance at law and economics seminars.

Despite these efforts, regulation remains an accepted principle, and judges and bureaucrats eviscerate it as usual. Whether reinforcing "symbolic reassurance" or permitting genuine amelioration at times, the consensus-building potential of Progressivism has been preserved. Over large areas of practice, there is little difference between "conservative" and "liberal" policies. However, democracy does not triumph when so much power resides in an unaccountable, elitist judiciary.

8

Social Change Organizations

> Mr. Rockefeller could find no better insurance for his hundreds of
> millions than to invest one of them in subsidizing all agencies that
> make for social change and progress.
> —Frank Walsh, "The Great Foundations"

Philanthropy suggests yet another explanation for the decline of the 1960s' and 1970s' protest movements. Radical activism often was transformed by grants and technical assistance from liberal foundations into fragmented and local organizations subject to elite control. Energies were channeled into safe, legalistic, bureaucratic and, occasionally, profit-making activities.

The pluralist view of the U.S. political system maintains that democracy is vindicated through the interest group process. Aggrieved minorities have simply to organize and put pressure on the system through lobbying, influencing public opinion, and electoral work. By forming coalitions and compromising, they most likely will gain some of their demands, at which point they can continue to work for further action.

Critics of the pluralist interpretation of U.S. politics argue that the system is not, as it is claimed, open to all interests, for the powerless rarely organize. They are deterred by lack of resources, the demands of everyday life, the rational calculation of cost and benefits, a culture of passivity, and/or a hegemonic ideology that prevents them from even recognizing their grievances.[1] Furthermore, they may have no way of knowing others similarly situated, as there are no mailing lists of poor defendants or abused children. In the rare cases when organizations of the powerless arise, their demands may never appear on the political agenda; alternatively, their few apparent victories often are "symbolic" only.[2] In the interest group process, as well as all others that contribute to policy determination, elite groups win whenever it is important to them.[3] On the national or local level, "business" is not just another group but part of the governing system.[4]

Those who criticize pluralist theory often note that organizations of the disadvantaged are rare and generally weak, yet they assume that such groups are autonomous in origin and development. Studies in resource mobilization theory suggest that, on the contrary, an organization's initiation and destiny are heavily dependent on resources. These may be mustered from membership, conscience constituency, corporations, unions, churches, foundations, and/or government.[5] Nevertheless, most social scientists view both the universe of groups and the universe of patrons in a highly individualistic, atomistic light. Here it is claimed that much that appears to be "pluralism" often is merely a mask. Citizen and grassroots groups are far less autonomous than is generally assumed and often are subject to elite control in their goals, structure, and activities.

Furthermore, their actual and potential sponsors are not an independent collection of "banks," each seeking to make an "investment" in a cause for its own idiosyncratic reasons. Support for citizen groups largely has been provided by an interlocking elite group of liberal foundations. Groups may begin with few outside resources, but those that survive tend to seek grants. In recent years, activists also have been supported by religious organizations and "alternative" foundations that attempt to promote radical change; these will be considered in the second half of this chapter. However, the liberal foundations exert strong influence on the entire universe of social movement donors, including not only the radical ones but also conservative and corporate funders.

These foundations and their allies want change to occur. As Progressives, they strive for rationalization, centralization, and bureaucratization in public policies. They have promoted many reforms to reduce threats to capitalism arising from our archaic and local traditions, such as segregation, police brutality, and dumping raw sewage into rivers. Their reformism contrasts with the right wing of the elite, which may stubbornly attempt to prevent all change. Nevertheless this does not put them on the "left," as they do not defer to the democratic process.

It sometimes is necessary to create "grassroots" organizations to generate adequate political pressure for change, or to overpower competing initiatives. Earlier Progressives helped destroy mass-based political organizations through city charter revision requiring "at-large" instead of "ward-based" city council elections. In a similar way, today's social engineers promote only the activism that they can control. A Ford Foundation executive has said:

> [W]e may feel that public policy is neither well formed nor well carried out, in which cases we try to support responsible critics despite the risk that they and the government may perceive each other as adversaries. We sometimes have supported institutions and individuals in an adver-

sary role (especially as they employ litigation and other active means short of lobbying and political campaigning) when we felt the public interest would be served.[6]

When an organization such as Ford, with assets of approximately $15 billion, decides to throw its weight behind one cause rather than another, it is no small distortion of democracy.[7] This steering prevents threatening alternatives from appearing on the serious political agenda. Those who see our travails arising from corporate power and wealth gradually are excluded from political discourse; they are labeled "irresponsible," "unrealistic," and "unfundable." The kind of organization favored by foundations, the professional reform organization, is initiated, managed, and supported by elites and approaches "social problems not in terms of a political conflict of interests, but as amenable to the application of social-science knowledge and expertise."[8] A further instrument of control arises from the form that grant making assumes, for example, providing support for specific projects rather than organizational infrastructure.

One way that the liberal foundations can exercise hegemony in the philanthropy world is through peak organizations such as the Council on Foundations and Independent Sector. Alternative funders such as churches, unions, and social change foundations are tempted to join this resource-rich and legitimating mainstream. Co-funding, by alternative and liberal foundations, buys "a piece of the action."[9] For example, the Funding Exchange (a coalition of alternative foundations) received a $95,000 grant from the Ford Foundation for women's travel to the Nairobi United Nations Conference on Women.[10]

A relatively new development is corporate foundation sponsorship of activist groups. In the past, corporate philanthropy had been closely tied to either public relations (e.g., donating a skating rink to a city) or the propaganda needs of a particular industry (e.g., health institutes set up by tobacco companies). Today corporations are collaborating with liberal foundations to fund projects designed to save capitalism "in general." They give grants to citizen organizations, neighborhood activists, and institutions such as the Martin Luther King Jr. Center for Non-Violent Social Change. Frank Koch, a publicist for the Syntex Corporation (birth control pills), stated:

> An exciting new partnership is waiting to be established—a partnership among thousands of corporations all over the country and the hundreds of thousands of non-profit organizations, mostly operating on a community level, that have shown energy and initiative in dealing with pressing social problems.[11]

He later explained how his company gained influence with organizations concerned with family planning and women's health issues by financing and organizing workshops on women and health and suggesting speakers on birth control and related issues.

As might be expected, large institutions can easily dominate fledgling organizations led by volunteers. A foundation providing only 10 percent of a group's budget can nevertheless exert decisive control (as a minority shareholder of a corporation might), especially if the funds are for new initiatives. "Grassroots" organizations may have a considerable portion of their budget supplied by foundations, sometimes by a single one. Beginning in the late 1960s, both the ACLU and the NAACP-LDEF received crucial support from foundations.[12]

Grants are not the only way organizations are controlled; "technical assistance" is provided through centers, conferences, consultants, and publications (all financed by the liberal foundations). Unfunded groups also can be influenced as they design their projects and structure their organizations to qualify for grants. Even if they fail to receive any, groups may nevertheless proceed with other resources. Of course, organizations that do not seek grants may be able to retain their independence as long as they are self-funding.

Sponsors may influence citizen organizations' choice of leaders. The boards of citizen groups sometimes include foundation personnel and, in any case, must be attentive to sponsors' interests. Funding has created and sustained a universe of overlapping and competing social change organizations, resulting in the fragmentation of protest. Multiculturalism as an ideology reinforces this atomization. There is a well-observed tendency in the United States toward a multiplicity of associations; nevertheless, funding practices can encourage or discourage consolidation. In addition, "grassroots" organizations created by foundations add to the confusion. It is to the elite's advantage to be countered by a "mass movement" consisting of fragmented, segmented, local, and nonideological bureaucracies doing good works and, furthermore, being dependent on foundations for support. Diverse organizations emphasize differences among the disadvantaged: ethnic, racial, sexual, rural-urban, or age, and they discourage a broad left recognizing common interests.

Why support such organizations at all? Might it not be better if only the elite and its supporters were organized and the disaffected deprived of resources? This is not an optimal solution, for several reasons. First, the disadvantaged might organize anyway using their own resources, thereby making elite control difficult. Second, the existence of poor people's organizations legitimates the political system, even more so as they can obtain both material and symbolic benefits. The "trilateralists" warned that too much participation may stress democracies.[13] On the other hand, political withdrawal where there is considerable discontent can have a destabilizing effect.[14] Third, leaders of these groups, considered former or potential troublemakers, have status, salaried positions, and opportunities to be co-opted into government and private bureaucracies. There develops a mutual interest in the existence of many well-funded organizations. Much time and energy must be devoted to fund-raising and organizational maintenance, while goals both recede and become more aligned with the funders' ideology. Repeated interactions between activists and foundation executives, especially on elegant turf, can in itself create mellowing. Finally, elite sponsors see organizations as containment vessels. They fear violence because of the 1960s' protests and the persistence both in the United States and internationally of the oppressions that ignited them.

In 1969, McGeorge Bundy, president of the Ford Foundation, testified at a congressional hearing on foundations. He was asked why Ford supported radical organizations. He replied:

> [T]here is a very important proposition here that for institutions and organizations which are young and which are not fully shaped as to their direction it can make a great deal of difference as to the degree and way in which they develop if when they have a responsible and constructive proposal they can find support for it. If they cannot find such support, those within the organization who may be tempted to move in paths of disruption, discord and even violence, may be confirmed in their view that American society doesn't care about their needs. On the other hand, if they do have a good project constructively put forward, and they run it responsibly and they get help for it and it works, then those who feel that that kind of activity makes sense may be encouraged.[15]

We can see this pattern of patronage in the decline of the New Left and the associated radical protest movements of the 1960s and 1970s. This included the Students for a Democratic Society, the Student Nonviolent Coordinating Committee, the Southern Christian Leadership Conference, the Congress of Racial Equality, the Black Panther Party, Chicano and American Indian militants, the anti-Vietnam War coalition, poor people's organizations, confrontational-style neighborhood groups, environmental activists, and radical groups in health care and other professions. Anti-capitalist, anti-bureaucratic, and anti-imperialist ideologies were pervasive in these movements, although many activists were non-doctrinaire, and heterodoxy prevailed.

The observers and scholars of these movements have noted the decline in radicalism in general as well as the demise of particular groups.[16] Explanations are legion. Sidney Tarrow indicates that there are "cycles of contention"; here we seek some specific mechanisms.[17] For example, some point out that there were internal contradictions in the goals of the Students for a Democratic Society, and that it was unable to create an alliance with workers.[18] Movements, such as the Student Nonviolent Coordinating Committee, that sought redemptive goals rather than pragmatic gains found the going rough in the American political system.[19] Many of the activists were students who grew older and moved on to other things; others dropped out when they reached the stage of mortgages and babies. The harassment of activists, infiltration by informers and agents provocateurs, and other repression also took a heavy toll.[20]

In order to know what political groups are thinking and doing but also to prevent momentum from developing that would make repression much more costly, the police put people inside, not simply spying, but playing an active role—disrupting, discrediting, misdirecting, and neutralizing the state's opponents. . . .

FBI documents released under the Freedom of Information Act indicate that, in the 1960s, a bogus Black liberation organization in St. Louis was used to misdirect other Black organizations in the U.S. and, interestingly, to spy on Vietnamese revolutionaries.[21]

Some activists were lured into lotus-eating by drugs, wild sex, and the pleasures of consciousness transformation. For others, the conflict between making the revolution and trying to live an ordinary life was wearing.[22] Members of the elite, on the other hand, rarely experience conflict between the demands of daily life and helping to sustain the system. Commentators have emphasized the importance of the media and the availability of outside resources in the rise and decline of protest.[23] Some mention co-optation, and this will be given more attention later.

Another possibility is that the movements died because their objectives were achieved. There were some successes. The anti-war protest had been bolstered by draft opponents; its end may have reduced some activism. The military is now a high-tech opportunity arena, especially for minorities, and there is less dipping in "the big muddy." The Vietnam War ended. South Africa now has a multiracial government. Legal segregation in the United States is gone; middle-class blacks and other minorities participate in the affluent society, and minority politicians hold office on the national and local levels. Public and private institutions now hear the voices of the previously excluded (e.g., student trustees of universities, citizens' advisory boards, interveners in public utilities hearings, etc.). Women are miners, TV news anchors, and national security advisors. Environmental laws have been passed.

Yet how much has really changed? We are intervening against liberation movements and supporting dictatorships throughout the Third World. Current activities in several nations parallel aspects of our intervention in Vietnam; both counterinsurgency and "low intensity democracy" are foreign policy techniques.[24] Worldwide bombing and sanctions cause massive death and destruction and clearly violate treaty obligations, including the United Nations Charter.

Corporations, as well as government, have been shown to have poisoned and maimed workers, consumers, and communities beyond anything suspected by the radicals of the 1960s. Military bases at home, in the lands of our allies, and in our colonies are deserts of toxic pollution. Neighborhoods are being destroyed by neglect or gentrification. Poverty and degradation are rampant in urban and rural ghettos. The "Harvest of Shame" semi-slave conditions of migrant farm workers pervade every agricultural region.

Militarization has spread throughout society by "defense" contracts, the political influence of the military and retirees, limited civilian opportunities for many youths, propaganda use of the space program (especially involving school-children), and the intensification of jingoistic celebrations. Inner-city and suburban youth violence is rampant, fueled by violent electronic media and handy access to guns. "Participatory" democracy and a society based on peace, love, and justice are barely aspirations any more.

The 1960s seem like almost a golden age from today's perspective! Protest activity is not a direct function of deprivation, as many scholars have discovered.[25] A decline in radicalism, in addition to the reasons cited above, may be attributed to elite manipulation and the co-optation of radical movements.

Almost all foundations serve in some way to sustain the system; here we will concentrate on the work of the large liberal foundations (principally, Ford, Carnegie, and Rockefeller) in promoting and channeling reform by funding social change organizations. For example, in its *Report* of 1949, the Ford Foundation pledged to use its vast resources to promote democracy and fight the challenge of communism, which could find a seedbed in "maladjusted individuals, lack of political participation and intergroup [i.e., racial] hostilities." By the late 1960s, Howard Dressner, secretary of the Ford Foundation, reiterated the role of the elite:

> American society is being strained at one extreme by those who would destroy what they oppose or do not understand, and at the other by forces that would repress variety and punish dissent. We are in great need of more—not fewer—instruments for necessary social change under law, for ready, informed response to deep-seated problems without chaos, for accommodation of a variety of views without deafening anarchy. Foundations have served as such an instrument.[26]

The foundations fostered genuine reforms. The Carnegie Corporation sponsored the extensive study of U.S. race relations by Gunnar Myrdal, published as *An American Dilemma;* many foundations supported civil rights measures and major improvements in the criminal justice system. Policy innovations, as in the earlier period, were proposed by "buffer organizations," such as the Metropolitan Applied Research Center, or litigation firms, such as the Mexican-American Legal Defense and Education Fund. This method had the advantage of avoiding mass mobilization while engaging radical leaders in research, managerial, and legalistic activities. Foundation ideology considered radical protests as symptoms of defects in pluralism. Disadvantaged groups, such as blacks, Chicanos, women, children, and the poor, needed help obtaining their rights. Grant money and technical assistance would enable them to participate in the interest group process, and then they would no longer waste their energies in futile, disruptive actions. The poor were considered just another minority group. "Troubles" were not to be linked, and organizations and movements that found systemic causes for poverty, military intervention, racism, and environmental degradation would be ignored, transformed, or destroyed.

The universe of organizations has been influenced in a number of ways. Moderate organizations were generously funded. This gave them legitimacy as well as resources; their constituencies gained benefits, and leaders attained salaried positions. Some generally moderate groups may have had radical factions; by funding certain projects rather than others, donors threw their weight behind the more moderate tendency. Various stipulations, formal and informal, could be attached to the grant. Foundation trustees who were board members of funded organizations could keep a close eye on activities.[27]

To ensure that there would be an adequate number of attractive, well-funded moderate organizations enlisted in the appropriate causes, foundations also created organizations that appeared to be of "grassroots" origin. For example, the Ford Foundation started the Puerto Rican Legal Defense and Education Fund, the Women's Law Fund, the Environmental Defense Fund, the Natural Resources Defense Council, and many others. Sometimes these "paralleled" radical groups, such as Central American solidarity or nuclear disarmament organizations. In addition, "umbrella" organizations were created (e.g., the Youth Project, the Center for Community Change) that provided integrative services and technical assistance to the frontline groups. They emphasized that with the right managerial or legal techniques, benefits could be gained from the system.

The liberal foundations (and even some corporations) sometimes funded radical organizations as part of a transformative strategy, and they thereby muted the criticisms of the left. When they were criticized by the right for aiding these strange bedfellows, the foundation spokespeople explained how useful it was to have a "piece of the action." Bob Nichol, a consultant to foundations, advised: "Prepare your boards. . . . You're moving into a new funding arena. These are people dealing with social change. . . . It is buying into a movement," which is "what America is all about."[28]

Groups genuinely independent of elite control are to be feared. Consequently, *Foundation News* articles emphasized how important it was to co-fund projects sponsored by alternative foundations and religious organizations, and that the wildest appearing groups were essentially pragmatic.[29] Ignore their rhetoric; all they want is to obtain benefits or their "rights" from the system.[30]

"Leadership training" is another project of foundations that sought to tame radical protests. Here influence was exerted not on specific organizations but on activists and potential leaders. Domestic programs paralleled foundation and CIA Cold War efforts to identify activists in the Third World, preferably at the high school level, and to capture them for our side, through conferences, scholarships, and extended stays in the United States. For example, the CIA channeled $1 million through the Kaplan Fund to an institute training political leaders for the democratic left in Costa Rica and in the Dominican Republic.[31] The

Parvin Foundation, which came into the spotlight because of its questionable connection to Justice William Douglas, had a similar mission: saving young Latin American activists for capitalism.

A related steering mechanism can be seen in the domestic programs that direct politically conscious young people into the appropriate forms of activity: model Congresses, internships in the major parties, and even foundation-funded American Political Science Association programs. Basically, the lure of these programs is that they are well funded; "alternative" service can rarely offer comparable internships, travel, publicity, and the prospect of paid employment.

The turmoil of the 1960s increased the number and sophistication of foundation leadership programs. These sought to identify militants from various ghettos and to persuade them that responsible leadership means giving up the idea that the power structure should be changed. They must instead be taught how to obtain "tools" to improve the quality of life in their domain. Typical was the Leadership Development Program of the Ford Foundation, which spent more than $11 million between 1967 and 1975 to develop new rural leaders.[32] Generous grants allowed 700 fellows to pursue projects of their choice while acquiring the means to function better within the system (e.g., learning how to testify at congressional hearings, to apply for grants, and to use videotape to publicize their cause). Most were tamed, and after leaving the program, they found their personal careers enhanced; in addition, good works with concrete results (e.g., local clinics) did occur.

A useful discovery made by Ford was that middle-class radicals (sometimes involved in the training operations) tended to be intractable and saw "the system" and not merely the lack of tools as the enemy.[33] The program then increased its efforts to concentrate on recruits from poor backgrounds who would be initiated into the ways of the world by solid, system-supportive bureaucrats.

Since 1967, hundreds of millions of dollars have been invested by foundations, corporations, and government in "Community Development Corporations" that have as one of their objectives the development of leadership in minority communities. From these programs came models of responsible leadership, demonstrating that the system works. These leaders included W. Wilson Goode, mayor of Philadelphia, Franklin Thomas, president of the Ford Foundation, and Jesse Jackson, presidential candidate. This also relates to the transformation of "black power" into black capitalism, described in chapter 4.

Elite hegemony was exercised through the foundations' technical assistance activities that affect grantees, organizations hoping for grants, and perhaps even those groups that choose to avoid foundation money. Assistance was available through peak organizations, such as the Council on Foundations, the National Committee for Responsive Philanthropy, Independent Sector, the Association of Black Foundation Executives, the New York Regional Association of Grant Makers, and Women and Foundations/Corporate Philanthropy; resource centers, such as the Grantsmanship Center in Los Angeles, the Foundation Center in New York, and foundation libraries located throughout the country; publications, such as *Foundation News* and *Grantsmanship Center News;* conferences sponsored by these entities; and satellite organizations created or "adopted" by foundations to aid and guide grantees (e.g., the Southern Regional Council, the Center for Community Change, the National Council of La Raza, and the Youth Project). In addition, individual foundations engage in varying amounts of technical assistance and sponsor conferences intended to be widely influential. Consultants to nonprofit and activist organizations also provide help with long-range goal setting, management, fund-raising, and the facilitation of meetings.

The techniques taught include the use of computers; fund-raising strategies; how to participate in legislative, judicial, and administrative processes of government; publicity; and building coalitions. An example of the latter follows:

> [T]he Ford Foundation will support activities to bring such groups together and to help them identify common concerns around which coalitions and joint efforts can be organized. For example, the Foundation may convene a planning group composed of representatives of civil rights organizations serving blacks, Hispanics, Native Americans, and women to develop a list of topics for discussion. Later, support may be provided for a series of meetings of these groups to discuss these topics in depth. Possible topics include occupational segregation, health care, political participation, and media portrayals of minorities, women, and immigrants. Foundation staff will also work with various coalition-building organizations to strengthen their effectiveness, encourage dissemination of information on common problems and crises, facilitate better coordination, and encourage joint projects.[34]

Examples of the transformative process will now be examined in more detail, by looking at civil rights, poor people's, and neighborhood organizations; the process is similar for foreign policy and environmental activism. Excellent detailed studies of the latter have been made by Brian Tokar and Mark Dowie.[35]

CIVIL RIGHTS ORGANIZATIONS

Foundations and corporations have from the outset had a deep interest in the civil rights movement as well as in black higher education. They favored the NAACP, with its concentration on litigation, leadership by an elite, rejection of mass mobilization, and assets invested in stocks and bonds. The litigation campaign that led to the Supreme Court's *Brown v. Board of Education* decision of 1954 was aided both by the Carnegie Corporation's underwriting of Gunnar Myrdal's *An American Dilemma* and by Ford Foundation support of the NAACP.

The growth of mass-based black protest in the postwar period created a problem for the elite, partly because there were communist ideas and organizers in the movement.[36] Activists were relating the liberation of blacks in the United States to the anti-imperialist movements of the Third World. The Communist Party line was that blacks were a "semicolony" in the United States; their deliverance would come not through integration but by joining the revolution spreading throughout the colonial world. These ideas even gained some currency within the NAACP; there were purges and repression during the McCarthy era to extirpate this virus. W. E. B. du Bois was expelled from the NAACP not only for his hostility to its capitalist sponsorship but also for supporting a petition to the United Nations condemning U.S. racism as a threat to international peace.[37]

There were close connections between the Rockefeller philanthropies and Martin Luther King Sr., but the rise of the Southern Christian Leadership Conference (SCLC), the Student Nonviolent Coordinating Committee (SNCC), and the Black Panthers portended movements independent of elite control. In the late 1960s, the combination of militant mobilization, protests, and riots in the ghettos spurred the foundation world into a more active role. The "black power" slogan, which emerged from the SNCC, was perceived as both enormously threatening and capable of deflection into harmless channels. Under the leadership of the Ford and Rockefeller foundations, the National Urban Coalition was created in 1967 to transform "black power" into black capitalism. Foundations donated $15.6 million in 1970 to moderate black organizations, mostly to the National Urban League, the NAACP, the NAACP-LDEF, and the Southern Regional Council.[38] In contrast, the total outside support of the SNCC was $25,000, and by 1972, the SNCC had disappeared. There were internal weaknesses; on the other hand, competing, well-funded, rival organizations reduced the pool of potential members.

CORE, an organization with strength in the northern ghettos, was the most radical group to receive significant funding. They endorsed the "black power" slogan; however, CORE leaders were amenable to interpretations that were not threatening to the elite.[39] The Ford Foundation's $175,000 voter registration grant to Cleveland CORE in 1967 helped elect Carl Stokes, the first black mayor of a major Northern city. Stokes then initiated job training programs for dropouts and encouraged black-owned local businesses. "Black power" was becoming increasingly acceptable to major American corporations, which financed black power conferences in Newark in 1967 and in Philadelphia in 1968.[40]

The SCLC, founded in 1957, received income both from church contributions and from elite funding, especially through the Rockefeller philanthropies, which had a close connection to M. L. King Sr. Despite its direct action tactics, the SCLC often was regarded as moderate by elites because of its religious connection, its philosophy of nonviolence, and its integrationist goals. The increased militancy and radicalism of M. L. King Jr. in the late 1960s were accompanied by a steady decline in the SCLC's outside income.[41] King had taken the forbidden step of linking the plight of the poor, black and white, with the struggle against unjust economic institutions, the Vietnam War, and the immiseration of people in the Third World.

After King's assassination, elites set about to sanitize his memory. In 1968, the Martin Luther King Jr. Center for Non-Violent Social Change was established in Atlanta.

> Its principal goal is to preserve and advance his unfinished work through teaching, interpreting, advocating, and promoting, nonviolently, the elimination of poverty, racism, violence and war in quest of the Beloved Community. The King Center envisions itself as being an agent for nonviolent social change.
>
> Its responsibilities, therefore, are catalytic in nature and made operational through research, development and testing of model or pilot programs which can impact upon improving the quality of life for all people. As a catalyst, the King Center focuses its resources and capacities on the provision of extensive training and educational services involving the dynamics of interpersonal, intergroup and interracial relations.[42]

The Center was financed by the liberal foundations as well as by the corporate foundations of Ford Motor Company (which contributed $1 million for its establishment), Atlantic Richfield, Levi Strauss, Xerox, Amoco, General Motors, John Deere, Heublein, Corning, Mobil, Western Electric, Proctor and Gamble, U.S. Steel, Monsanto, Johnson & Johnson, Morgan Guaranty Trust, Union Pacific, and Johnson's Wax.[43] It is officially a "complex" that has been declared a national historic district with National Park Service tours. Coretta Scott King, its first president, had a staff of sixty-two and an operating budget of $2 million. The Center maintains the King Library and Archives of the civil rights movement, a conference center, and a gift shop. Programs include a day care center, basic skills training for youth and adults, workshops on conflict resolution, cultural performances, housing rehabilitation, voter education, information on how to celebrate Dr. King's birthday, and similar innocuous fare. "The King Center's approach is to utilize the existing human service delivery systems of government and the private sector in carrying out its mission."[44] Two of its projects reflect a selective memory of King:

> The King Center works closely with the United States Department of Defense, the Armed Forces Chaplain's Board and others, on a variety of programs including its Chaplain's Program. The Center works directly with military chaplains on interracial, interpersonal, human relations and conflict resolution programs. The Center, through the Chaplain's

Program, jointly sponsors King Week Birthday Observance services at hundreds of military installations in the United States and overseas and provides technical support as requested.[45]

The King Center co-sponsors with the University of Georgia an annual Martin Luther King Jr. Lecture Series entitled, "The Free Enterprise System: An Agent for Nonviolent Social Change." The series provides representatives of the nation's basic institutions with a platform from which to respond to the needs of a nation undergoing rapid change and a world coming to grips with its destiny. The aim of the series is to translate thought into action and to improve the lives of all members of society. The lecture series began in 1983 and is now entering its second year of presentation.[46]

Meanwhile, other civil rights organizations, including the SCLC itself, found themselves in the shade of this dazzling complex. "Much of the criticism within the civil rights movement comes from leaders who say the center has monopolized resources that could have been spread among other organizations. This feeling is particularly strong within the Southern Christian Leadership Conference."[47]

Foundations also supported redistricting, voter education, and registration projects to encourage the election of moderate black officials. These often were financed through the Southern Regional Council, which received large grants from the Ford, Rockefeller, and Carnegie foundations. Political office enabled leaders to distribute genuine benefits to followers (e.g., in public services, jobs, health care, day care centers, etc.). There also were significant nonmaterial benefits, such as more respectful treatment of black citizens. Black officeholders served to legitimate the system while providing a channel for social mobility or national prominence. For many of the less successful, employment was found in crime or the military; for the least successful, in prison industries.

There are similar stories to tell of other minority movements. The Ford Foundation created the Mexican-American LDEF, the Native American Rights Fund, and the Puerto Rican LDEF, which like all public interest law activities tend to absorb the energies of activists and focus on incremental legal and bureaucratic remedies. The Southwest Council of La Raza and the National Council of La Raza (NCLR) were projects of the Ford Foundation, transforming and containing what were originally militant movements of Chicanos in the Southwest.[48] East Los Angeles was torn by riots, United Farm Workers were agitating, and similar militancy appeared in Colorado and in Texas.

Twenty years later, the grassroots activity consisted of community development activities on the Ford Foundation model: housing, local capitalists, and a franchise in McDonald's, financed by Ford, corporations, and government antipoverty programs. On the national level, the NCLR acted as an advocacy organization in the traditional interest group process. It "lacked a constituency, but was supported and validated by the Ford Foundation."[49] In the process, both on the local and national levels, steady rewards were offered to "pragmatic" activists who were acceptable to the minority group as well as to the dominant society. Reasonable people such as Gilbert R. Vasquez, president of the California Board of Accountancy, served as directors. The staff of the NCLR had opportunities to move into government positions and to serve on national task forces with groups such as the League of Women Voters, the American Association of Retired Persons, and the American Bar Association.

Foundations' work with Chicanos is a good example of the promotion of "identity politics." Some have claimed that "Hispanic" identity was a product of elite social engineering:

> MALDEF won its first major victory on behalf of Hispanics in *Serna v. Portales* (1972), a case that won Spanish-speaking children in New Mexico the right to bilingual education.
>
> MALDEF's efforts on behalf of bilingualism continued with its support for the 1974 Supreme Court Case, *Lau v. Nichols*, which forced school districts to remove language barriers that prohibited linguistic minorities from fully participating in public education. Working with the Court's definition of "linguistic minorities," MALDEF and other Hispanic groups took the final steps to institutionalize an "Hispanic" identity (as opposed to an assimilated Mexican-American one) and to gain recognition for Hispanics as a federally recognized minority by amending the Voting Rights Act of 1965.
>
> As a result of Ford Foundation money and direction, Hispanic activists had achieved the miraculous: status as a federal minority that previously hadn't existed.[50]

Now Hispanic activists could become absorbed in calculations regarding redistricting and proportionate shares of federal benefit programs. Elite financial activism has similarly channeled other minority groups by supporting or creating factions that focus on benefits and identity politics. The benefits have been considerable; on the other hand, in the process, militant groups have been repressed, defunded, or converted.

POOR PEOPLE'S ORGANIZATIONS

Poor people's organizations shared major concerns with civil rights and neighborhood organizations. Three examples will indicate styles of foundation penetration.

The Center for Community Change (CCC) was founded in 1968, absorbing an earlier organization, Citizens Crusade against Poverty (created by the Field Foundation and United Auto Workers). The CCC originated

with major Ford funding; today it is supported by many foundations and corporations, including Mobil, Chevron, Aetna, and Heinz. Its aim is to coordi-
nate all grassroots poverty organizations through technical assistance and
grants to local groups.

> If community groups are to survive and increase their capacity to serve
> their constituents, they will have to gain added leadership skills,
> become more competent and sophisticated in their approach to com-
> munity development, and find new strategies for tapping philan-
> thropic resources. They will require additional research and analytical
> tools, as well as good sources of information about public and private
> economic programs and the strategies that can improve the economy
> of their neighborhoods.
>   Organizational assistance . . . includes training an organization's
> board and staff; helping an organization develop strategies to broaden
> its constituency and leadership; and helping a group assess its needs, set
> goals and priorities, plan, budget, evaluate and improve its management
> and internal efficiency.[51]

The Community Development Corporation approach is favored, which means a
partnership among the poor, government, and corporations, with local businesspeople on the poverty organizations' boards. The phasing out of federal government welfare benefits has led to a "privatization" of welfare. The CCC consequently has persuaded groups that it is realistic, productive, and functional to
request grants from major corporations. In 1981, the CCC was one of fifty-two
organizations, including the Heritage Foundation and the National Association
of Manufacturers, sponsoring a conference on small business as a cure for
poverty.[52] The CCC's influence extends much further than its own budget, for it
helps organizations obtain grants and loans from all public and private sources.
It also sponsors special projects funded by others, many in the public policy field,
such as the Black Teenage Pregnancy Project and the Coalition on Block Grants
and Human Needs, and it serves as the fiscal agent for the National Committee
for Responsive Philanthropy and the Rural Coalition. It is not an exaggeration
to say that the CCC is a vast holding company in the "grassroots" poverty organization business. It performs good works, on the assumption that capitalism is
the cure for poverty. A participant in this evolution commented: "One day I was
an anti-poverty worker [in North Carolina]. The next day I discovered I was a
shopping mall developer."[53]
    Similar to the CCC but operating on a smaller scale was the Youth Project,
fostered by liberal foundations in the late 1960s "to assist young people working
with social action projects at the community level."[54] It provides seed funding and
technical assistance (e.g., management development programs) for grantees. Like
the CCC, it evaluates grantees for outside donors, acting as a broker between

activist groups and foundations. It continues with its technical assistance even after grants have ended. Among the groups sponsored have been some with radical goals, for example, opposition to U.S. militarism in Central America, or challenges to government nuclear programs. However, the majority of the grantees are engaged in unthreatening work (e.g., leadership development, community economic development, voter registration, etc.). Radicals are contained by being embedded in the larger network of "reasonable" organizations, represented by tiny groups operating on the local level, and helped to "devise realistic goals, formulate feasible strategies, and choose appropriate tactics."[55]

Another poverty organization, the National Association for the Southern Poor (NASP), was created by Donald Anderson, a former Capitol Hill lawyer.

> Black Belt counties . . . are organized into individual community action groups called Assemblies. Problems are dealt with on an individual basis. . . . A member of the community fills out a "problem" sheet and gives it to his conference representative. If the representative has no solution, it goes before the Assembly leadership or executive council, consisting of 10 to 12 chairmen assigned to different categories of problems, such as welfare, housing, health, education, employment, and so on. . . .
>
> The Rockefeller Foundation invested $350,000 in establishing an Assembly in Norfolk, Virginia, the first in a large city. According to Anderson, "Norfolk is a test. The Rockefeller Foundation feels that if the Assembly concept works in a city it could be a very important answer to urban poverty. So they've hired an anthropologist who's watching the organizing very closely."[56]

Anti-poverty initiatives are not limited to steering existing organizations or creating "grassroots" groups. Foundations have undertaken projects to correct the mistakes and omissions of the invisible hand, discussed in chapter 6.

NEIGHBORHOOD ORGANIZATIONS

Neighborhood organizations include many middle-class groups interested only in protecting their property values. However, the 1960s and 1970s saw a more disruptive neighborhood movement of the poor, which absorbed many former anti-war protesters and civil rights workers. It was supplied with an ideology, "neo-populism," here described by S. M. Miller, a former Ford Foundation official:

> One of the advantages of neo-populism is that it is a locally oriented, democratic alternative to centralized socialism. It departs from socialist

notions of increased statism and nationalization of industry that leave power in the hands of bureaucrats and politicians. In moving toward this alternative to nineteenth-century visions of socialism, neo-populism Americanizes radicalism by connecting radical efforts to the American past, to American values.[57]

To emphasize the nonthreatening nature of this orientation, Miller states that it has no clear goals, no economic program (other than consumer issues), and no national outlook. It emphasizes traditional values and institutions, decentralization, and personal transformation as a means to empowerment. Thus it was a safe movement for foundations to promote and colonize. One might expect an anticorporate bias from populists, but the foundation ideology gradually dissolved radical implications and claimed:

> Community organizations have essentially a pragmatic approach to their task. The members want to save what they have, win some improvements in services and opportunities, invent some new community resources, break down some barriers between them and the realization of the American Dream. As I have said on other occasions, no one shows more desire to reach for that Dream than poor people in our cities, and without such resources as community organizations no one is less likely to get there. Outsiders do no favors to such citizens by attributing to community organizations a more exotic politics that isn't there.[58]

In contrast, one historian remarked:

> [T]he original Populists would make it their first order of business to secure the major plank of their 1892 platform: measures to bring the nation's banking system under democratic influence. A populistic—that is, democratic—agenda for 1984 would deal with the fact that the financial "austerity" imposed on the developing world by the U.S.-dominated International Monetary Fund has become one of the most telling ingredients fueling revolutionary movements across the Southern half of the globe.[59]

The confrontational tactics of Saul Alinsky were not a major problem for the more farsighted corporate liberals. One militant group started in Chicago by Alinsky organizers was The Woodlawn Organization (TWO). It began in 1961, originally aiming at politicizing citizens and identifying sources of exploitation. Its first target was a citadel of "the third sector": the Rockefeller-founded University of Chicago, which wanted to expand into the Woodlawn community. Residents reacted by demanding some control over decisions affecting their lives.

Gradually, TWO became transformed into a social service agency, administering a variety of programs (e.g., Headstart, job training, and a drug abuse center), and it no longer sought its members' active participation. By 1971, it was peacefully coexisting with the power structure. Its director, Leon Finney, was at the same time the director of the local CDC, with a salary designated by the Ford Foundation.[60] The services and enterprises of TWO (it owned a supermarket and a movie theater) were increasingly financed by private foundations, as government funds diminished. It might be thought that this evolution was a measure of success, and that the technical assistance and leadership training had done just what the foundations claimed: enabled an organization to be effective. However, while there was no question that health care, housing, and other benefits had been provided to residents, in terms of the original objective, preserving the community, TWO was a failure. "In the meantime, the neighborhood was being burned down."[61] There were 1,600 fires in 1970, which were made to order for developers with their gentrification plans. The population of Woodlawn was 65,000 in 1967; by 1971, it was 35,000.

In regard to national elites and multinational corporations, TWO illustrates precisely powerlessness at the local level. Perhaps this is one reason foundation grants and technical assistance have nurtured neighborhood organizations and helped create networks, coalitions, and intermediaries (Citizen Action, Association of Community Organizations for Reform Now [ACORN], National Training and Information Center, Midwest Academy, and the like). Many of the early organizers considered themselves socialists; however, their public pronouncements became increasingly timid:

> Citizen Action's preliminary economic program was critical of military spending and corporate waste and called for higher incomes, an industrial policy and greater control over capital. But others within Citizen Action, including Hayden and . . . Ira Arlook have argued that the organization's program should focus more on growth and downplay confrontation with corporations in some instances.[62]

Gradually, these groups narrowed their issues. They were likely to protest against utility rate hikes, termination policies, and the siting of power plants rather than challenge the rationale for privately owned utilities. Organizations such as ACORN fought against toxic waste dumps, concerns that have become part of the current environmental justice movement, which is struggling to make a difference.

ENVIRONMENTAL GROUPS

Leading environmental organizations have either been created or vitally sustained by the foundations, for example, Resources for the Future, the Natural

Resources Defense Council, the Environmental Defense Fund, the Sierra Club Legal Defense Fund, and the Environmental Law Institute (funded also by Atlantic-Richfield, G.E., and other major corporations). Although environmental issues fueled the 1960s protests, such as pesticide toxicity dramatized by Rachel Carson's *Silent Spring,* organizing around these issues never attained the status of a mass movement (in terms of numbers or class).

Grassroots organizations also are supported by the liberal foundations. One conduit is the Environmental Grantmakers Association (EGA), which includes the major liberal foundations (e.g., Ford, Rockefeller, MacArthur, and Mott), along with conservative funders (e.g., Pew, Smith Richardson, Packard, and Hewlett). Among the many corporate foundations in this group, we might expect Ben and Jerry's and Patagonia, but also here are BankAmerica, Heinz, Merck, and Philip Morris.[63] The EGA has been increasing its environmental justice grants in recent years and, according to environmental sociologist Dan Faber, it has become a "terrain of struggle" between the more radical and traditional liberal grant makers.[64]

The transformation of environmental protest into "sustainable development" has been furthered by foundation-supported NGOs, think tanks, and UN conferences. The story will not be told here; it has been well described in several major works, including Mark Dowie's *Losing Ground* and Brian Tokar's *Earth for Sale.*

A small but significant anti-nuclear power movement arose in the 1970s and has not been welcomed, destroyed, or co-opted by the elite. In any case, the demise of nuclear energy probably would not threaten the continuation of corporate capitalism. In the meantime, the heat is removed from the general toxicity of the system.

FOREIGN POLICY GROUPS

Liberal foundations have spent heavily abroad to develop elites sympathetic to capitalism and the economic penetration of the Third World. The Carnegie Corporation has long supported many peace organizations. Foundations also have created and/or funded the major organizations that attempt to influence public opinion on foreign policy issues: the Council on Foreign Relations, the Foreign Policy Association, the Asia Society, the United Nations Association, the RAND Corporation, the Overseas Development Corporation, the Trilateral Commission, and others.

Foundations support anti-war organizations; by 1984, foundations contributed about one-third of the peace movement's income.[65] Most of it went to university and think tank research programs and to education for high school and college students. In funding grassroots organizations, foundations distinguish between "acceptable and unacceptable activism."[66]

The Rockefeller Family Fund, for example, made its first grant, $20,000, to a fledgling organization called Physicians for Social Responsibility in 1979. The money went to hire PSR's first executive director and to open its first office. In 1980 the Fund followed with $33,000 for the executive director's salary and the first test direct mail appeal. It was a classic example of "seed" money at work. PSR took root and flowered. Last year it reported 100 local chapters, 16,000 members, 30,000 supporters and an annual budget of $500,000. Moreover, its "establishment" credentials undoubtedly created a credibility that sped the growth of concern over the issue.[67]

This was a safe group to inject with funds as "the role of corporate profit-making in the arms race is a concern that receives little emphasis in PSR . . . activities."[68] This serves to remind us that the Carnegie Endowment for International Peace had a substantial brigade of war industry executives on its board of trustees.[69] Favored groups maintain a single issue focus, which:

[O]bscures many of the political and economic underpinnings of militarism. The profit motive leads corporations to develop and sell nuclear weapons, nuclear power, toxic chemicals, and fossil fuels. Third World nations and national minorities in the United States suffer underdevelopment and economic exploitation by multinational corporations. In support of corporate interests the U.S. government intervenes militarily with conventional weapons throughout the world, and U.S. military planners contemplate the use of theater nuclear weapons in such regional conflicts. Yet, from the respectable point of view, the complexities and interrelatedness of these issues are not a proper concern of the peace movement, since any deep analysis would call attention to the profound corporate contribution to the risk of nuclear war. Corporations and their affiliated philanthropies look favorably on peace groups that strictly limit their attention to nuclear war, no matter how unrealistic and misleading the single-issue focus may be.[70]

Groups formed primarily to protest against U.S. policy in the Third World tend to make the forbidden "link" between capitalism and imperialism. Consequently, foundations may attempt to fund them in the hopes of exercising control (e.g., grants from the Ford and MacArthur foundations to the North American Congress on Latin America). In addition, foundations create activist organizations that restrict their concerns to safe issues.

"Solidarity" groups, which relate the poverty and rebellions throughout Latin America to U.S. corporate penetration backed by overt and covert military action, are potentially challenging to the system. Foundations have attempted to counter this perspective by creating Americas Watch and many other human rights organizations. These regard the troubles arising from a lack of respect for human rights throughout Latin America. They hope to improve the situation by such means as bringing human rights violations to the attention of the media and international organizations and encouraging human rights groups throughout the hemisphere. The problem with this legal approach is that abuses are regarded as "deviations," even when a regime is using terror as an instrument of policy. With a similar rationale, the Ford Foundation established Asia Watch. Again, its emphasis on rescuing individuals obscures the causes of state repression, including training received through the benevolence of foreign aid. Amnesty International is also funded, a group that condemns torture but does not investigate the causes.

In the case of South Africa, foundations promoted activism based on opposition to apartheid, avoiding the issue of the monopolization of economic resources by the white minority (national and multinational). They created organizations promoting a legal approach, such as the Lawyers Committee for Civil Rights under Law, which provided legal aid to South Africans accused of violating apartheid laws. The Ford Foundation sought to educate all Black African leaders in exile, but it is not known whether this philanthropic endeavor actually was executed. (See chapter 9 for more about South Africa and foreign policy activism.)

Dissent and protest are rare enough in our society; it seems that the little that appears and survives is far more orchestrated than most would imagine. Those organizations of the powerless that are ideologically and tactically acceptable to the elite are generously funded and provided with technical assistance to keep them true to the path. Organizations that link racism, repression, imperialism, and militarism to the practices of corporate capitalism may be ignored and often atrophy from lack of resources and/or legitimation. An alternative tactic is to fund them for special projects in the hopes of weaning them away from their untoward obsessions and supporting their moderate factions. Those with no "reasonable" or "constructive" tendencies frequently have been eliminated through disruption by the FBI and the IRS, harassment of leaders, and/or violence.

"Grassroots" organizations may be less independent and atomistic than they appear to be; nevertheless, elite attempts at manipulation do not always succeed. There are groups that survive without being co-opted, some which have even accepted grants. Overall, however, co-optation of funded groups is common. Members of several different types of citizens' organizations have admitted to changing policies or staff because of donor pressure; it is likely that much more occurs than is acknowledged.[71] A more subtle process seems to be in effect: groups increasingly emphasize those projects that are fundable and those tactics and goals declared "effective" and "realistic." Members are attracted to groups with resources and deterred from groups that are ignored and/or repressed.

The very proliferation of organizations also serves the elite well, and funding policies encourage a multiplicity of small local organizations engaged in good works and providing many niches for ambitious leaders. At the same time, significant reforms and genuine empowerment have occurred. Furthermore, one can make no certain assumptions about what the current quality of life in the United States would be like had foundation intervention in social movements not occurred. What can be said with some certainty is that what is hailed as pluralism is often only a surface appearance.

SOCIAL CHANGE FOUNDATIONS

In addition to the liberal foundations, bent on reforms that will contain and channel social change, there are foundations dedicated to the promotion of radical change. How is this form of philanthropy faring?

Early twentieth-century radical funds give us a preview of contemporary dilemmas. The "Garland Fund," formally called the American Fund for Public Service, began in 1922; Charles Garland had inherited $1 million. As he was a radical anti-capitalist, he decided to use the money for left-wing organizing and created a foundation that would be administered by a board of trustees. It was not so strange that a millionaire's son would be a socialist; Marx had a grantee relationship with Engels, and Schumpeter warned capitalists to take precautions against such defections.

The Garland board included Roger Baldwin, Norman Thomas, William Z. Foster, Scott Nearing, Sidney Hillman, Morris Ernst, Freda Kirchwey, Louis Gannett, Elizabeth Gurley Flynn, and James Weldon Jones—a panorama of the left.

> Roger Baldwin and his hand-picked associates had been given an opportunity to decide what would best advance America toward a new social order. For reasons both internal and external, they did not take full advantage of that opportunity. Serious and effective strategies would have required a comprehensive social and political philosophy agreed to by a majority of the board, which actually had no strategy at all. Devotion to experimentalism made each proposal a new contender for counterhegemonic status and caused the directors to scatter their resources without giving each enterprise realistic funding or the time to become effective.[72]

The scatter-shot approach was not a consequence of ineptitude. There were, as implied earlier, divisions on the board, which made a "pluralist" approach to funding seem fair and natural. Second, although they created the Vanguard Press, they did not want to engage in "vanguardism" and attempt to direct the revolution from above. Counter-revolutionaries have no moral scruples about plotting, social engineering, or researching good strategies. Those whose aims include democratic restructuring often will feel obliged to await initiatives from the oppressed. For related reasons, Garland did not fund communist activities. The Communist Party was not only a "vanguard" movement, but it would have no truck with the "pluralism" represented on the Garland board.

The Fund subsidized many radical popular publications and created a left-wing news service, the Federated Press. Grants and loans went to the United Mine Workers, Brookwood Labor College, the NAACP, and the Brotherhood of Sleeping Car Porters. Workers' education was a primary interest. There were many barriers to socialist organizing during the 1920s. In addition to repression and racial and ethnic separatism, there were the distractions: "radio, movies, spectator sports, . . . celebrities . . . automobile . . . and installment payments."[73] Increasing home-ownership was another one; in addition to keeping up with the payments, there was the time required for storm windows, lawn mowing, and clearing gutters, and some who had finally achieved a couch were jolly well going to potato on it. Scott Nearing blamed the meager impact of the Garland Fund on philanthropy itself:

> Private philanthropy, even when it is directed with the best intentions, is not an answer to economic injustice. It may help tide an individual over emergencies, but subsidies to institutions make the subsidized satisfied with handouts, and eager to come back for more as soon as possible. The Garland Fund aimed to put left-of-center institutions "on their feet." What the grants did was make them permanent beggars from the Garland Fund and other foundations.[74]

Others have a more charitable view of the impact:

> Even if the assistance that the Fund gave to many of the organizations had no appreciable long-term consequences, it nevertheless demonstrates that a considerable number of leftists and militants continued to operate through radicalism's lean years. The Fund served as clearinghouse, rallying ground, and, in many instances, life support. Most significantly, however, the Fund's contributions to "Negro Work" and workers' education eventually produced important long-range changes in American society, most important, the end of *de jure* segregation and the initiation of industrial unionism in mass production industries.[75]

The Fund also contributed both to ameliorative measures and to the reduction of labor militancy; at the same time, it gave radicals the hope that the ground was being prepared for further struggle to change the system.[76]

Garland was liquidated in 1941; other early radical foundations, such as the Schwartzhaupt (which funded the Highlander Folk School), Stern, and Field foundations, were usually designed to spend out and terminate rather than become eternal entities. Social change philanthropy of the 1930s, 1940s, and 1950s had a clear target—destruction of the apartheid system. Most considered its mission "to empower disadvantaged groups in our society."[77] Its practitioners were emphatic that empowerment was different from traditional charity, which primarily served to maintain ruling classes. Yet it is not clear that these funds differed greatly in the methods and aims from those of the Carnegie, Rockefeller, and Ford foundations, which also sought to eliminate, not to relieve, poverty and discrimination.

Starting in the late 1960s, new foundations were created by civil rights, environmental, anti-war, anti-nuke, and anti-imperialist activists, many of whom were also anti-capitalist. These included regional funds, such as Haymarket, North Star, Crossroads, and others, which were to join in the Funding Exchange, and national foundations, such as Tides, Resist, and the Peace Development Fund. They usually arose from a core of inherited wealth and operated as public charities, supplementing their endowments with annual donations from rich and middle-class sympathizers. They were committed to funding grassroots activists and to including grantees in decision-making processes; Haymarket grant decisions were made by boards of activists. Church-based funds, such as the Catholic Bishops' Campaign for Human Development and the Unitarian Universalist Veatch Program, also were part of this burgeoning radical philanthropy. Almost all were dedicated to promoting social change.

This goal creates many problems. A major one is that it is not clear what social change entails; foundation statements do not describe objectives in much more detail than empowerment, rights, and justice. There are some good reasons for this imprecision.

First, even sociologists are not sure that there is any useful or accurate concept of social change; one president of the American Sociological Association expressed hopes that "catastrophe and chaos" theories would provide tools for studying social change.[78] Literature on this concept frequently relates only to the transformation from agrarian to commercial societies.

Second, while few in the alternative foundation network are Marxists, certain Marxist concepts still have strength among leftists. Marx and Engels predict in *The Communist Manifesto* that from the workers' unions for mutual aid, strike funds, and confrontation of employers there will develop a "national [political] struggle between classes." This may suggest to the social change philanthropists that grassroots organization and demands by oppressed and disadvantaged groups ultimately will create coalitions for radical change. This need not require a violent revolution. It could proceed the way the Fabian socialists suggested (and failed to implement): education and gradual legal restructuring that would eventually result in a total transformation.

The Haymarket People's Fund echoes this strategy:

> Haymarket helps people channel their money to groups that galvanize
> and empower their constituencies to work for progressive social, eco-

nomic, and political changes. . . . [E]ach victory won by a community group, a victory that transforms even in a small way the status quo, adds another link to the "chain of change" and renews people's energy and hope. To ensure that such victories are not reversed, change-oriented groups must address the problems inherent in the inequitable distribution of power and resources in our society.[79]

If groups have been steadily organizing and winning small victories, and no change has occurred, it could be that the theory is wrong, and that another tack must be taken. Perhaps Gramsci must be heeded and more attention must be given to the creation of a counterhegemonic movement. Another possibility is that it is too soon to know; major change has not occurred, but the seeds have been planted, and it is on the way. On the other hand, it may be that the Marxian idea is sound, except that those who wanted to prevent radical changes in power and wealth got there first and instituted measures to make sure that empowerment did not go too far. They heeded Gramsci by incorporating all new trends and disturbing elements and by turning rebels into honored intellectuals of the establishment.

Social change philanthropists have other disadvantages. The self-emancipation of the oppressed precludes utopian blueprints of the future. It also excludes paternalism or vanguardism (as the Garland board recognized), such as goal definition by donors or trustees. This makes it difficult to evaluate the impact of social change philanthropy by measurement against stated objectives. However, these philanthropists are in a bind; they do not have the freedom to engage in central planning. They also may hesitate to imitate a method used by the liberal foundations: creating "grassroots" organizations. Thus the Green Mountain Fund of Vermont has socialism as one of its goals, but it does not appear to fund any socialist organizations, probably because few exist that would seek or qualify for grants.

Another dilemma arises concerning the investment of funds; many alternative foundations have their assets in the stock market. This can lead to contradictions such as the following:

> The New York-based New World Foundation is one of the most prominent funders of progressive social activity in the country. . . . According to its IRS filings, the New World Foundation granted Silicon Valley Toxics [Coalition] $50,000 in 1992 and $50,000 more in 1993. At that time, New World also held stock in several Bay Area computer companies the toxics coalition had been fighting. . . . New World's other investments include companies such as Louisiana Pacific, Nike, Freeport-McMoRan, and Philip Morris—none of which is exactly a progressive-community darling.[80]

The Green Mountain Fund did not want to own any stocks and considered putting its endowment into affordable housing. While this is politically correct, it is not likely to promote socialism, or even activism (once people have the place to put the couch). Alternative foundations may have difficulty producing change because, often, they were not created to *counter* the effect of liberal philanthropy but to *supplement* it. Some claim that they will support the homeless, the disabled, the surveilled, and the transgendered: those disdained by other foundations. Thus with resources provided, which included not merely funds but also training in organizing, each would get rights. This approach again reinforces fragmentation and multiculturalism, setting a limit on change. It excludes the possibility that a better route to social change might be the creation of a national political party or movement, or funding a counterhegemonic cable TV channel. The political climate influences all, and this is especially the case because grantees operate in a universe where some organizations of the disadvantaged succeed in getting substantial grants from liberal foundations.

Thus for all of these reasons, alternative funds slide toward pluralism. Because of the diversity of boards, and the boards' opposition to vanguardism, the climate of opinion in our society, and the requests of grantees, it is easiest to provide groups with resources, directly for social services or for demanding compensatory measures from government. Yet this fits in with the ameliorative measures promoted by liberal foundations that allow the system to continue. Both the mission statements and the actual grants of the alternative funds seem to be moving toward the liberals.

The creation in 1978 of the National Network of Grantmakers "committed to social and economic justice" may have contributed to this isomorphism. Members included Haymarket, Kroc, Ford, Playboy, the Peace Development Fund, AT&T, the Appalachian Community Fund, Ben and Jerry's, the Rockefeller Brothers Fund, and the Avon Products Foundation. Large private foundations and corporate foundations dominate "social movement" philanthropy in terms of the amounts granted. One estimate finds that alternative foundations contribute only 2 percent to 3 percent, with movement-based public charities, such as the Ms. Foundation and Nader's Public Safety Research Institute, responsible for about 14 percent of grant money.[81] A further difficulty is inherent in the patronage relationship between donor and grantee. Some ardent supporters of movement philanthropy, echoing Scott Nearing, question whether democratic political action should be dependent in this way.

MEASURING SOCIAL CHANGE

Despite the fuzziness of the "social change" concept, we can suggest some ways that the impact of alternative foundations might be measured, using clues from the social movement literature. We could attempt to measure outcomes against stated goals. On the other hand:

While it is certainly true that social movements are rational efforts aiming at social change, their consequences are often unintended and are not always related to their demands. Furthermore, such unintentional consequences may be positive as well as negative for a given movement. . . . To identify the range of potential changes that movements can provoke unintentionally is a major task of research in this field.[82]

The "traditional" goals of social movements, as identified by William Gamson, are acceptance of the group and gain in benefits. To this must be added benefits for others, which constituted a large objective of the 1960s' movements: anti-imperialist, prisoners' rights, animal welfare, children's welfare, and anti-surveillance; or benefits for all: environmental and consumer rights and the democratization of the political system.

Goals might include difficult-to-measure effects on the lives of the participants (creating habits of participation or assertiveness or, alternatively, a predisposition to duck) or changes in the attitude or behavior of the general public. Encouragement or discouragement today easily crosses national boundaries.

Movements also leave political by-products that lie outside their programs and sometimes even contradict them: new police personnel and practices, the generation of rival movements and organizations; alterations in laws of assembly, association, and publicity; co-optation of activists and their organizations by governments or political parties; transformation of social movement organizations into pressure groups; the creation of legal precedents for subsequent challenges by other social movements.[83]

If we concentrate on the goals announced by alternative philanthropy, the outcomes have been discouraging. For example, the vision of the Funding Exchange, a network of alternative regional foundations, follows:

Of all the causes of social problems in the United States, from environmental damage to crimes, the most fundamental is the increasing disparity of wealth and power. A history of exploiting human and natural resources, along with the undue influence of wealth on our political system, perpetuates and strengthens a destructive dynamic within our country, and between the U.S. and the rest of the world.

We believe these conditions must be fundamentally changed in order to have true democratic economic justice and lasting peace. Through our funding, we seek the goal of a society characterized by:

• A more equitable distribution of wealth, resource, and political power both within and between national borders;

- The exercise of political power by historically disempowered peoples and communities;
- Placing the well-being of people and the environment above sheer profit and the accumulation of private wealth;
- A dedication to peace, justice, and internationalism;
- The affirmation of diversity; freedom from institutional and cultural discrimination, particularly those based on class, race, gender, sexual orientation, disability, or age, and respect for the dignity and inherent value of all individuals.[84]

Diversity and empowerment of the previously excluded clearly have increased in the last three decades. Not merely tokenism but also genuine inclusion in decision making, especially on the local level, are more likely today. The social change foundations have undoubtedly contributed to these effects, not only because of their grants and training but also because they goaded the more establishment funders into action on these fronts. To discover the extent of participation in decision making and how much it has changed would require more data. On the other hand, there has not been much progress in the more radical goals.

There is some evidence that funding organizations themselves have been transformed, often moving from system-challenging aims to more system-sustaining pluralism and multiculturalism. The Peace Development Fund (PDF) began in 1981 to support "grassroots groups around the country that focused on issues of antimilitarism, nuclear proliferation, and Cold War politics."[85] However:

> In the late '80s, PDF's focus changed considerably due to the shift in global politics that came with the end of the Cold War and the diversification of our staff and board. We began to think of peace not merely as the absence of war or militarism, but as the presence of equitable relationships among people, nations, and the environment. This new understanding of peace allowed PDF to take a social, environmental, and economic justice perspective in our work, a perspective we maintain today.[86]

The PDF emphasized its commitment to its activist grantees to support a democratic process that avoids "vanguardism." Now it funds the Native American Youth Association (NAYA) in Portland, Oregon:

> NAYA throws open many doors to draw children into the center according to their needs and interests. Tutoring, a hugely popular basketball program, and space "to hang" attract the kids. Staff members can then work intensively with them one-on-one through formal and informal counseling, a Native American Family Healing Circle that addresses domestic abuse, advocacy in the schools, and a vibrant Indian cultural program. A youth leadership development program focuses on

job development and community service, building skills for long-term community involvement. Some young people come to the center searching for their identities.[87]

This is certainly a worthy program, but it replicates a Ford Foundation model and leaves too few holding the peace bag. When, understandably following a democratic process, agendas are derived from the concerns of Native Americans and other low-income and minority communities, militarism may not seem a salient problem. On the contrary, the military not only employs but often enhances the status of the poor. It is not clear how this dilemma can be resolved. It seems to indicate that the "invisible hand" does not work in the nonprofit world; just because there is injustice does not mean that organizations will arise and persist to counter it.

The fragmentation of protest (originally promoted by the liberal foundations) makes the continuation of solidarity movements problematic, although the American Friends Service Committee, based in a strong, conscience community, remains dedicated to this work.

Another anti-militarism philanthropy is Resist, which began in 1967 to oppose the Vietnam War and to support draft resistance. Today, it describes itself as:

1. An activist foundation that strives for social change and works against injustice.
2. A grantmaker for groups defending the rights of lesbians and gay men, workers, women, the poor, native people, people of color, the disabled, and immigrants.
3. A different kind of funding organization seeking out groups that withstand reactionary government policies, corporate arrogance, and right-wing fanaticism through organizing, education, and action.[88]

Resist now funds Native American cultural programs, abortion rights, environmental concerns, gay rights, and the whole spectrum of progressive causes. However, it continues to award grants to the solidarity and anti-war movements, including such organizations as Mobilization for Survival, Fellowship of Reconciliation, Veterans for Peace, and Chiapas support groups. Clearly, some funds and organizations have maintained their radical heritage, but whether there are enough remaining to turn the tide may be in doubt.

PILOT STUDY OF SOCIAL CHANGE GROUPS

Systematic research is scarce on the social change effects of radical funding. In 1986, I undertook a small pilot study of groups that had received grants from the

Haymarket People's Fund (HPF) during its early days (1974 to 1978) to discover outcomes approximately a decade later. My status was participant-observer, as I was then a member of the Haymarket New Hampshire Funding Board, which also, at that time, included policy-making participation in Haymarket's semi-annual meetings. Like all board members, I was an activist, in my case in Central American solidarity and Green movement organizations. The novel idea of the HPF was that the activist community (rather than staff or trustees) made the funding decisions.

My major purpose was to discover whether radical funding could promote significant changes in the distribution of political, social, and economic power in contrast to the frequent "deradicalization" resulting from liberal funding. However, as suggested in the earlier discussion of social movement outcomes, during the study additional questions became salient. Aside from unintended effects, there were issues of organizational survival, and in some cases, I could not track down either the organization or any former members.

Providing an operational definition of social change was a major hurdle. In the vast literature on the subject, it usually is associated with "modernization." More useful for this study is "a long-term change in the structures of political decision making or the allocation of power and wealth."[89] "Empowerment" is not necessarily social change. It may amount to individual or group social mobility that does not alter the hierarchical nature of the system. Others, perhaps less visible, remain at the bottom.

Another problem was bias. First, the major sources of data were the reports from the groups studied. There may be a tendency for such respondents to exaggerate their success, although the opposite effect sometimes occurs. Second, I have a strong commitment to social change and possibly unduly high standards for signifiers of change. However, William Foote Whyte, an experienced social researcher, suggests that action-inspired research may be both scientific and useful.[90]

Haymarket, created in 1974 by people of inherited wealth, funds groups based in New England; some have national or international objectives. Haymarket announced the following goals in 1986:

> ... [T]o help people understand the sources of social and economic injustice and how to change them; to support people trying to take control of their lives through challenging established power, learning how to use leadership, and developing self-respect; and to work towards the shared vision of a non-oppressive society with economic and political justice.[91]

Haymarket literature, at that time, typically stated that: "There must be fundamental changes in the distribution of power and wealth in our society." A minimum indicator of social change, for the purposes of this study, was finding a change in power and wealth favoring the groups that Haymarket has supported. One sign that this has occurred would be the inclusion of a group into the decision-making process rather than the mere granting of benefits.[92]

Haymarket's strategy for promoting social change is to award grants to eligible groups. These should be self-organizations of the oppressed, although this is not required of solidarity movements. Grants are made to groups, not individuals, and they primarily supply seed money for organizing purposes. However, some organizations have been vitally sustained over years with the help of the HPF. Organizations likely to be supported by liberal foundations or United Way usually are excluded, as are those with large budgets. As with all 501 (c) 3 organizations, Haymarket cannot fund political parties, referenda campaigns, or lobbying on behalf of specific legislation. During the period I studied, grants ranged in size from a few hundred dollars to $3,000; groups were expected to develop their own funding as soon as possible. Haymarket also provided technical assistance to its grantees, for example, in fund raising, dispute resolution, media use, and facilitation. Furthermore, the regional and general meetings and special events created synergy among diverse activists; this was especially stimulating for outliers who rarely experienced local conclaves of world changers.

The organizations that I investigated were selected from the *Annual Reports* of grants for the period 1974–1978. Forty-six were chosen, which included all of those that appeared to have social change as their primary goal. Groups that were social-service oriented and media projects were not used as subjects. It could be that services and/or media are the best ways to promote social change, but it was not feasible to measure their outcomes.

The next step was to review the grant applications and other materials in the files of these groups to discover their goals, and to note the names, addresses, and telephone numbers of group members (addresses and phone numbers of the organizations themselves generally were obsolete). Detective work in telephone directories and inquiries of current Haymarket board members resulted in current addresses for people connected to thirty-seven of the groups; no survivors were located for nine of the groups.

A questionnaire (see Appendix A) was sent to members or former members; some of the groups were still very active. For most organizations, only one person was queried, but in a few cases, two or three were contacted. The cover letter (see Appendix B) stated that a telephone or personal interview might be arranged if mutually satisfactory. In some cases, both a completed questionnaire and an interview were obtained. Twenty-two groups were surveyed one way or the other. Fifteen groups either ignored my letters and calls or refused to be interviewed.

For nine of the groups, no person could be located who had been identified as a member from data in Haymarket files, or noted as such by informants. In fifteen other cases, the questionnaire probably found its target, as the letter was not returned by the post office, but no response or interview ensued. In one case, the subject was averse to reporting a negative experience; this may have been the situation of some of the other nonrespondents.

I received no response from any member of a Puerto Rican solidarity organization (four such groups had received grants) or from anyone from a Western

Massachusetts group. Perhaps the Puerto Rican groups had been subject to more repression than others, and their members had dispersed or were wary of being studied. It is not the case that in Western Massachusetts groups die without leaving a trace. My research in the archives of the University of Massachusetts showed that "12-1" had been instrumental in unionizing clerical workers, and materials in Smith College's library indicated that the Valley Women's Union had evolved into a feminist newsletter collective, the *Valley Women's Voice*. The Nuclear Information Commune of Montague mutated into Green Mountain Post Films.

It is hard to draw any conclusion about nonresponses. Obviously, some people just do not want to be bothered, but why Western Massachusetts people are more busy or reclusive than others is not clear. Of course, with unlimited time or staff (I had neither), one could have stalked one's prey at rallies and conferences.

In many respects, the results were positive. First of all, survival. At least fourteen of the groups (including some nonrespondents, which I knew were there) had continued to exist or had evolved into organizations related to the original goals. In other cases, groups fostered the creation of current organizations and movements, for example, PACT (tenants' rights) in Burlington, Vermont, laid the groundwork for the Sanderistas. Nuclear Reaction and the Gay Task Force, both in Maine, set the stage for current strong organizations in these areas.

Second, almost all of the respondents reported many positive achievements, especially in consciousness raising and specific reforms. For example, the [South] African Liberation Support Committee of Boston had ignited similar movements throughout the United States. Inclusion of blacks in the government of South Africa qualifies as a change in the power structure. The Lewiston Tenants Union had obtained subsidized housing and greater legal protection for tenants. In many cases (e.g., the Clamshell Alliance and Friends of the Filipino People), there had been success in placing issues on the public agenda.

Third, more often than not the leaders and members remained active in social change movements. This was the case even in one of the most negatively reported groups, the Public Power Project of New Haven, which created a food co-op that vitally nourished the progressive community. The transformation of people's lives through activism is not an entirely unintended goal, but it may escape from evaluations that concentrate on "success" only.

Fourth, in some cases, organizations evolved into political interest groups that have had a voice in the political process; they became recognized interests (e.g., City Life in Jamaica Plain and the National Alliance against Racist and Political Repression in Hartford).

Fifth, the very survival of these groups and their goals during a period of repression and reaction had kept the ground fertile for the "seeds" of social change.[93] Nevertheless, few have achieved marked "social change" in decision-making structures or in the allocation of resources. Certainly individuals have been empowered to achieve social mobility and/or to mitigate oppression. Homeworkers Organized for More Employment (H.O.M.E.), a low-income women's employment project in Maine, is an impressive example of this. Perhaps the greatest changes in structure and resources occurred in the Penobscot Nation in Maine, where a successful fight for monetary and land restitution has given the tribe new options for determining its direction and goals. It also served as a model for other tribes throughout the country.

Other outcomes included consciousness raising, either among the general public or the victims of oppression, or both, reported by nineteen of the twenty-two groups. For example, the Maine Feminist Health Project stimulated women to demand more control over the provision of medical care. Another type of consciousness raising can occur when the victims generally are not visible to U.S. citizens. This is the case with a group such as Friends of the Filipino People, which over a long period tried to make U.S. policy toward the Philippines an issue for the general population, which at best had noted the media attention focused on the wicked Marcoses rather than the underlying dynamics.

The Clamshell Alliance not only kept the Seabrook nuclear plant on the public agenda in New Hampshire for fourteen years, but its example and methods have spread throughout the country and abroad. Participants in the Clam coalition, such as the Upper Valley Energy Coalition and Nuclear Reaction, educated the population in their local areas about the environmental dangers, health hazards, and high costs of nuclear power (including civil liberties costs) and suggested better alternatives for the production of energy. It is unusual in our political system for a consumer or an environmental interest to be sustained for such a long period, especially when the participants have little material incentive in relation to the efforts expended.

In the four tenants' organizations studied, the consciousness raising occurred primarily among the tenants. Housing activism can unite a diversity of low-income people and illustrate the many ways in which the poor suffer (e.g., in the employment, health, education, and environmental pollution of their communities). Yet it is difficult to sustain these organizations; usually the problem is resolved for some, and the others move away. Furthermore, difficulties in fighting gentrification discourage many. Slumlords can be held to higher standards, and more units of low-income housing can be provided. Land trusts and co-ops are fine models, but radical, large-scale changes in housing provision appear necessary.

Reforms achieved were reported by ten groups. The Abenaki Support Committee obtained better jobs, housing, and education, primarily by pressuring the federal government. Healthy Vermont contributed to the development of home health care and to free or nearly free dentistry for low-income older people. The National Alliance against Racist and Political Repression helped obtain the release of some political prisoners and fostered improvement in the way police treated people of color. In addition, H.O.M.E. was able to change state and federal mortgage policies so that houses in land trusts would be eligible. Insofar as these achievements demonstrated how ordinary people can influence the political system, they may contribute to a sense of empowerment and may inspire others.

Interest groups were created in ten cases, which were accorded some voice in the processes concerning their members. In addition, the press recognized the groups as valid participants in the debate. Voices were heard, even if sometimes softly and without immediate effect. The United Farm Workers Support Group of New Haven is an example of this recognition; many New Haven people based their boycott activity on the group's recommendations. The Mental Patients Liberation Front of Boston obtained representation on official committees. Mobilization for Survival, on the national level, testified before congressional committees.

Social change was hard to detect, except in the Penobscot Nation. Even here, the organization was not attempting to change the larger society. However, by obtaining benefits, in the form of land and financial restitution, and generous scholarship provisions, the Nation increased its power of self-determination.

In some cases, goals were transformed. Groups that persisted and experienced successes tended to move toward single-issue objectives. In the early 1970s, activists often had a multi-issue approach, linking American imperialism, racism at home, destruction of neighborhoods by real estate developers, exploitation of the workforce, and environmental degradation. Gradually, radical analysis became muted. Mobilization for Survival was a notable exception in retaining its multi-issue approach.

By the late 1980s, one saw little of the typical goals of the early 1970s, such as: "The profit motive should be removed from the health care arena"; "We wish to discover and expose those people both in and out of state who determine how [the state] will be used and exploited as part of the consolidation of large financial empires"; "Our goals and purposes are to build a mass-based organization to fight fascist and political repression in all its manifestations"; and "[We aim to bring] about public ownership of the local electricity distribution monopoly."

Goal reduction is not surprising in view of the long-term frustration awaiting those seeking major transformation. Political scientist Betty Zisk's empirical study of peace and environmental activist groups, *The Politics of Transformation*, has shown that: "Organizations pursuing short-range, tangible, incremental goals were markedly more successful (and even on goal attainment, somewhat more so) than those seeking long-range structural change."[94]

Group survival seems to have been affected by location; the intense activity in the Boston area had a sustaining influence. Yet groups succeeded and survived in other cities, and in Vermont, New Hampshire, and Maine. Churches were cited as both negatively (before 1980) and positively helpful later on. In a number of groups, religious people and organizations formed the backbone. Increasing social activism by religious groups crossed the entire spectrum of social issues. Church buildings, sponsorship, and grants have been significant resources for activists. The New England Puritan tradition, Quaker peace and justice work, and Catholic liberation theology have stimulated and sustained conscience movements.

Volunteers in Service to America (VISTA) workers also were helpful to several organizations, including the Penobscot Nation. On the other hand, some activists believed that volunteer efforts were discouraged when paid staff was available. Nevertheless, the presence of full-time staff seems to make an enormous difference in the ability of small organizations to succeed and survive. There is a paradox here; the professionalization of movements often has defanged them. On the other hand, volunteers may not be able to sustain activity indefinitely, especially in peace and justice movements, where the results are on the far horizon.

Newsletters, especially statewide, seemed to be an important rallying point and activism sustainer. Groups that provided emotional support to members were more long lasting (achieving the status of a "functional dysfamily," a term used by the later Monadnock Greens). Those with regular meeting places or offices seem to have done better. However, it could be that offices were the consequence of groups' success.

Organizational decline may have occurred in some cases because the original activists grew older; they married, had children, and both worked full time to support, among other things, the rent or mortgage. The cost of housing, both in time and in money, may be a major factor in American "exceptionalism." The same might be said of inadequate public transportation, thus necessitating expensive private transportation. Days are spent paying them off and evenings fixing them up.

Social change movements are subject to generational cycles, yet to sustain themselves they must keep recruiting younger people. Younger people often are "into" something else, and they do not share the grievances of their elders. In any case, children of dissenters may dissent from their parents' causes, because they were brought up to question authority. Groups reported frustration with their goals of changing major centers of power (e.g., the media, the medical-industrial complex, or the real estate development industry). They experienced the backlash against popular agitation that began in the late 1970s. There has been outright repression and various ways of neutralizing dissent. These include the promotion of jingoism, the yuppie culture, and the high costs of life's necessities, such as education, housing, medical care, and transportation. The media ignore or ridicule dissenting individuals or movements, the military entices low-income young people, and children do not receive the kind of education that would lead them to question the powers that be. The cause of human liberation is made to seem irrelevant.

Under the circumstances, radical funding, while not promoting immediate change, may well be nurturing the "seeds of the future." Yet one must conclude that far more investigation and thought is needed on *how* to build an effective counterhegemonic movement.

9

International Activities

Because NGOs [non-governmental organizations] generally depend on foundations, their reputations as being legitimate and representative may be undeserved—more a product of funding than actual connections with constituencies. NGOs clearly benefit from the widely accepted notion that they represent "civil society," yet both private businesses and democratic social movements will dispute the notion.

Just who benefits from that assumption is clear, but it is critical to point again to who loses: those social movements and political formations out to challenge and transform the fundamentals of economic and political power. There is a competition of sorts to shape the framework of discussion and the civil debate, and those with greater funding have an easier time setting the agenda. By limiting discussion and education to narrow issues, NGOs and NGO funding often constrain political partisan/electoral involvement. Illusions of influence notwithstanding, the result of much NGO activity in the South is demobilization and disempowerment.

—Alejandro Bendaña, "Which Way for NGOs?"

Foundations spent $1.6 billion on international activities in 1998, much for the support of friendly NGOs.[1] This may not seem like much, but the money works in concert with United States Government funds from the National Endowment for Democracy, the Agency for International Development, and covert sources; and grants from the other NATO democracies. Furthermore, even a few thousand dollars is a huge pot in most countries being made safe for capitalism. One consequence is that without foreign donors, local projects, organizations, and research can rarely compete.

Just as the twentieth-century foundations built upon and transformed the traditional Christian charities in their domestic work, they have absorbed and extended earlier missionary goals in their foreign activities. For example, American Protestant missionaries began traveling to Bulgaria in 1834. Their leader, Elias Riggs, wrote, "Look for a moment at the Bulgarian field. A whole people is there presented to us just awakening to a desire for education, earnestly desirous of books, but having no means of obtaining them, and no press in the country."[2] Books, sewing machines, and other technology were supplied. Riggs estimated this intervention to have considerable consequences: "Directly or indirectly, however unintentionally, American missionaries fostered nationalism and the breakdown of the Ottoman Empire." He then stated:

> Missionary detractors at home and abroad have discovered "missionary imperialism": the Cross-Dollar-Flag syndrome. . . . Related to such "Bible imperialism" was what might be called "language or cultural imperialism." . . . The missionaries themselves equated the more advanced technological standards of living of their homelands with Protestantism, religious freedom, and the "Truth," as they saw it, and therefore, the obligation to spread this divine purpose throughout the world.[3]

The Bulgarians avidly accepted scientific apparatus and textbooks for their schools; the religious doctrines made no headway. However, the influence of missionaries in Bulgaria continued through their founding of a Bulgarian newspaper, *Zornitsa*, and from their base at Robert College in Constantinople. In the early twentieth century, the Rockefeller Foundation, the Carnegie Endowment for International Peace, the Near East Foundation, the American Red Cross, the YWCA, and the YMCA heavily invested in philanthropic activities in Bulgaria. Toward the end of the century, democratization and marketization missionaries were bringing blue jeans, skateboards, pop music, and Internet connections. Today, philanthropists are again creating new universities and financing an independent press.

International philanthropy was at first primarily in education and health; indeed, the Rockefeller Foundation eradicated malaria in Bulgaria. In 1921, it created a Western-type medical school in Asia, the Peking Union Medical College. This was not for training "barefoot" doctors who might provide basic health care for the population. Instead, it sought to

> create an infrastructure it believed necessary for China's development along Western lines. . . . [T]he foundation officers expected their medical education program to help "modernize" China, to develop an elite professional stratum to transform Chinese society in ways suited to the needs of the industrialized, capitalist nations.[4]

This model for medical education was then incorporated into foundation, foreign aid, and UN programs throughout the world.

Also in the interwar period, the Phelps-Stokes Fund of New York, with financial support from the Carnegie and Rockefeller foundations, "facilitated the transference of the theory and practice of nonacademic education designed for southern Negroes (the so-called Tuskegee philosophy) to their African counterparts" in the English-speaking colonial areas.[5] More recently, Phelps-Stokes has brought African students to the United States for seminars on the virtues of economic privatization. Exchange programs involving promising students or future leaders remain an important part of "cultural diplomacy." A related operation, the initiation and funding of international studies institutes in the United States, carries on the missionary tradition while serving foreign policy goals.[6]

Creating international institutions, for example, the League of Nations, had been one objective of the Carnegie/Rockefeller-sponsored Council on Foreign Relations. However, after 1945, these processes became world and issue encompassing, aiding U.S. economic and cultural domination. The new institutions also mitigated challenges arising from the counterhegemonic agents of nationalism, neutralism, and communism.

Planning for the United Nations began in 1943, by a steering committee consisting of Secretary of State Hull and five CFR members. One, Isaiah Bowman,

> first suggested a way to solve the problem of maintaining effective control over weaker territories while avoiding overt imperial conquest. At a Council [of Foreign Relations] meeting in May 1942, he stated that the United States had to exercise the strength needed to assure "security," and at the same time "avoid conventional forms of imperialism." The way to do this, he argued, was to make the exercise of that power international in character through a United Nations body.[7]

One might wonder why the UN was so readily accepted worldwide at a time of raging anti-imperialism. One explanation is that in 1945, the United States was identified with New Deal policies of security and progress.

> America was the liberator with the power and money this time to prevent war from recurring. . . . Virtually the entire communist movement from America to Russia to the European and Asian parties believed that America was coterminous with Roosevelt and the New Deal. Ho Chi Minh was so taken with America that he made the American Declaration of Independence the model for Vietnam's own declaration of independence from France. At the end of World War II, the dominant sentiment in the advanced countries was a yearning for peace and security, not for revolution. . . . At the end of World War II, people did not yearn for class struggle but for an end to struggle. War was so horrible an evil that nothing could be worse. No other nation seemed so dedicated to and capable of providing the security that the world wanted than America.[8]

John D. Rockefeller Jr. gave an $8.5 million gift enabling the UN to buy the land for its East Side New York headquarters. The component parts of the UN (e.g., the World Bank, International Monetary Fund, Food and Agriculture Organization, Human Rights Commission, etc.) also have served foundation interests, and they receive grants for special projects.

The European Union was another U.S. government-foundation enterprise.

> Washington's main tool for shaping the European agenda was the American Committee for a United Europe, created in 1948. The chairman was William Donovan [former head of the OSS] . . . the Vice Chairman was Allen Dulles [future CIA director]. . . . The documents show that ACUE [American Committee for a United Europe] financed the European Movement, . . . in 1958 it provided 53.5 percent of the movement's funds. . . . ACUE's funding came from the Ford and Rockefeller foundations as well as business groups with close ties to the U.S. government.
>
> The head of the Ford Foundation, ex-OSS officer Paul Hoffman, doubled as head of the ACUE in the late Fifties.[9]

Nongovernmental organizations parallel to intergovernmental institutions also were created, adopted, and/or supported by foundations. Human Rights Watch is one (evolving from Helsinki Watch); its original mission was to monitor human rights in both Eastern and Western Europe. Now it has affiliates such as Americas Watch, Asia Watch, and similar groups, and there are international NGOs for the rights of children, women, minorities, refugees, and indigenous people.

Environmental protest has been incorporated into the foundation network with many new organizations, such as the Centre for Our Common Future in Switzerland. The NGOs at the "Global Forum," adjunct to the United Nations Conference on Environment and Development in Rio de Janeiro in June 1992, were mostly funded (and some were created) by foundations.[10] They function to transform protesters into advocates for "sustainable development." Parallel conferences began as confrontations to official conferences, for example, TOES (The Other Economic Summit) to the G-7 (richest nations' annual meeting). However, outsiders have been domesticated and are now invited in or set up nicely in the backyard. Well-funded organizations can afford the transportation to international conferences; others may receive special travel grants if they are civil and pragmatic.

The 1992 Rio Conference was accompanied by an indigenous people's convention. Leaders had previously met at UN committees, but Rio was a full-scale conference with large delegations of Sami, Australian Aborigines, Maori, New Guineans, North and South American Indians, and Africans. It included political networking, creating an extensive joint declaration, and cultural performances; one spokesperson, a Brazilian Indian, was permitted to address the formal UN Conference.[11] Subsequently, the world's indigenous peoples, who often oppose militarization, nuclear power, colonizers' land claims, and national boundaries, were included in the world of NGOs, international conferences, UN Declarations, and attractive Web sites, all of which require generous foundation support.

International NGOs have multiplied by the thousands. Some are broad based, such as the well-known Amnesty International or Greenpeace. Others are specific to countries and issues, often concerned with human rights, democracy promotion, environment, or development, such as the Empower Foundation in Thailand (concerned with prostitutes' rights), the Kenya Rural Enterprise Program, or the Press and Society Institute of Peru.

Current activities entwine foundations, government programs, "QUANGOS" (quasi-non-governmental organizations), non-governmental organizations, and international governmental entities. They embody the international side of Progressivism—public-private partnerships on a world scale. There also are vestiges of Progressivism's ethnic attitude in contemporary democracy promotion, implying that the Anglo-Saxon nations are uniquely qualified to teach the rest of the world about democracy, human rights, and good government. According to the promoters, the precondition for such benefits is a "free market" economy, or the adoption of "neoliberalism," which entails the privatization of most government functions, deregulation of business, abolition of subsidies and welfare, and availability of all assets (land, TV stations, national newspapers, etc.) for purchase by any corporation, regardless of nationality. Freedom also means that foreigners can start any business anywhere, such as a new university or a radio station. Sometimes democratization is even associated with the right of foreigners to be candidates for national office, but it does not abolish immigration restrictions for the unmonied.

Foundation-government partnerships have a long history. In early days, they were cemented through shared personnel, for example, among the Council on Foreign Relations, presidential advisory teams, and the State Department. The post–World War II Cold War accelerated institutional interconnections. The CIA used foundations and organizations as "pass throughs" for its international operations. In 1967, there was a brief period of indignancy after these transactions became public:

> Press reports indicated that the CIA probably had used at least 46 foundations in an involved method of funneling funds to certain organizations. Under a method of transfer known as a "triple pass," the usual procedure was for the CIA to convey funds to "dummy" foundations established by the CIA to act as fronts for its activities. The "dummy" foundations then made grants to legitimate foundations. The legitimate foundations—which also handled other funds—then made grants to

certain CIA-designated organizations, using the funds from the
"dummy" foundations. However, the pattern varied in some instances.
Press reports disclosed that there were some examples of direct grants
by the "dummy'" foundations to organizations and at least one example
of grants by legitimate foundations (using CIA funds) back to a
"dummy" foundation. A tabulation of press reports shows at least
$12,422, 925 was channeled to organizations by the CIA.[12]

Among the legitimate foundations used were the Appalachia Fund, the J. M.
Kaplan Fund, and the Norman Fund, which generally were considered "progres-
sive" foundations. The organizations serving as covert channels included the
American Newspaper Guild, the Asia Foundation, the Congress for Cultural
Freedom, the International Confederation of Free Trade Unions (ICFTU), the
National Council of Churches, the National Education Association, and the
National Student Association. The last organization was fatally wounded by this
revelation. The ICFTU was no great surprise; funding via the AFL-CIO to
teach the world how to run free trade unions has been well documented, and the
Polish Solidarity movement also was supported through this agent.
    The Congress for Cultural Freedom (also funded by the Ford Foundation)
had been under suspicion from the start. Its mission was to discredit Marxism,
especially among European intellectuals. It tried to convert as many eminent
intellectuals as possible, while getting the young aspiring academics, writers, and
artists on track with travel to conferences, assured publication, and (frequently
unmerited) early recognition. (See chapter 5 for more about the CCF.) Covert
funding violated the CIA's legal obligation to avoid domestic operations (rarely
enforced), and it disturbed some obsessive-compulsive sticklers for morality and
legality. Ultimately, the technique lost its potency, because it blew covers and
damaged "civil society" associations.
    The CIA found other ways to support foreign "citizens'" groups, including
the use of Marshall Plan "counterpart" funds in Europe. Congress eventually created a new institution—the National Endowment for Democracy—in 1983 to
put a different face on this type of intervention. This was a QUANGO like the
Asia Foundation mentioned earlier. It was modeled on the private foundation.
The NED initiates some projects, distributes grants (mainly to its designated
subsidiaries), and directly funds some nonprofit organizations or for-profit subcontractors. The subsidiaries or "core grantees" of the NED are the Center for
International Private Enterprise (an affiliate of the U.S. Chamber of Commerce),
the American Center for International Labor Solidarity (affiliated with the
AFL-CIO), and, affiliated with the parties, the National Democratic Institute
(NDI) for International Affairs and the International Republican Institute. Thus
all of the U.S. political tendencies (that matter) are represented. The NED is
technically a private corporation, like the Corporation for Public Broadcasting,
although almost entirely funded by Congress. Some private foundations chip in,

for example, Smith Richardson and Mellon-Scaife. The Mott Foundation gave the NDI $150,000 in 1998 "to increase public confidence in democratization and the transition to a market economy in Ukraine"; it also donated $50,000 for election monitoring.[13]

Private foundations are deeply involved in co-funding the foreign organizations that receive pass-through government funds. Thus also supported by the Lilly Endowment and other foundations,

> the Institute for Liberty and Democracy in Peru, run by Hernando de Soto, is known globally for its research on the informal sector and its free-market solutions to underdevelopment. ILD owes its worldwide reputation to the funding and public relations efforts of the U.S. Government. The institute was set up with AID funds, [and] is currently backed by AID and NED.[14]

The U.S. public and private "democracy" enterprises abroad frequently were modeled on those of the German political party foundations. While technically these are nonpolitical charities:

> Reality, however, is different. Not only are the West German foundations genuinely linked to political parties, but they can also be considered as the "executive organs" of their political mother organization, allowing the party to participate to a certain extent in the domestic politics of another country at a non-governmental level without violating the rule of non-interference in inter-governmental relations.[15]

The Konrad Adenauer Foundation (of the Christian Democrats) and the Friedrich Naumann Foundation (of the Free Democrats) shore up conservative parties and NGOs:

> [T]he Konrad Adenauer Foundation has been widely known for its manipulation of the political processes of Latin American countries such as Chile in the 1960s and Guatemala and El Salvador in the 1980s. Furthermore, from the 1960s onward, it has been legendary in Latin America for its role as a laundry for CIA funds. A recent example of this role was in the 1984 presidential campaign of Christian Democrat Jose Napoleon Duarte in El Salvador, when the Adenauer Foundation acted as a conduit for $350,000 in CIA funds designated for Duarte's campaign.[16]

The Friedrich Ebert Foundation (Social Democrats) and the Heinrich Böll Foundation (Greens) work at reinforcing the "noncommunist Left" throughout the world, which does not include the Sandinistas: "By 1957, the Friedrich

Ebert Foundation . . . was using money provided by the West German foreign ministry for its work with ORIT, the organization of anticommunist trade unions in Latin America."[17]

Other NATO democracies now have government foundations similar to the NED and work cooperatively (e.g., the Canadian Rights and Democracy and the British Westminster Foundation for Democracy). France, the Netherlands, Greece, Italy, and Sweden fund party foundations on the German model, especially active in Latin America and Africa. The European members of the Socialist International (an association of socialist and social democratic parties worldwide) have their own foundation, the European Forum for Democracy and Solidarity, which distributes "democratization" aid.[18]

That is not all. The European Union has worldwide grant programs for sustainable development and democratization. UN agencies such as UNICEF, WHO, UNESCO, or FAO have long operated this way. The UNs' Department of Peacekeeping Operations has an Electoral Assistance Unit, which helped organize the Nicaraguan 1990 election, among others.[19] The Adenauer Foundation played a large role in that operation, working with U.S. agencies to support Chamorro's election.

> NED's partisan activities in Nicaragua have been a textbook example of the use of "political aid" to complement other instruments of U.S. interventionism: military aggression, economic destabilization, and anti-Sandinista propaganda. From 1984 to 1990, NED organized, sustained, unified, and promoted the political forces which became UNO.[20]

The 1990 election in Nicaragua was judged by all of the official and NGO observers to be a free one; neither threats of physical annihilation nor millions of foreign dollars violated the purity of that process.

Another UN entity, the World Bank, has a grant-making foundation side that sponsors, guides, and coordinates grassroots poor people's organizations. Many U.S. agencies are engaged in similar work, for example, the United States Agency for International Development (USAID) and the United States Information Agency support and create foreign NGOs and media. United States NGOs, foundations, and the CIA continue their traditional direct connections abroad and cross-fund. These activities are not secret. However, they create a thicket that few researchers care to penetrate, especially as the rewards for this type of research are meager.

Even those who approve in principle of missionary-style democracy promotion take exception to the NED's activities:

> Managed since its creation by a small band of neoconservatives who use government funds to wage their own foreign policy, the foundation bears a troublesome past. It has assisted groups with agendas

other than the promotion of democracy, such as a thuggish far-right outfit in France and a Costa Rican policy institute that schemed to unseat an elected president. Past government audits have found lax financial management.[21]

Critics of the NED often find that, on balance, it is a threat to democracy here and abroad. For example, in addition to supporting new "democratic" partners such as the Cultural Council of the Afghan Resistance, the NED meddles in the politics of our allies; Northern Ireland's Social Democratic and Labor Party and an affiliated think tank have received NED grants for organizing and outreach efforts.

A Costa Rican research institute associated with the United Social Christian Party (PUSC) received $434,000 from 1986 to early 1989 funneled through [the Republican Party Institute]. In the 1990 election the PUSC ran the winning contender against the party of President Oscar Arias, whose peace initiative in Central America won him disapproval in Washington.[22]

The private foundations often are more skillful operators, although they work closely with the U.S. government. The Rockefeller Foundation and Rockefeller family enterprises were deeply involved in political projects and cultural diplomacy throughout Latin America. John J. McCloy, for many years chairman of the Ford Foundation's trustees, "thought of the Foundation as a quasi-extension of the U.S. government. It was his habit, for instance, to drop by the National Security Council in Washington every couple of months and casually ask whether there were any overseas projects the NSC would like to see funded."[23] Although Ford's overseas staff and fellows did some jobs for the intelligence people and were subject to "debriefing" upon their return to the United States, the foundations' foreign interventions bore a friendly mask and were mostly accepted by foreign elites. This was partly because of the exquisite, tasteful gifts, such as Ford's publication in India of Indian religious classics, and Rockefeller's public health projects. However, although some programs may have been window dressing, many functioned to extend U.S. domination (cultural, political, military, and economic) and to counter or reverse attitudes and movements that threatened such domination, whether they were nationalist, neutralist, populist, or communist.

Ford's work in Indonesia was a major example of this strategy, and one replicated elsewhere. This incredibly resource-rich area was, at the end of World War II, ready to oust the Dutch colonial masters. One problem for the United States, which wished to become the new influence, was that it was not quite a nation. The rhetoric of self-determination had stirred up the many ethnic groups that had been collected into a Dutch colony; fragmentation and nationalism could make future control difficult. Another problem was that the main nationalist forces in Jakarta were crucially supported by the well-organized and numerically strong Communist Party. This did not mean that they were waiting for the opportunity to invade the United States and take over its high schools, as is popularly assumed (perhaps wishful thinking). Rather, the sticking point was the ownership and control of those vast resources, and the labor power of this exceedingly populous area.

The Ford Foundation, working with the U.S. government, was able to gently insert itself into the picture:

> Education had long been an arm of statecraft, and it was Dean Rusk who spelled out its function in the Pacific in 1952, just months before resigning as Assistant Secretary of State for Far Eastern Affairs to head up the Rockefeller Foundation. "Communist aggression" in Asia required not only that Americans be trained to combat it there, but "we must open our training facilities for increasing numbers of our friends from across the Pacific."
>
> The Ford Foundation, under the presidency of Paul Hoffman (and working closely with the Rockefeller Foundation), moved quickly to apply Rusk's words to Indonesia. As head of the Marshall Plan in Europe, Hoffman had helped to arrange Indonesian independence by cutting off aid funds to Dutch counterinsurgency and by threatening a total cutoff in aid to the Dutch. As the United States supplanted the Dutch, Hoffman and Ford would work through the best American universities—MIT, Cornell, Berkeley, and finally Harvard—to remold the old Indonesians hierarchs into modern administrators, trained to work under the new indirect rule of the Americans. In Ford's own jargon, they would create a "modernizing elite."[24]

Ford established a U.S.-type economics program at the Indonesian university and trained faculty at the U.S. universities to run the Indonesian program. There were similar operations at the Bandung Institute of Technology, where the University of Kentucky was "institution-building." To round things out, high-level Indonesian military officers were being trained in the United States, learning counterinsurgency skills from the military and business and public administration at Harvard and Syracuse universities. When the coup was instituted to overthrow Sukarno, well-trained leadership was available to run the country and to negotiate reasonable deals with multinational corporations. One more group of assets was important. As the army had no popular support, student mobs were assembled to provide the illusion of a mass uprising. Some had been "American Field Service" exchange students or had been in other leadership training programs in the United States; others were technology students who had studied at the University of Kentucky. "Students in all of Indonesia's elite universities had been given paramilitary training by the Army in a program for a time advised by an ROTC colonel on leave from Berkeley."[25]

Asian regions with fewer or less accessible resources also have to be kept in line, as rebellions can spread. The Afghanistan Foundation is a "private" non-profit organization, with honorary Co-Chairmen Dr. Zbigniew Brzezinski and Gen. Brent Scowcroft. Among its principals are RAND and CFR members, and Dr. Frederick Starr, the former president of Oberlin, who is now at the School for Advanced International Studies of Johns Hopkins University. One of the Foundation's programs is the Afghanistan Charter Project:

> The Charter will be a declaration of principles, drafted by Afghan scholars and leaders around the world, based on common values and essential elements of culture, history, national unity, education, and economic development. The Charter will represent an historic effort to define the ideals that will help to shape, strengthen, and unite Afghan society now and in the future.[26]

Many NGOs worked in Afghanistan in support of the mujahedeen, including the Mercy Fund and the Council for International Development. Another, the Afghanistan Relief Committee, is funded by the NED and others. It ran schools in the mujahedeen-controlled areas:

> The texts provided by ARC were designed to combat the Soviet "indoctrination" of Afghan youth. This project was monitored in Afghanistan by Médecins sans Frontières, a group which received funding from the staunchly anticommunist U.S.-based NGO, the International Rescue Committee.[27]

Not all NGOs are hard right. Emerging trends must be incorporated, which everywhere in the world includes feminism. The Revolutionary Association of the Women of Afghanistan operates an elaborate, music-enhanced Web site based in Pakistan. It rejects the Taliban as well as communism, and it strives for "peace, freedom, democracy, and women's rights."[28]

In Bangladesh, NGOs supported by foundations and today's expanded circle of donors work to counter disruptions brought about by both modernization and neoliberalism. Traditional redistributive relations and subsistence agriculture are disappearing. At the same time, economic planning and government welfare, which were policies of the nationalist Bengali movement, are being eliminated by neoliberal governments. Women who demand rights might be tempted into an alliance with radicals.

"By 1982, the country was considered 'the aid capital of the world.'"[29] Development projects became the dominant aid model: "NGOs, especially those tied to the rural hinterland, also create new frontiers for resource extraction, provide access to sources of cheap labor and markets for imports, and aid in the privatization of all social relations."[30] An important prototype is Ford's Grameen Bank project, which distributes resources especially to poor women and organizes groups to ensure loan repayment. A number of researchers have found that these poverty-alleviation systems promote "depoliticization":

> No longer do citizens need to organize on their own behalf and engage in various forms of opposition, including social movements, rallies, and other forms of dissent. Instead, the NGO sector, legitimized as a controlled, organized arena of public debate with institutional and financial support from the donor community, has come to speak on behalf of the citizenry, particularly those groups that have been targeted among the needy, women, and the poor.[31]

While persistent poverty can be dangerous to stability, especially if there are surplus unemployed activist-intellectuals about, the nouveau-pauvres also have to be mollified. People in Mongolia, as in many former communist countries, have lost their welfare and health care systems, and the free market has not had enough time to provide affluence on the U.S. and European models. Private Agencies Collaborating Together (PACT), a U.S.-based NGO, is working to foster economic and civic development of the Gobi region, in coordination with Mercy Corps International and Associates in Rural Development. To provide a strong market economy, the group is developing and promoting information technology use throughout the region.[32] Mongolia's Soros Foundation, as those elsewhere, attempts to organize the desocialized economy and society. Information technology and media enterprises associated with Soros also are becoming the major sources of information about these countries.

LATIN AMERICA

Latin American foundation programs help mold an elite serving U.S. interests. Undergraduate and graduate training in the United States and academic programs throughout Latin America create:

> [A]n international community of scholars that the philanthropic foundations ... have been instrumental in shaping. Their behaviors and attitudes eventually are shaped by expectations as to what professionals with North American graduate degrees should know and how they should act. Rewards and gratifications as professionals derive from publishing in international or regional journals, in attending conferences forming part of the international peer network, and in engaging in scholarly activities for which they have been trained. ... [T]he effects of

foundation sponsorship are such that individuals become increasingly attached to viewing themselves in certain ways and conducting research which accords with Ford views of appropriate scholarship.[33]

Until recently, this research often employed radical paradigms, such as dependency theory:

A Kafkaesque situation exists where information, produced by the Latin Americans on situations of internal and external domination, is flowing to the alleged source of oppression—rather than toward those who need the information to defend themselves against exploitation. . . . The research is not threatening probably for two reasons: (1) it is not intelligible to the masses, for certainly, if the same sentiments were expressed not in academic journals but from a street corner or as part of a political movement which mobilized large numbers, the individuals would be jailed or exiled; and (2) the regime itself benefits from the knowledge generated, while simultaneously enhancing its international image by permitting academic freedom.[34]

Containment became more urgent when radical ideas spread beyond university intellectuals, who sometimes *did* become leaders of popular revolt. The Cuban and Nicaraguan revolutions inspired insurgencies in Central America; throughout South America (e.g., Colombia, Ecuador, and Peru); and the aborted Grenada revolution. Counterinsurgency tactics such as death squads often were counterproductive; people joined the resistance *because* family members were killed or had disappeared.[35] In addition, genocide was frowned upon in the civilized parts of the world, so its employment was a diplomatic liability.

Cultural, social, and economic changes also fueled insurgencies. Women were no longer being kept in line by the Church, as education and feminism had loosened its hold. Furthermore, the Church itself became divided with the advent of "liberation theology"; most of the lower clergy and some bishops and archbishops joined the anti-capitalist, anti-imperialist forces. Women were further radicalized by the disappearances of their children and increasing hardship resulting from neoliberal economics, which curtailed food subsidies, health care, and similar frills deemed inflationary by the International Monetary Fund.

An intervention attempting to lure women away from revolutionary movements was the creation and support of Christian Socialist political parties and organizations, in which the German Adenauer Foundation played a leading role. Another was the foundation sponsorship of NGOs. Sociologist Jim Petras claims that these functioned to "raid popular communities and direct energy toward self-help projects instead of social transformations and . . . introduc[ed] a class collaborationist rhetoric packaged as 'new identity discourses' that would discredit and isolate revolutionary activists."[36] The NGOs emerged by the thousands in the last three decades of the twentieth century. Some promoted small-scale economic development, as in microcredit or aid to the "informal economy," while others managed health clinics or financed home ownership in shantytowns.

Human rights NGOs were extensive, sending the message that neither women's equality nor police due process required radical transformation. "[T]hese humanitarian NGOs, however, were careful not to denounce the role of U.S. and European complicity with the local perpetrators of human rights violations."[37] The foundation-created organization, Americas Watch (now Human Rights Watch/Americas), did not relate U.S.-supported militarism (including death squads) to the abuses in Latin America. It found the chief problem to be "a lack of respect for human rights." Its remedy was publicizing human rights violations to media and international organizations and encouraging human rights groups throughout the hemisphere. Abuses were regarded as "deviations," even when a regime used terror as an instrument of policy. "The demand by human rights organizations that a regime account for human rights abuses against its people tends to legitimize the regime by acknowledging that the regime is still the place to seek redress."[38]

Latin American NGOs served a further important purpose. Many intellectuals lost their jobs at universities or other government employment when military dictatorships and neoliberal governments took over, as in Chile under Pinochet. Some were dismissed as being "too radical"; others, regardless of political views, were surplus in the era of austerity policies. The NGOs and research centers supported by Ford, Rockefeller, and other foundations took these people in—even the radicals. Gradually, their radicalism declined:

> NGOs foster a new type of cultural and economic colonialism—under the guise of a new internationalism. Hundreds of individuals sit in front of high powered PCs exchanging manifestos, proposals and invitations to international conferences with each other. They then meet in well furnished conference halls to discuss the latest struggles and offerings with their "social base"—the paid staff—who then pass on the proposals to the "masses" through flyers and "bulletins." When overseas funders show up, they are taken on "exposure tours" to showcase projects where the poor are helping themselves and to talk with successful micro-entrepreneurs (omitting the majority who fail the first year).[39]

Right- and left-wing NGOs have become increasingly similar. For example, agricultural development groups promoting small organic farmers run up against agribusiness:

> In the face of the broader constraints of the international market, structural adjustment, state policy, and the general political bias against the

interests of small producers, the "alternative" strategies advocated by progressive NGOs often end up looking not too different from those of neoliberal groups.[40]

This report is from the North American Congress on Latin America (NACLA), an organization which itself has been transformed and is now heavily funded by the Ford Foundation. Likewise, the Latin American research institutes no longer criticize imperialism or discuss dependency theory.[41] Latin American social scientist Carlos Vilas explains this:

> Since the end of the 1960s, we have been giving increasing attention to the role of endogenous factors in the formation and development of our society and their multiple dimensions in an effort to go beyond studies inspired by a more traditional Marxism, which reduced everything to production relations and put what now seems to us excessive emphasis on exogenous factors.[42]

Another reason for changing ideologies might be that moderation led to a comfortable existence and future possibilities for high rank. "[T]he NGOers were strategically placed as 'democrats' who would be available as political replacements for local ruling classes and imperial policy makers when repressive rulers began to be seriously challenged by popular mass movements."[43]

Multiculturalism and identity politics also have overtaken class analysis:

> [T]he great majority of NGOs operate on the basis of identity politics and argue that this is the basic point of departure for the new (postmodern) politics. Identity politics does not challenge the male dominated elite world of IMF privatizations, multi-national corporations and local landlords. Rather, it focuses on "patriarchy" in the household, family violence, divorce, family planning, etc. In other words, it fights for gender equality within the micro-world of exploited peoples in which the exploited and impoverished male worker/peasant emerges as the main villain.[44]

This perspective is central in Latin American women's organizations; another example is the Philippine women's group, discussed in chapter 5. Furthermore, in international women's NGOs (whose gatherings and participation in UN conferences are heavily subsidized by foundations), "domestic violence" has become the "common denominator" target, while government and corporate violence are deemed too difficult or controversial as a focus.[45]

Fragmentation and isolation in thousands of funded organizations also have a moderating effect. For example, grants are given throughout Latin America to AIDS prevention groups. However, economic policies may make prostitution, like drug growing, a subsistence activity. "Free trade" makes many legal activities uneconomical, such as producing corn and beans, which now cannot compete with agribusiness in export or local markets. Both also may be important sources of "currency" for foreign exchange. Sex tourism and exporting women who remit earnings back home give some nations their stake for the international trade game, yet these structural causes of AIDS are rarely taken into account.

Currently popular resistance to trade liberalization has been subdued, although the Chiapas revolt is an exception. Perhaps one reason is the incorporation of NGOs into trade summits.

> At the Miami Summit [1994], the region's leaders (except for Cuba's) agreed that their trade ministers would meet periodically to complete negotiations for the FTAA hemispheric trade agreement by the year 2005. CSOs [i.e., NGOs] have attended every trade ministerial following the Miami Summit; . . . in 1997, CSOs from 18 different countries assembled in May in Belo Horizonte, Brazil.[46]

Ford and other foundations, along with USAID, provide travel funds so that even groups with few resources may participate; however, support is limited to their own regular grantees.[47]

The NGO world presented here may seem as though it is on another planet, but that is because critical views are rare and nearly invisible to the partaker in "common wisdom." One explanation is:

> It is symptomatic of the pervasiveness of the NGOs and their economic and political power over the so-called "progressive world" that there have been few systematic Left critiques of the negative impact of NGOs. In a large part this failure is due to the success of the NGOs in displacing and destroying the organized Leftist movements and co-opting their intellectual strategists and organizational leaders.[48]

SOUTH AFRICA

The role of NGOs in Africa is similar, with the additional problem of a serious "brain drain." Both critics and professionals in general often migrate to the developed world, and many end up in menial work. Those who remain in Africa "are tempted away from public institutions by the NGOs who can afford to pay ten times what governments can afford."[49] Similarly, indigenous NGOs cannot offer attractive salaries. Some observers see a new colonialism emerging, including white expatriate consultants treated as "bosses," enjoying luxurious lifestyles, and engaging in sexual exploitation.[50]

South Africa required deft treatment. United States public opinion will support "authoritarian" anti-communist dictators, but apartheid was unacceptable to many here, black and white. Our allies faced the same moralistic pressures from their citizens, and Third World countries were critical of close U.S.–South Africa relations. On the other hand, the leading South African opposition was the African National Congress (ANC), although banned and exiled for many years, and the South African Communist Party was a major component. The ANC Freedom Charter of 1955 stated its goal of creating a multiracial socialist South Africa, with land and resources reverting to the people. Eschewing this rosy future, many whites left the country, emigrating to Commonwealth nations or South America. This may have strengthened racist elements in the destinations, but it eased the situation somewhat in South Africa; those remaining were not such hard-core separatists.

The challenge for the Western elite was to disconnect the socialist and anti-apartheid goals. Foundations, along with other actors, aided in this process, partly by framing the debate in the United States. In 1978, the Rockefeller Foundation convened an eleven-person Study Commission on U.S. Policy toward Southern Africa, chaired by Franklin Thomas, president of the Ford Foundation, and including Alan Pifer, president of the Carnegie Corporation of New York. Its mission "was to determine how the United States can best respond to the problems posed by South Africa and its dismaying system of racial separation and discrimination."[51] At the same time, it had to take into account the "full range of U.S. interests."

The Commission had a large staff and conducted extensive meetings in the United States with "representatives of civil rights, antiapartheid, religious, congressional, and student groups; university administrations, corporations, research and public policy institutes, and state and local governments; . . . and three former senior government officials: Henry Kissinger, Donald F. McHenry, and Cyrus Vance." It traveled to South Africa and met with all elements throughout the country and later conferred with interested parties in England, France, and West Germany.

The Commission's *Report,* which became a major policy document in the United States, concluded that there needed to be a genuine sharing of political power, acceptable to all races. United States strategic interests that must be protected included sea routes (for oil shipments), corporate investments, and access to minerals—not gold and diamonds, but chromium and ferrochrome, manganese and ferromanganese, platinum, and vanadium.

The *Report* warned of danger from the "growth of Soviet influence in the region, promoted by white intransigence in South Africa, growing political instability, rising levels of racial violence, and armed conflict."[52] It did not, however, emphasize that the Communist Party, as a major partner in the ANC, was an internal threat to capitalism, and not a "tool" of the USSR. Soviet "philanthropy" did help the ANC and was a major public relations benefit for the USSR vis-à-vis black Africa.

Among the *Report's* recommendations was support for an arms and a nuclear embargo. It advised against a general divestment process or economic sanctions. Corporations should be encouraged to improve black welfare and follow the Sullivan Principles, which was a pledge to promote equal opportunity in employment, decent pay, and human rights in general. At the same time, pressure should be put on the government to share power with blacks. United States private organizations were urged to "support organizations inside South Africa working for change, assist the development of black leadership, and promote black welfare."

Foundations had been working for some time creating NGOs as alternatives to the liberation movement approach. The Ford Foundation promoted public interest law firms concerned with civil rights, which helped people to whom the apartheid laws were unfairly applied, and assisted black trade unions, especially those developing power in the mining industry. A Ford publication quotes approvingly of Halton Cheadle, a partner in the largest human rights and labor law firm: "Only in unions have blacks had an opportunity to exercise democracy—the practice of electing your leadership and holding your leadership accountable." It then notes: "Perhaps not coincidentally, the leader of the mineworkers union, Cyril Ramaphosa, was recently elected Secretary-General of the African National Congress, the nation's oldest political party."[53]

Ford also gave grants to the South African Council of Churches, scholarships to enable blacks to become lawyers, and generally helped the moderate reformers. When the apartheid system finally collapsed, there were many human rights organizations in place to draft the new Constitution (1996), which has a "state of the art" Bill of Rights. However, South Africa's resource distribution has hardly been altered, socialism evaporated from the ANC leadership, and the new black governments are content to participate in the world market and its leadership institutions, such as the World Economic Forum.

A South African scholar, Andrew Nash, has suggested that the ANC today is a hegemonic force that deflects or absorbs all criticism. The ANC now maintains that there is no alternative to global capitalism. It uses a "culture of human rights" to legitimate state power and incorporates hierarchical tribal practices, harnessing the masses' nostalgia "for a world in which personal ties of loyalty and obligation are not subsumed into commodity relations."[54] Furthermore, ANC leadership is increasingly comfortable and separate from the vast majority of impoverished citizens, as the black bourgeoisie settles into the previously white suburbs.

As in the 1960s' United States, "black power" is interpreted by some as "black capitalism." Now Cyril Ramaphosa, the Ford democratic hero, heads a consortium of black investors that has purchased "a large piece of the Anglo American Corporation" at discount prices. Many such deals exist to co-opt black leadership. They purchase support for the capitalist system in general, and also deter the enactment of anti-business corruption legislation, as even the *New York Times* attests:

Black empowerment, South African style, has critics. Some say that in a nation where black unemployment is about 40 percent and laborers may earn $12 a day, the deals mainly enrich well-connected business-men. Others call the deals cynical efforts by big business to buy the friendship of those in power.[55]

EASTERN EUROPE

Currently there is intense philanthropy in the former communist countries, serv-ing both to promote hegemonic ideology and to ease the pain of "transition." Eastern European revolutions have been largely attributed to: (1) dissatisfactions among citizens, paralleled by the decline of hegemonic ideology among the rul-ing elite; and (2) changes in the Soviet Union, and the perception of Soviet tol-erance (even encouragement) of radical change in Eastern Europe. In addition to internal weaknesses and external destabilizing attempts, we may posit a "pull," which included both material goods and public diplomacy of the United States and other Western nations. An important factor, validating Brzezinski's strate-gies (see chapter 1), was that engineering and managerial elites had unlimited respect for Western technology, in contrast to their own: "[The] distributive function of centralized planning has fared much better than the processes of technological advance."[56]

Cultural influence played a large role, as predicted. Gradually, English became the dominant foreign language in Eastern Europe, and "just as Ameri-can culture and scholarship began to dominate the attention of East European intellectuals, so American subcultures and countercultures began to prove irre-sistible to millions of East European young people."[57] Both intellectuals and workers saw "the West in idealized terms of liberty and prosperity."[58] The dis-tinctions remaining in socialist societies between "intellectuals" and "workers" ultimately helped their demise. High status was not enough; intellectuals (in the broadest sense, including teachers, doctors, and lawyers) resented the higher pay of manual workers.[59]

A more general source of dissatisfaction was the oversupply of educated people, historically an important factor in regime dissolution.[60] Rapid mod-ernization during the building of communist societies created an enormous demand for educated specialists. In addition, for ideological reasons, educa-tion was to be universally available. Once a moderate level of development had been attained, opportunities became scarcer. Those with power in the Com-munist parties often employed nepotism to ensure their children's careers; those without connections became resentful and identified "communism" with the corrupt Communist Party elite. Consumer goods were increasingly avail-able, and by the mid-1980s there often was too much food, drink, and tobacco floating around Eastern Europe. However, the intellectuals prized travel opportunities, and these were scarce except for people with either powerful Communist Party or Western foundation connections.[61]

Even more damaging to system maintenance was that egalitarianism faded from communist doctrine as a meritocratic "new class" became ascendant. The acceptance, even desire, among intellectuals for status and economic differentials made them look favorably upon Western liberal capitalism. Another destabilizer was Radio Free Europe, a U.S. propaganda operation, which not only painted a rosy vision of capitalism but also persuaded many that everything their own governments told them was false.

The Helsinki Accords brought East Europeans into closer contact with Western ideologies and organizations. These resulted from the USSR's request of Western Europe for an East–West European security agreement. The West agreed, with the conditions that Canada and the United States be included, and that economic and human rights standards be incorporated. An agreement was reached in 1975, which also provided for intellectual cooperation. Its emphasis on civil liberties substantively reinforced Western standards for political evaluation.

Helsinki Watch, an international NGO created by foundations to monitor the agreements, is now Human Rights Watch, with divisions for other continents. The Rockefeller, Ford, and Soros foundations are prominent supporters. Many other human rights organizations were then founded; for example, in 1988, the Merck Fund supported the Campaign for Peace and Democracy/East and West, which operated throughout Eastern Europe. Eastern European participants became socialized into the comfortable NGO world. At the same time, Western intervention into USSR and Eastern European societies to support human rights activists gained legitimacy. This was necessary, as some of the earlier "human rights" "NGOs," such as the Assembly of Captive European Nations (created by the CIA and meeting at the Carnegie Endowment), lacked respectability because of their prominent Nazi contingents.[62]

Scholarly exchanges, which began in the 1950s, also had been creating a transnational, Western-oriented elite. By the late 1980s, many of these scholars were "waiting in the wings" in East European governments, universities, and research institutes, hoping to apply their democratic-capitalist skills and knowledge.[63] The Rockefeller Brothers Fund (RBF) and others supported the American Center for International Leadership to identify and provide visits to the United States for "emerging young leaders" in any occupation.

The RBF was heavily involved in the economic side of the Helsinki provisions, especially in agricultural, environmental, and sustainable development projects. It helped establish the Foundation for the Development of Polish Agriculture and provided grants for Sierra Club involvement in USSR environmental protection exchanges.

Foundations have administered the exchange programs, even the overt U.S. government ones, such as the Fulbright scholarships, often through subsidiaries such as the Social Science Research Council, the International Research and Exchanges Board, the American Council of Learned Societies, and the Institute of International Education. In addition to the Ford, Rockefeller, and Carnegie foundations, the MacArthur, Bradley, McKnight, Mott, Mellon, and Soros foundations and the Merck and Rockefeller Brothers funds have supported East European scholars, universities, and institutes. The New School in New York held "Democracy Seminars" in the 1980s for Eastern European dissident scholars, a program supported by Pew Charitable Trusts and the Mellon, Ford, and Soros foundations. Currently it hosts a major democratization program for Eastern Europeans, which it regards as a direct descendant of its 1930s haven for anti-fascist refugees.[64]

Soros's "Open Society Institutes" are imperial in scope.[65] Foundations also have funded "East–West" integrative organizations, such as the Fondation Pour Une Entraide Intellectuelle Européenne (Paris), the Institute for East–West Security Studies (New York), and Salzburg Seminar in American Studies in Austria. These programs were to serve as a "civilizing mission":

> [T]he United States should expand relations with senior officials in all these countries and enlarge contacts with the technocracies and the scientific-intellectual communities, in order to learn more about them and even to help shape on the margin the decisions of these oligarchies which will inherit power over the next decade.[66]

The intellectual cooperation that the Helsinki Accords opened up went far beyond the exchange of scholars. For example, in 1988, the Rockefeller Brothers Fund and George Soros financed an International Management Center in Hungary, set up with the help of the University of Pittsburgh. By 1989, Soros was funding a totally revised edition of the *Great Soviet Encyclopedia*.

Private organizations were the channel for public diplomacy, not only because of their expertise but also because many believed that narrow-minded congressional interference would restrict the range of programs and create a U.S. foreign policy aura that would deter the participation of foreign scholars. The Eastern Europeans with Western connections were, after the abrogation of communism, able to open doors for money, contacts, and positions. It also was the case in Eastern Europe that academics were a greater proportion of the ruling elite than in the West.

Influence did not flow in one direction only. The International Research and Exchanges Board (IREX) programs enabled Westerners to study Eastern Europe in the manner of "history from the bottom up."[67] Ultimately these ethnographical and other empirical studies were not welcome to U.S. policy elites, who maintained that "totalitarianism" explained everything, precluding the need to know what was really going on. For example, Gerald Creed's work supported the heretical notion that Bulgarian farmers welcomed and benefited from collectivized agriculture.[68] The same phenomenon existed among South-east Asia policy makers during the Vietnam War era. They did not want to hear what the experts had to say, and many scholars were banished, as was Ralph McGeehee, an enthusiastic intelligence operative whose patriotism did not extend to distorting evidence as his masters wished.[69]

The Ford Foundation was a major supporter of the East European Cultural Foundation (EECF) in London, one of several new foundations begun in the 1980s promoting Western-style pluralism in Eastern Europe. The EECF states that it was:

> [C]reated in response to requests from Central and Eastern Europe for effective assistance in maintaining cultural, intellectual and civic life in these countries and to prevent their isolation from each other and from the West. The EECF encourages and helps to facilitate various forms of creative work by Czechs, Slovaks, Hungarians and Poles, and dialogue between Polish Solidarity, Czechoslovakia's Charter 77, the Hungarian democratic opposition and unofficial peace and human rights activists in East Germany, and between these groups and the West.[70]

The Foundation's journal, the *East European Reporter* (begun in 1985), focused exclusively on dissenting theories and leading dissenters. It was dominated by anti-communists and largely excluded reformist thought or those critical of Western democracy. Vaclav Havel was a prominent author. In his earlier writings, he had criticized both the capitalist and communist hegemons. For example, in *Power of the Powerless* (which appeared in 1985 in English), he speaks of

> . . . [t]he crisis of contemporary technological society as a whole. . . . Technology—that child of modern science, which in turn is a child of modern metaphysics—is out of humanity's control, has ceased to serve us, has enslaved us and compelled us to participate in the preparation of our own destruction. . . . We look on helplessly as that coldly functioning machine we have created inevitably engulfs us, tearing us away from our natural affiliations (for instance, from our habitat in the widest sense of that word, including our habitat in the biosphere). . . . There is no real evidence that western democracy, that is, democracy of the traditional parliamentary type, can offer solutions that are any more profound. . . . This static complex of rigid, conceptually sloppy and politically pragmatic mass political parties run by professional apparatuses and releasing the citizen from all forms of concrete and personal responsibility; and those complex foci of capital accumulation engaged in secret manipulations and expansion; the omnipresent dictatorship of con-

sumption, production, advertising, commerce, consumer culture, and all that flood of information: all of it . . . can only with great difficulty be imagined as the source of humanity's rediscovery of itself.[71]

Gradually his views shifted. By 1987, writing in the *East European Reporter,* he indicated that his major concern "about nuclear power stations is their centralizing aspect, which is why I am opposed to nuclear power in the hands of irresponsible bureaucrats, as is the case in totalitarian regimes."[72] Criticisms of Western political institutions or consumer culture had faded away. Similarly, the Czech "Charter 77" condemned militarization and the presence of foreign troops; this seems to have been forgotten in the later clamor for membership in NATO.

Similar views, by emigrés and dissidents, were featured in the *Journal of Democracy,* a publication of the U.S. government foundation, the National Endowment for Democracy. Challengers to the democratic-capitalist hegemony in the form of either democratic socialism or social democracy had no voice. The democratic revolution must be based on the "emancipation of civil society," which precludes government intervention in the affairs of citizens, unless they are foreign governments.

The British Jan Hus Educational Foundation reported in 1990 that it had been supporting the underground in Czechoslovakia. Among those financed was Tomas Jezek, chief advisor to the minister of finance, who "for many years, worked secretly with Pavel Bratinka on translations of the works of Friedrich von Hayek."[73] Other writers translated into samizdat editions included Alexis de Tocqueville and Karl Popper. The latter was George Soros's professor at Oxford, and the multitudinous "Open Society Institutes" are named after Popper's most noted work, *The Open Society and Its Enemies.* Cultural exchanges also supported the dissidents; in 1989, Joan Baez gave a concert in Bratislava, dedicating a song to Charter 77.

In Bulgaria, Western-style foundations have promoted intellectual cooperation. One of these, the Lyudmila Zhivkova Foundation (its name has recently been changed to the International Foundation St. Cyril and Methodius), began in 1982, with a stellar cast of founders, including Armand Hammer, United States; Pierre Cardin, France; Dr. Rifaat Assad, Syria; and Robert Maxwell, Great Britain. Many Bulgarian scholars worked with the foundation, and overseas branches were established; the Krupp Foundation initiated a German affiliate. An investigative foray to Sofia in 1989 and an interview with the Foundation's director, Dr. Evgeny Kirilov, yielded not much more than tickets to a delightful "Banner of Peace" International Children's Concert. One Bulgarian social scientist was of the opinion that the Foundation was mostly a cover for the transfer of funds abroad.[74] This may be the case; in Eastern Europe, as elsewhere, foundations also serve as contrivances for wheeling and dealing.

As Eastern European systems were crumbling under the pressures of human rights activists, frustrated intellectuals, and party reformers, and no longer maintained by Soviet intervention threats, the concept of "civil society" played a large role. A nonprofit sector barely existed, and it would not be politic to attack state welfare agencies, so the term was frequently used to designate dissidents and their activities, especially in Czechoslovakia and Hungary.

> For scholars of Eastern Europe, the term [civil society] often refers to the democratic opposition against communism, growing out of a strategy of self-organization in the 1970s and 1980s; for scholars of Western democracies, it typically refers to the "third sector" or nonprofit sector distinct from the state and the economy.[75]

Civil society connoted a rejection of communism, government, and formal political parties. The self-organization was mainly about publishing books and magazines, art exhibitions, rock concerts, lectures, seminars, and the like, rather than day care centers or retirement communities. This was convenient for the foreign funders, as they could continue their mission of creating and supporting NGOs, the media, culture, and education and avoid the taint and/or illegality of appearing to fund political parties.

Private donors and the U.S. government funded overthrow groups such as the Civic Forum in Czechoslovakia and Solidarity in Poland and, in later rounds, the Union of Democratic Forces in Bulgaria and Otpor in Serbia.[76] The situation became increasingly complex when more agents entered these operations. Overt U.S. sources included the Agency for International Development and a special fund for Eastern Europe: Support for East European Democracy (SEED). These worked in concert with German party foundations, the European Commission, and corporate and private foundations.

The pattern of both informal and formal cooperation continued during the next phase—creating a new hegemonic ideology and elite. For example, Partners for Democratic Change, formed to build civil society in Eastern Europe, the former USSR, and Argentina (all "emerging democracies"), includes directors from the Kettering and Eisenhower foundations, the United States Information Agency, the European Commission, and the Council on Foreign Relations, among others. The Civic Education Project, begun to assist universities in Eastern Europe and the former USSR, includes directors from the Soros-created Central European University, Boeing, Harvard, Yale, Princeton, and the German Marshall Fund. Its contributors include Mobil Oil, the European Commission, the Ford Foundation, the MacArthur Foundation, NATO, IBM, and several Soros foundations.

George Soros is perhaps the single most significant private funder. His enterprises, often called Open Society Institutes, are supplemented by many special projects. For example, he supported at Eotvos Lorand University in Hungary students and professors who organized an alternative college named for Istvan Bibo, an earlier dissident. They formed the core of the new political party—FIDESZ.[77]

When the revolution started, the members of the bibo-colleges organized FIDESZ as a base for enlisting the participation of Hungary's
younger generation and urban masses in the movement.

After the success of the Hungarian revolution, members of
FIDESZ crossed the border into Czecho-Slovakia without authorization to participate in the pro-democracy demonstrations taking place in
the center of Prague.[78]

In a number of places, the staging of revolters required that mobs be moved
around to convey the notion of mass support. Perhaps this was for TV watchers,
as everyone who is concerned about such things knows that revolutions are made
by small groups. Similarly, students in Sofia were called upon to protest the 1990
elections, although all observers attested that they had been won fairly by the
Bulgarian Socialist Party (the reconstituted Communist Party).

They led chants of "strike, strike! We'll never work for the Reds." A
"City of Truth" tent encampment to harass the government was set up
near the parliament in Sofia and continued for months. Student strikes
were called. By the same Autumn, the leaders of these student strikes
were studying on scholarships at American universities.[79]

FIDESZ is a particularly interesting example of incorporating new trends
into hegemonic institutions. In 1990, a delegation from this group was invited to
Japan by a Japanese Foundation, the Sasakawa Peace Fund. The program officer
awaited them at the airport; he saw only a "foursome resembling a rock band."
They could recognize him, and the leader, Fodor Gabor, introduced himself. "His
attire was the most rock-bandish of the bunch: Slim and with long hair, he wore
a summer sweater over a T-shirt and blue jeans full of holes."[80] Two years later,
here is one of the visitors, according to Tina Rosenberg:

On the floor of the Hungarian parliament, Zsuzsa Szelenyi wears black
hot pants, black tights, black boots, and a red sweater. A member of
parliament since 1990, she is twenty-five years old and still at work on
her undergraduate thesis. The headquarters of her political party, the
Federation of Young Democrats (FIDESZ) . . . look like the green
room at MTV.[81]

The party originally was limited to those between the ages of sixteen and thirty-
five and prohibited membership in any other politically based youth group.
When FIDESZ reached the stage of running candidates for parliament, it
formed a political media-consulting firm, the Image Group, which convened
focus groups. The Image Group advised running Tamas Deutsch, "a six-foot four,
drop-dead-handsome, twenty-two year old law student with shoulder-length

hair and a denim jacket." After a successful election, Deutsch posed for a Levi's ad, and also was offered a Harley-Davidson plus cash from that company. The party's campaigns included rock concerts, where the candidates sang along onstage. Despite all of this jazz, "FIDESZ is a Potemkin party; there is little behind the impressive parliamentary group seen on television—no well-established organization, no cadre of grassroots activists."[82]

It does have political positions, originally advocating for a parliamentary democracy and market economy, along with a "social policy . . . needed to set aright the social disadvantages that develop and to create equality of opportunity."[83] By 1998, FIDESZ had become right wing and was renamed the Hungarian Civic Party. It no longer was restricted to the young but represented the new entrepreneurial class as well as traditional conservatives. It now leads governing coalitions and leans toward Lockheed-Martin products for its NATO kit. Its leader, Viktor Orban, had studied at Oxford on a Soros grant; back in 1989, he had been noted for his boldness in telling the Soviet Union to remove its troops from Hungary.

After the successful collapses, Western forces had to create new hegemonic ideologies, elites, and institutions. There was already a core of dissidents, reformers, human rights activists, and exchange scholars. More Western friends were being produced at the Soros-created Central European University in Budapest (with branches in other countries), the new Soros American University in Bulgaria, and thousands of "civil society" organizations. However, activists of the overthrow period were not all reusable. The new ideology declared democracy and free markets inseparable; everything must be for sale to anyone, including national universities and newspapers. The board chairman of Soros's Bulgarian foundation, Professor Bogdan Bogdanov of Sofia University, argued that the university should be converted to a private, joint stock company.[84] The democratization ideology exported to Eastern Europe excluded the concept of a "middle way," or European social democracy. Ultimately the knights of democracy would be consecrated in the humanitarian league of nations: NATO.

> The dissidents—the New Forum people in Germany, the Havels, the Hungarian Network activists—came of age in an Eastern Europe of the Prague Spring and "socialism with a human face." Some wanted only to reform Communism, or at least to preserve its few charms of solidarity and social equality. They disdained the shallowness and greed of capitalist society.
>
> This generation of dissidents is all but irrelevant today. The East German dissidents, who opposed unification, were the first to go.[85]

Likewise, the environmental activists, such as the Bulgarian Ecoglasnost, have been dismissed as interfering with economic development.[86]

Massive funding is available; how, then, can it be used to remake Eastern Europe? Social scientists have been developing models of "transitology" to predict and guide transitions to democracy. Often these are based on Chile, Argentina, Spain, and Portugal; their applicability to Eastern Europe is not considered impressive. However, there is broad agreement that "non-state" actors play a major role in promoting democracy. These might include human rights groups and other international NGOs, foundations, and even multinational corporations.[87] Other factors are demonstration effects, whereby citizens and elites associate the "good life" with the adoption of a democratic-capitalist system; coercive measures, such as bombing, a contra war, or refusal of International Monetary Fund (IMF) loans if the socialist parliamentarians win majorities; and inducements, such as membership in the European Union, dependent on the adoption of a democratic-capitalist system. Covert actions might operate along with any of these democracy promotion methods. For example, secretly funded political parties could be converted into mobs should they fail to win the election and thereby prevent the "undemocratic" winners from exercising power. This frequently happened in Bulgaria, requiring the application of historic "democracy promotion" techniques:

> The protest movement in Bulgaria was beginning to feel and smell like the general strike in British Guiana to topple Cheddi Jagan in 1962, and the campaign to undermine Salvador Allende in Chile in the early '70s—both operations of the CIA—where as soon as one demand was met, newer ones were raised, putting the government virtually under siege, hoping it would over-react, and making normal governing impossible.[88]

Some have suggested that democracy promotion would be a wasted effort, as the West had so much power over Eastern Europe that it did not matter what kind of political systems it had or which political parties won elections.[89] Political scientist Claus Offe opined that democracy would hurt a market transformation, as it needs an iron hand. It was only because Western capitalism came into being before democracy that its requisite inequality and hardship could be imposed.[90] Nevertheless, foreign policy elites in Canada, the United States, and Western Europe regarded the creation of a new hegemony as important. For foundations, it was a new challenge in their normal line of work; it also has become a growth industry for private corporations. Foundation executive Kevin Quigley explains:

> Why did U.S. private foundations respond to the events in East and Central Europe? Part of the explanation lies in the sector's self-image. Foundations see themselves as society's research and development sector. In that way, philanthropic investments are the building blocks for

important social and economic change. Historically, the philanthropic sector has identified and piloted innovative solutions that have helped to solve many critical problems, such as funding the Green Revolution, which addressed many of the problems of global hunger.[91]

While foundations have participated in every aspect of democratization, they have special "expertise in the independent sector and development of civil society." Between 1989 and 1994, the private foundations spent $450 million in Eastern Europe.[92] A small sample of their activities follows. One democratization technique was direct support for advisors to Eastern European governments:

> For example, the Ford Foundation supported a Polish-American economist who served as a key advisor to the first postcommunist Polish finance minister, Leszek Balcerowicz, the architect of Poland's stabilization and economic restructuring program. Balcerowicz himself has acknowledged this individual's role in drafting Poland's initial plan for the transformation of its economy.[93]

The Pew Charitable Trusts funded an advisor in the Economics Policy Ministry in Czechoslovakia and with the Ford Foundation supported advisors throughout Czech and Slovak Republic ministries: finance, trade, central bank, social service and others. Mott financed an advisor to the Bulgarian prime minister. Soros widely supports this type of technical assistance, including Jeffrey Sachs, the Harvard prophet of "shock therapy" for capitalist transition. Kevin Quigley pointed out that private foundation funding of advisors "removes any suspicion that the advisor is 'in the pocket' of some foreign government or organization whose interests might be antithetical to those of the host country."[94]

Another approach is "leadership training," by which future elites are educated in democracy while becoming part of networks. The internship program of the National Forum Foundation, the Pew Economic Freedom Fellows, and the Eisenhower Fellowships are examples. Conferences and workshops also further democratization. For example, the Mott and Rockefeller Brothers Fund held workshops throughout Eastern Europe on how to create an independent sector.

Much activity is devoted to the founding of new institutions. As local funds are lacking, foreign funding is considered the only way to produce a truly independent sector. By 1995, there were 29,000 NGOs in the Czech Republic, 20,000 in Poland, and similar numbers in other countries.[95] They were almost entirely supported by foreign corporations, foundations, governments, political parties, and international institutions such as the European Union and the World Bank.

Political parties are a favorite charity. Although some countries have laws prohibiting foreign funding of parties, these often were evaded in the interest of democratization.[96] Some foreigners complained of unfair interference. For example:

At issue is $400,000 that the National Endowment for Democracy in Washington has given to the [Czech] Civic Forum and the Public against Violence, the organizations that coalesced last November to lead the revolution against Communist rule. Both are now political parties running full slates of candidates in this country's first free elections in 42 years.[97]

Similar criticisms by Hungarians were defended by U.S. Ambassador Mark Palmer:

"I'm open about supporting the opposition parties, including getting money for them from the National Endowment for Democracy," he continued. "I think we should be proud of it."[98]

A member of the U.S. democratization elite, Larry Diamond, has devised a legal justification, claiming that there is an evolving international "right to democratic governance" that justifies intervention by international organizations, foreign governments, and NGOs.[99]

The U.S. Agency for International Development now spends far more money on democratization in general and support for political parties and NGOs than does the National Endowment for Democracy. It too has been accused of interference in the domestic affairs of sovereign states, as it helps all except Communist parties. It justifies such policies by claiming, for example, that such funding "does not violate Russian law."[100] The USAID also argues that its mission is to help "democratic" parties only, even though "[a] strict standard of organizational democracy would not be met by either of the two major parties in the United States."[101]

As a citizen of the United States and a political scientist, it pains me that my government engages in such democracy "doublespeak." Foreign money, or even domestic money used for elections "United States style," is a far cry from democracy, which we claim has something to do with "self-determination." In Bulgaria, it was the Communist Party that through a "palace coup" overthrew old-style communism and adopted an ideology not so far from the West's, of economic modernization, joint ventures with multinationals, parliamentary democracy, and a social safety net.[102] Renamed the Bulgarian Socialist Party (BSP), it enjoyed deep support throughout the country, where most continued to believe in socialism.[103] On the other hand, the Union of Democratic Forces (UDF), despite its millions in foreign funds and IMF threats on its behalf, had practically no support outside of Sofia students and intellectuals. This has been attested to by many observers, even those who were foundation people. The BSP was judged as being more fair in process, more willing to compromise, and more observant of the new constitution than the UDF; in addition, as it enjoyed popular support, it was much more democratically based.[104] Election observers, funded by the West, looked for flaws only on the BSP side, and they could not find any. The BSP also was unduly supportive, at a great cost to Bulgaria, of U.S. sanctions on Iraq and Yugoslavia.

Party money from all sources is used for coalition building, by which all of the monarchist, free market, Christian, environmentalist, and other groups opposing Communists or Socialists are persuaded to unite, at least for election purposes. It also is used for polling, focus groups, image building, and message development. These techniques "allow for party leaders to reach out to their constituents to discover what issues matter most to them, and create new platforms and campaigns based upon such popular opinion."[105] Money is used to hire major Western advertising companies to manufacture party and candidate image. There is much spent for the orientation of candidates and those elected; for example, "the Ford Foundation pioneered a training program for new parliamentarians."[106]

Modern communications equipment, media expenses, and headquarters also are funded. Furthermore, travel for conferences or special missions often is required. The National Democratic Institute (now supported by U.S. AID and private foundations as well as the NED): "[O]rganized a program to bring Serbian opposition party leaders to Poland to receive advice and guidance from Polish party activists on their current political situation, based on the similar experiences of the Poles in recent years."[107] Above all, the money goes a long way in buying friends in impoverished countries and enables the principals to bestow gifts or contracts on many others.

New media institutions are another way of promoting democratization, through independent press centers, the training of journalists, and supplies and equipment for radio and TV stations. Libraries and electronic databases are generously supported by the Soros and Mellon foundations.

Think tanks, which help shape policy, as in the United States, also have been developed throughout Eastern Europe, such as the Ford Foundation-supported Gdansk Institute for Market Economics.[108] Other NGOs by the thousands are supported. Some are concerned with policy issues, some with market supplementation that has become urgent in "shocked economies," and all provide status and salaries for intellectuals. For example, the MacArthur, Ford, Eurasia, and Soros foundations support women's groups throughout Russia and a Center for Gender Studies in Moscow. The Network of East–West Women helps women's groups in the entire former Soviet bloc, supplying computers, training, and Internet access, among other assistance.[109]

Human rights NGOs now support every type of minority; notable are the new organizations for Roma that receive considerable Soros money. Here a great need arose; whereas communist governments had squelched particularist sentiment with the dogma of international brotherhood, the strategists of rollback encouraged nationalism and heaped scorn on communist "unity." Thus Soros, aware of the anti-Semitism that accompanied anti-communism in Hungary, designed the FIDESZ party to minimize nationalistic elements. Its image was to be that of a "capitalist international," with youth, MTV, Harleys, and denim instead of workers and peasants with hammers and sickles. Another unpopular minority is the Bulgarian military officer group; it was not deemed suitable for the anticipated NATO relationship, and an NGO has been created to find suitable occupations for these officers.

The Foundation in Support of Local Democracy, funded by Mott and others, is a Polish NGO, created in part because of complaints that all of the money was going to elites in large cities. This organization provides training for local government officials and study visits throughout Poland, Western Europe, and the United States, where the NGO has its headquarters at Rutgers University. The Mott Foundation also has endowed community foundations throughout Eastern Europe, with similar roles to those in the United States.

Environmental protection was another interest; the democratic free market parties generally show even less concern for the environment than the former communists. In Bulgaria, the new hegemons forced the decollectivization of agriculture. "[The] restitution of agricultural land led to the almost complete abandonment of measures aimed at preventing water and wind erosion, soil flooding, acidification and salinization."[110] In addition to very specific groups, such as the Bulgarian Society for the Protection of Bats, some organizations work throughout Eastern Europe, for example, the Institute for Sustainable Communities. This group, headquartered in Vermont and supported by the Rockefeller Brothers Fund, Mott, and others, has brought to localities environmentally friendly technologies of watershed protection, sewage treatment, and solid waste disposal. For example, a Community Environmental Action Project was conducted in Bulgaria beginning in 1992:

> The purpose of the two-year project was to demonstrate how local governments in Bulgaria can set environmental priorities, develop action plans, and implement cost-effective strategies to address the most serious problem in the community through a participatory planning and decision-making process. The demonstration community of Troyan, Bulgaria (population 40,000), implemented the country's first leak-detection program for water conservation, launched an environmental audit program for local industries, and significantly enhanced public understanding and commitment to addressing environmental problems. ISC's Bulgarian partner, the National Movement of Ecoglasnost, has replicated the project in five additional communities. At the conclusion of the project, ISC hosted a national conference for municipal environmental specialists to review the results of the project and distributed a guidebook on how to implement a community action project based on the Troyan experience. The Minister of Environment distributed copies of the Troyan Action Plan to communities across Bulgaria.[111]

Many programs exist for the "creation of civil society," that is, to further the proliferation and support for NGOs in general. Both the Open Society Foundation-Sofia, and the Civil Society Development Foundation, supported by the European Union, have in recent years added another goal: to prepare Bulgaria for integration into the European Union and NATO.

There is evidence that many of the "civil society" organizations operate mainly to build clientele relationships between foreign donors and grantees; the NGOs themselves have few constituencies.[112] Soros Open Society funds are notable for being spread around widely, providing many small grants to individuals with little accountability required.[113] Some believe that "huge amounts of Soros money [are] wasted," but the buying of friends among the intellectuals and proliferation of NGOs is functional, as it is in the United States.[114]

New educational institutions were another aspect of democratization; donors also facilitated extensive curriculum revision at existing schools and universities. The Central European University (CEU) in Budapest, founded in 1991, enjoyed $65 million in Soros money. It is considered by one scholar "the jewel in Soros's crown":[115]

> Every student from Central Europe that is accepted is given a full scholarship that includes room, board, tuition and a monthly stipend. Students can also apply for scholarships that allow them to study abroad for a portion of their tenure at CEU. The emphasis at CEU, however, is on training *in the region* the next cohort of leaders and on convincing them to take positions in their own country after graduation. . . . For example, the economics department's goal is to train economists from the region in how to deal with problems arising from the transition from a command to a market economy. All of the courses are conducted in English by faculty both from the region and from the West.[116]

There have been tensions, because salaries are four to five times that of local universities; nevertheless, the CEU remains an important source of transition ideas, techniques, and leaders.

While microcredit programs and economic policy think tanks are supported by private foundations, major economic restructuring required for democratization has mostly been funded by governments and intergovernmental bodies such as the European Union. About $80 billion in aid was given to Eastern Europe between 1989 and 1998.[117] Much of it was for economic privatization, a matter that had earlier received less attention than constitution writing and party building. There were few guides, a situation somewhat similar to that facing Lenin when going in the other direction. It was most important for ideological reasons to demolish the large industrial complexes with associated health, sport, and other facilities; and collectivized agriculture.[118] These were symbols of socialism. In Poland, four glass-making firms were privatized in a process that required over $900,000 in aid for each.[119]

There was much corruption, East and West. Former communist managers often purchased their firms or brokered deals with Western corporations that left them sitting pretty. The USAID operates by tendering contracts to profit-making firms, including the "Big Six" accountancy firms and new specialized businesses:

> Nowhere is aid a bigger business than in the Washington area, home to dozens of development groups that feed off USAID and compete for contracts. Many of these companies are staffed by retired USAID employees skilled in writing proposals to appeal to their erstwhile government colleagues. Some employ spouses of current USAID officials.[120]

Consultants have sometimes appraised Eastern enterprises, after which they were purchased by the consultant firm's Western clients. The term "Charles Dickens" capitalism has been used by observers; others call it "vulture capitalism," whereby enterprises have been set free to deteriorate, or in some instances, bombed, after which Western firms obtain them at bargain prices. "For instance, the Copper Metallurgical plant near the town of Pirdop [Bulgaria] producing gold and platinum as well as electrolytic copper was sold in 1997 to Union Miniere, Belgium for next to nothing."[121] No type of enterprise is exempt from foreign ownership: "Today, almost all the big Czech banks have been taken over by foreign institutions, from Erste Bank of Austria to GE Capital."[122] Newspapers, TV and radio stations, telecommunications, and news services are all available; Internet Securities, a Boston-based firm, acquired Kadiev News Service, "a full-service Bulgarian news provider."[123]

Apart from skullduggery, economic desocialization has lent little support to another goal of the democratizers: creating a new hegemonic ideology. The process employs enormous subsidies and economic planning, both violating the "free market" idea: "Now the Western donors replaced the Communist Party in the role of enlightened planner, albeit a capitalist one."[124]

The new ideology is meeting resistance, because despite talk about "winners and losers" and the ultimate benefits of "globalization," massive poverty is occurring. Social benefits, such as pensions for the elderly, health care, maternity leave with pay, or child care, and in some places, even free education, have been dismantled. Downsizing and lack of funds for investment or maintenance have produced high unemployment rates. News and cultural institutions subsidized under communism, such as the Hungarian film industry, have now collapsed or been purchased by foreign firms. These effects have been attested to by the USAID itself.

> Social sector issues in the E&E (Europe and Eurasia) region differ from those in most developing countries. In a number of countries, the realities of transition are creating a new class of chronically poor

rather than the large and stable middle class that the shift to market systems was expected to engender. Many citizens have lost benefits (such as housing and utilities) previously provided by the State and social services such as education and health care have deteriorated. An estimated 50% of Eurasia's population and 24% of the Southern Tier were living in poverty in the mid-1990s, compared with 4% and 5%, respectively, in the late 1980s. Those countries that have experienced the largest and most sustained drops in GDP and have been slowest to regain their 1989 income levels have also suffered the biggest increases in income inequality. These losses, combined with limited employment opportunities, create resentments that threaten social cohesion and prospects for continued transition. It is essential to deal with social issues in order to build support for economic and political change.[125]

Future aid programs may concentrate more on "market supplementation." Eastern economies may come to resemble the actual, not theoretical, "free market" United States, including a healthy dose of "military Keynesianism" provided by NATO membership.

It is hard to know how much democratization has occurred; information is best gleaned from specialist scholars. News services for Eastern Europe have been acquired by Western corporations, including Internet databases now owned or supported by Soros's Open Society foundations. Two anthropologists have suggested that the strongest democratic effect was produced in those wary of the new big brother:

[S]ince many Western initiatives claimed to be about establishing democratic participation and getting local people to take initiative away from top-down planners, the resistance generated by the conditions and requirements of aid programs may be their greatest success.[126]

WORLD CONCLAVES OF NGOs

The last quarter of the twentieth century saw a huge increase in NGO international conferences, networks, and coalitions. They had roots in earlier transnational human rights activity, including the anti-slavery movement, but the vast scale is something new in the world.[127] Communications technology and more efficient travel make this work feasible; however, the process has been stimulated and guided by globalization elites, who organize and fund most of it. This often is denied. Thus, CIVICUS, a world alliance of citizen action organizations, contrasts its structure with that of churches and socialist internationals: "In both cases, the global drive was promoted by a centrally organized institution, be it a church or a political organization, spreading its compass to the periphery."[128] The CIVICUS constituents, on the contrary, are said to be spontaneous actors, motivated by values, who create associations from the "bottom up." Today's movement "is not being promoted by one all-encompassing structure." Perhaps not a structure but an elite with shared understanding dominates.

The expensive conferencing tends to incorporate all protest, dissent, and even reform energies into a fragmented, pragmatic, NGO model dependent on foundation funding and attractive enough to draw away partisans or potential recruits of structural change movements. A leading *promoter* of NGOs, Thomas Carothers, vice president for Global Policy at the Carnegie Endowment for International Peace, had this to say:

> [M]ost of the new transnational civil society actors are Western groups projecting themselves into developing and transitional societies. They may sometimes work in partnership with groups from those countries, but the agendas and values they pursue are usually their own. Transnational civil society is thus "global" but very much part of the same projection of Western political and economic power that civil society activists decry in other venues.[129]

The United Nations Universal Declaration of Human Rights (1948) was created by an international group of human rights specialists: government officials, legal experts, and executives of national organizations. What is different about current conclaves is that in addition to elites, many ordinary activists attend, from rich and poor countries. It is a heady experience to participate in workshops, to compose declarations, and to later sit around in the café with counterparts from the Australian Outback, Tajikistan, Botswana, and Finland. Friends and family of conference attendees also may be drawn into the system. For example, an early gathering of this type was the 1975 United Nations Conference for Women's Rights in Mexico City. A "parallel" NGO conference was organized, and my mother attended as a representative of the United Nations Association. In addition to the enthusiastic reports upon her return, she had been given a special pin: a female symbol superimposed on a peace dove. I have inherited that pin and probably my daughter will some day; it could blur critical evaluation of UN projects.

The current conference scene emphasizes networks that differ from more conventional organizations by their lack of formal hierarchy, centrality of information sharing, and diversity of membership:

> Major actors in advocacy networks may include the following: (1) international and domestic nongovernmental research and advocacy organizations; (2) local social movements; (3) foundations; (4) the

media; (5) churches, trade unions, consumer organizations, and intellectuals; (6) parts of regional and international intergovernmental organizations; and (7) parts of the executive and/or parliamentary branches of governments.[130]

It may appear that no one is in charge, but a resource mobilization perspective could yield a different picture, as few NGOs are membership funded. Conferences of women's, children's, or indigenous peoples' rights activists require large sums for travel and infrastructure; coalitions formed also are sustained in between conferences by UN committees and foundation funding. Even alternative summits and parallel conferences protesting the official ones are supported by foundations, such as the Rio UN Environmental conference and the Free Trade Area of the Americas summits, discussed previously. At the 1999 World Trade Organization meeting in Seattle

> controlled and financed by official donors and research foundations, the hidden agenda is to install a "politically correct" Citizens' Summit, namely to ensure that the various teach-ins and public rallies in the streets of Seattle conform to the dominant "counter discourse." The latter consists in pressing for the inclusion of token environmental, labor and human rights clauses, "poverty alleviation" schemes as well as "institutional reforms" without defying the central role of trade liberalisation.[131]

The information-sharing aspect of transnational networks facilitates control by consent. Information may be gleaned from the very grass roots, but it is then filtered through centralized newsletters and reports and promulgated worldwide on Web sites and in other media. For an example of this process, we can examine a scholarly article by Éva Kuti, a specialist on Eastern European civil society organizations. She reports that:

> [I]n some Eastern European countries, the majority of the third sector's revenues come from abroad. . . .
> The figures for Hungary, where the nonprofit sector probably has a relatively low general level of foreign funding, seem to prove that the extent of the dependence of some nonprofits' activities on foreign support is alarming even there.[132]

However, when she prepares a country profile on the Hungarian nonprofit sector for a CIVICUS handbook, there is no mention of foreign funding.[133] Just as transnational financing of political parties is considered irrelevant by the democracy promoters, so the outside donor control of civil society is not worth mentioning.

Another integrative network is the World Movement for Democracy, organized by the National Endowment for Democracy, and its sister organizations, which now have their own network. Dutch, Australian, French, British, German, Swedish, Norwegian, and Canadian cognates are involved in financing political parties, policy institutes, trade unions, media, and many types of NGOs in other countries. The Second Assembly of the World Movement for Democracy was held in São Paulo and included "more than 400 democrats representing the non-governmental sector from more than 80 countries."[134] Predictably, the representatives from Serbia were from B-92, the Soros- and NED-funded radio station, and two from Otpor. The latter, according to the *New York Times,* was financed by the United States; "[n]o other opposition force was as unsettling to the regime or as critical to its overthrow."[135] The NED aspires to integrate the "hard right" and CIA front organizations with liberal foundation spokespeople and authentic democratic groups. This convergence has been occurring since the "shocking" revelations in 1967 of CIA national and international NGO funding. Such transborder manipulation has become so "normal" that it is rarely discussed, even by political scientists concerned about "money in politics," or those who consider themselves on the "left."

Now the World Bank is convening the world's poor:

> There is a wide disconnect between poor people's realities and global decision making. To address this gap, a group of nearly 100 representatives of poor people's membership-based organizations, multi-lateral organizations, foundations, government, Executive Directors, and staff across the World Bank and International Finance Corporation came together at World Bank headquarters [on] December 11–13, 2000, for a workshop of "Local-Global Connectivity for Voices of the Poor."[136]

Attending were representatives from poor people's networks, such as the Self-Employed Women's Association and the National Slum Dwellers Association, both of India; the Liberal Women's Brain Pool of Mongolia; foundation-supported venture capitalists such as the Ashoka Foundation and Enterprise Works Worldwide; Grameen Bank (microcredit); firms that link native craftspeople to customers via the Internet; the International Confederation of Free Trade Unions; Grassroots International; and a large contingent of World Bank poverty specialists. Conferences such as these, supplemented by a Web site, PovertyNet, and electronic conferences, aim to create a permanent World Bank-guided coalition of poor people's organizations.

To reveal what the poor are thinking, the World Bank gathered together "the voices of 60,000 poor men and women from 60 countries" in *Poverty Trends and Voices of the Poor.* The report documents that poverty is increasing in most places and that

[i]n all areas the income poor are systematically worse off than the non-poor. Poor people's experiences with government institutions are largely negative, even when government programs were rated as important. Corruption, rudeness and poor quality services seemed to be the norm, whether in health care or in programs of social support.[137]

The report indicates that small gains for the poor often are eroded: "Life story patterns showed that the poor with few assets would, with great effort, slowly creep upward, only to be plunged back into poverty by illness, loss of employment, poor crops, or, for women, desertion."[138] The poor's voices do not suggest that corporations, free trade agreements, or austerity policies of multilateral lending agencies have any bearing on the problem. Personal and local factors, and climate, are blamed throughout. A slight hint of structural causes is buried in the following statement:

> Most blamed governments for mismanaging the economy and for high taxes, inflation and privatization; declining agricultural productivity and declines in affordability of agricultural inputs; lack of cheap credit; corrupt government services; or simply lack of government care for the poor.[139]

The World Bank's own commentary steers away from discussions of neoliberalism; on the contrary, it asserts that international trade barriers are causing poverty. The statistical documentation of poverty is copious, and the steep declines in well-being in the "transition" economies are noted. For example, "In Bulgaria, in 1997, over 84 percent of the Roma lived below the poverty line (compared to a national poverty rate of 36 percent)."[140]

Despite the lack of analysis, the report's own documentation might create dissonance with the elite's assurance that the "wealth of nations" results from globalization. According to the World Bank, throughout the co-prosperity sphere

> livelihood strategies for the poor are primarily in the informal sector, and are sometimes illegal. People survive through an enormously wide range of activities—small-time vending, doing odd jobs, carrying brick and sand, working in quarries and mines, "shuttling" (the name given to constant movement while trading in Eastern Europe), borrowing from neighbors and moneylenders, working two or three jobs, growing vegetables on little plots, returning to subsistence agriculture in countries such as Bulgaria, Russia and the Kyrgyz Republic, collecting grass, herbs, and bamboo shoots, catching wild animals, selling cooked food, making crafts, working in factories, begging, washing blankets and carpets, putting children to work, praying for rain, selling assets one by one,

surrendering to prayer, reducing the number of meals, changing their diet, selling their own blood, and in desperation engaging in criminal activities, including prostitution.[141]

The foregoing has revealed only a tiny slice of the international pie that has been well larded by Western donors. The story can be repeated for every part of the planet; the evidence is easily accessible to researchers, although it might well be supplemented by translations from non-Western-financed local presses.

10

Conclusions and Questions
for Further Research

Democracy is fundamentally rooted in the proposition that political
sovereignty originates with citizens. The authority of the state is
anchored in the will of the people, and just and legitimate government
can only be based on their explicit consent. . . . Access to alternative
and competing sources of information is an important prerequisite for
ensuring effective political competition. . . . The empty exercise of
"free choice" in the absence of competing sources of information and
open debate on different courses of action confers no legitimacy on
the "elected" government.
—U.S. Agency for International Development,
Democracy and Governance

The masses are sufficiently enlightened to let their affairs be handled
by a national steering committee consisting of artists, scientists, and
industrialists, which would have ample qualifications to deal with all
matters of public interest, and to efficiently direct the general interests
of society.
—Claude-Henri de Saint-Simon,
De l'Organization Sociale

PURPOSE REITERATED

I wrote this book primarily to reveal the power that has been largely obscured
both in popular accounts of our society and in the more specialized political science literature. The liberal foundations try to hide their hands and do not
encourage critical research. They also become invisible by working through

197

buffer organizations such as the Social Science Research Council or the Brookings Institution. Foundations themselves are buffer institutions, serving the corporate interests of their origins, their trustees, and their investments.

They further obscure themselves and their subsidiaries through ideological mystification, for example, the concept of the sectors: government, business, and the independent one. This masks power, as crucial decisions are made in institutional and informal settings where elites from government, business, foundations, think tanks, academia, and the media interact. Those with the greatest influence are generally people who are simultaneously or serially corporate directors, trustees of universities, foundations, and charities, and top government officials.

I also have tried to demonstrate that acknowledging power (by which I mean the source of important decisions) would provide a more accurate account of politics, or history for that matter. Foundation wealth and connections are used to pursue interests directly and also to maintain hegemonic control via consent. Sometimes these goals appear to conflict. To right wingers with short-term perspectives, foundations that give grants to environmental organizations seem to be traducing their capitalist founders' intent.

Often the strategy is mutually reinforcing; civil rights for blacks served corporate interests and also helped produce consent. Some policies may work both ways. Free trade may mollify the populace with cheap T-shirts, but the moral and economic costs of maintaining an "open-market" world could backfire, as Brzezinski suggests. Not all system-maintenance activities involve government policies. Consent can be attained when nonprofit organizations are sustained, and their leaders are assimilated into "higher circles."

The liberal foundations and their associated think tanks have major influence over policy. However, it is not total; some matters are not pursued, and in other cases, no leverage has been obtained. Here is one topic for systematic research. We could start with the "Government's 50 Greatest Endeavors," based on the Brookings Institution's survey of 450 political science and history professors.[1] The resulting hit parade of policies, which includes both laws and treaties, could be explored for foundation input. A similar exercise might investigate state and local government policies. Here we will want to calculate the influence of foundation-sponsored public officials' organizations such as the National Governors Association, the International City Management Association, and the League of Cities. These groups help shape federal legislation as well, for example, in welfare reform. Foundations have been somewhat more visible when it is a matter of policies relating to themselves and the nonprofit sector, but even here more study is needed.

HEGEMONY

A major argument herein has been that foundations are prime constructors of hegemony, by which it is meant that they act to promote consent, and its corollary, to prevent effective dissent against capitalist democracy. Coercive institutions also have their role, but attracting flies with honey can get them stuck good.

Foundations induce consent by creating an ideology that appears to be common sense and incorporates all newly emergent or challenging trends. They also institute reforms against the resistance, indifference, or incapacity of political institutions. In addition, they integrate into their networks persons who are ambitious, or who threaten to lead counterhegemonic movements. They can accomplish this by offering funding, positions, legitimacy, access, and even social events, at the highest and lowest levels. The CIVICUS World Assembly, the World Social Forum (in Brazil), and community foundation workshops all aim to make outsiders insiders. Foundations and think tanks are today diverse, and groovy World Bankers mix with the "slum dwellers'" NGO. All of the processes of hegemony are now being exercised globally, as leading critics of foundations have noted:

> [T]he foundations sustain the complex nerve centers and guidance mechanisms for a whole system of institutional power. To a remarkable and not accidental degree, this power has both characterized and defined American society and its relations with the rest of the world in the 20th century.[2]

Just as advertisers have appealed to similar psychological needs in the world's populations, so mollifiers of dissent have recognized universal longings. Even among those who want to transform society, there is a need for self-esteem, pleasure, acceptance and, sometimes, rent money. People in protest movements expect to rough it in material terms, but they also may face rough interpersonal relations (not just between men and women). Dissenters often are angry people; they have not adjusted. So there is some truth in the Ford Foundation's 1949 *Report's* characterization of maladjusted people as potential troublemakers. They need anger to fight the suits, but it sometimes spills over onto their own people. The elite milieux not only include excellent hors d'oeuvres, but people usually are nice. The bombees are far away.

Hegemony is further maintained by fragmenting potential opposition into a multiplicity of specific advocacy groups that are rewarded for being pragmatic. The powerful, on the other hand, can work collaboratively. They have the resources to be wherever decisions are being made, the information to have answers ready before questions arise, and the skills to "frame" issues for others. This occurs at the top, for example, in the War-Peace Studies Project of the Council on Foreign Relations. It also is attempted at the local level, for example in the Public Issues Fora of the Kettering Foundation. More research is needed to determine if the latter has had any effect; few small towns have destabilizing grassroots activism.

The production of consent has been largely successful; nevertheless, hegemony can be threatened. It may not last forever, despite the proclamation of "the end of history." A weakness lies in the disparity between ideology and reality. Poverty intellectuals, such as those on the World Bank staff, could lose their faith because of the very richness of their data. They also know that the description from *Voices of the Poor* (chapter 9) omitted another way that people scrimp and save: by selling body organs.

Some leading capitalist ideologues are having second thoughts: *Lingua Franca* noted the conversion of John Gray, author of *False Dawn*, and Edward Luttwak, author of *Turbo-Capitalism*.[3] Even George Soros has written about capitalism destroying itself.[4] Those participating in U.S. foreign democracy assistance programs note its imposition by force, bribes, and bought elections. They also admit that the United States' democracy standards for others are not met in the homeland. Brzezinski believes that in the long run, democracy and imperialism may not be compatible. The great icons of behavioralism recently have indicated that they ignored the important issues; perhaps they will revisit them some day.

Another potential splintering in the hegemonic scheme may occur when the milder reforms that foundations promote reveal a need for further transformation. If children need equally funded education, maybe they also should have equally funded food, medical care, toys, and sports equipment. Or perhaps they need less food and equipment and fewer toys. Maybe they need a stable home situation. Is it possible that the family, the "sector" that is not looked at too closely, also is, in most cases, dysfunctional?

There are these and other stresses on the democratic capitalist consensus. Nevertheless, as long as ambitious and energetic young people of all races enjoy opportunities for social mobility, they are not likely to become leaders of the disaffected. The organic intellectuals who Gramsci thought would play a counter-hegemonic role are snapped up through leadership training programs before they can even think of it. Their counterparts are the organic farmers who are rapidly being incorporated into agribusiness and are now producing frozen organic TV dinners for export or cross-country shipping.[5]

DEMOCRACY

Foundations define democracy, changing the concept as needs arise. In the early twentieth century, they promoted guided democracy. This left most decision making to experts; the public's role was to elect leaders and to join interest groups for further representation. In the early twenty-first century, local associational activity is deemed the heart of democracy. In neither case do political parties have much of a role, except as they may be used to overthrow governments overseas.

One reason foundation definitions can attain legitimacy is that the U.S. Constitution (formal and informal) is ancient and leaves many issues unclear. Political science and public opinion emphasize voting, but the question of who or what should formulate policy is less discussed. The Constitution leaves the formal source of policy vague: should it be the president, congress, the courts, or the state or national government?

The ancient concept of democracy is derived from the experience of a small city-state, Athens. More recent exemplars are Iceland and Denmark. Even with modern communications, it is difficult to implement democracy in a huge country. There are other contrasting factors. In Athens, the majority was poor, so majority rule was assumed to promote the poor's interests. There were no elections or parties. Widespread participation was obtained by direct democracy and selection by lot which was, in theory, representative. However, there was not much innovation or expansion of citizenship to women, those not free born, and those not native born. Furthermore, the Athenian imperialistic policies cast doubt on the democratic experiment and lent support to Platonic elitism.

In modern times, political parties have been vehicles for democracy. Their degree of representativeness can be roughly estimated by the number of voters that they attract. Of course, when party strength is based on money because voters can be bought with spin, they primarily represent the party financiers. Parties could become legitimate vehicles of policy initiation if they were funded by members and supported their own policy institutes. They might be kept responsive to members through national and local conventions and/or electronic communication. People may be willing to pay substantial dues to parties producing benefits as they now do for unions, because they get something out of the deal. This is an approximation of the British Labour Party's operation in a less decadent time. Another possibility is the Canadian system, whereby moderate donations to political parties entitle one to a tax credit.[6]

The liberal foundations support campaign finance reform, but this would not expunge the influence of money. Furthermore, elections themselves give preference to certain personality types and occupational categories. This would be obviated in a representative system based on selection by lot, somewhat like the Athenian one. Direct democracy in tribal and local governments was a training ground for participation in the Athenian assembly. Local assemblies also were educational institutions for children, as politics was a big deal, and public schools did not exist. Today, education for citizenship could start in kindergarten, and teenagers, as in France, could have an auxiliary role in local councils. Using current voting rolls, every 100th or 1,000th person might be selected to serve in town councils or new local boards in large cities. After two years of service, the person would be eligible for selection by lot for state government and subsequently for national service. Pay could be either a reasonable sum or what the person is currently earning (as in Cuba), with a generous minimum wage for previously unemployed legislators. Employment status would need to be protected. No corporate funding, or junkets to the Greenbrier Hotel, would be permitted, and as in Athens, people would have to rotate off when their terms expired. Such an approach to democracy leaves vague matters of policy initiation and the control of nongovernmental institutions, whether profit making or nonprofit.

Furthermore, even with a fair and representative system, whether attained by lot, or through citizen financing, responsible parties, and proportional representation, there would be a problem foreign to ancient Greek democracy. It is now the case that only a minority in most capitalist democracies is poor, and it is not clear how its interests would be recognized with majority rule. The minority would be too weak to threaten revolution and if restive could be jailed or drugged by those who enjoy power. Maybe it already is.

Currently policy ideas and issue framing rest with foundations and think tanks. This might suit the elitist conception of democracy, in which people can exercise some choice after all of the challenging options have been filtered out. However, voters mostly select politicians who offer no clear policy or party program commitments, so even the passive choice among presifted policies is quite remote from citizens. Partly because of the time spent fund-raising, many elected representatives are only vaguely informed about the legislation they are enacting, especially that concerning foreign policy, where there may be no array of interest groups indicating the complexities of a situation. Even when interest groups are vocal and polls indicate strong majority opinion, it often happens that these have no effect. One such case was the U.S. invasion of Nicaragua, using mercenaries and election money, which defied even the resolutions of Congress.

A co-producer of policy in our system is the judiciary, including the U.S. Supreme Court, the lower courts, and the state courts. This characteristic enables foundation-supported litigation firms to steer the agenda. Whether or not they achieve the desired decision, the litigators focus public attention on what they think is important. Political debate is limited to controversy over which judges should be appointed and which policies should be proclaimed by the Court, not whether these Platonic guardians are consonant with democracy. Perhaps if we believe that judicial policy making is essential, the judges should be chosen in a separate election in which they offer their ideologies to the voters and serve for fixed terms. We also would have to ensure that the education of judges (whether or not they were lawyers) represented a broad spectrum of philosophies and interests.

.   CIVIL SOCIETY

In recent years, Alexis de Tocqueville's ideas have come into fashion, among both conservatives and liberals, especially those of the "communitarian" movement. The concept that local associations are the most vital centers of democracy is reflected in Putnam's "social capital" idea and in the "civil society" approach to Eastern European transitions. The earlier pluralist interpretation of U.S. politics also emphasized voluntary associations; currently there is more of an emphasis on local rather than national NGOs.

Problems with the civil society model of democracy abound. Many NGOs, whether local or national, wear the mask of pluralism. They are controlled by elites via funding, integration into coalitions, and overlapping personnel. In addition, not all interests can organize and represent themselves, and some, such as the poor, can do so only with great difficulty. Excluded from self-representation are the environment, and people in foreign countries who are vitally or fatally affected by U.S. policies.

Some NGOs with resources may enjoy visibility, but they never achieve power over decision making, for example, in the regulatory process. Here consumer interests, a vast majority, have little clout. Furthermore, most NGOs represent few citizens; their power is inordinately based on resources obtained from corporations and foundations. This may become increasingly the case as, just like parties, public relations and slick media can inflate organizations' images. In theory, the World Wide Web will provide an inexpensive communication medium for any cause. There is so far scant evidence that it counterbalances the resources available to elite-favored groups; this is a prime subject for research.

Civil society organizations are convenient instruments for imperialism because of their nonpartisan, neutral, and humanitarian images. The NGO model also is useful for ameliorating the market devastations of "transition countries." They are preferred to government-supported social services, culture, and education, as these constitute models of socialist production. If such enterprises manage to do anything that is effective and fair, there could be "blowback," as they could suggest to capitalist democracies, which are increasingly service economies, that there are viable alternatives to the market. The private service, as opposed to the public, keeps leaders, staff, and supporters mindful of the need to cultivate donors of surplus wealth.

The NGOs also co-opt leaders and movements for change. They provide fine jobs and travel opportunities to those who are reasonable and pragmatic. If they try to create an alternative public sphere, any sign of size or power will bring on the elite supporters. Subtle changes in mission toward the Progressive pluralist view are likely to follow. Grassroots organizations, often funded by both left-wing and mainstream foundations, lose their challenging edge. The need to distinguish their group from competing ones for grant-writing purposes draws activists away from structural change. Nationally and internationally, the human rights approach to reform displaces solidarity movements. It also has its use in legitimating the U.S. political system; among the few positive examples of civic participation that one can impart to (often cynical) college freshmen is the civil rights movement.

Furthermore, one must look inside of these organizations to see if their culture is consonant with democracy. How do fraternities and sororities contribute, with their exclusiveness, goose-stepping, torture initiations, and omerta codes? What about freemasonry, which has long served as an affirmative action plan for white men, especially in elective and appointive government positions, both national and local?[7] Do the National Rifle Association and the Boy Scouts cultivate democratic perspectives?

Among U.S. NGOs, religious institutions have great resources and members. They receive little in foundation grants, and they are largely self-funded. How do these groups contribute to democracy? The New England Congregational Church was the father of the town meeting, civil rights had a strong base in the black churches, and the liberation theologians (in all denominations) cry out for justice. What about the teachings and practices of most religious congregations? Why is it that democracy seems to flourish where atheists are plentiful, for instance, in Iceland, Denmark, Sweden, Norway, France, and northern Italy (where Putnam made his observations in the 1970s and 1980s)?

For that matter, if civil society is so important to democracy, why do we not hear more about bowling leagues, quilting bees, and bird-watching societies in Iceland, Denmark, Sweden, Norway, and France? Why is fascism so popular in Italy today when there are all those choruses and bocci clubs? Perhaps what has changed is the elephant in the living room that Putnam barely notes in *Making Democracy Work:* the Italian Communist Party, which now has splintered and faded.

A root problem of the civil society basis for democracy is that pluralism has always been a realm of great inequality. The most accessible form of participation, voting, becomes largely irrelevant in the interest group system, which is heavily skewed to the wealthy side.[8] One critic, David Rieff, suggested that the civil society system promoted and sustained by foundations is a new feudalism.[9] Donors, NGO leaders, and members are lined up in patron and client relationships; weak or strong alliances are formed vertically or horizontally by networking; resources and privileges are available for some at the ground level, for further dependency creation. We can see similarities among medieval barons, robber barons, and humanitarian barons.

Feudalistic autonomy has some virtues, for example, in allowing freedom for groups to practice their traditional culture and to create their own way of life, no matter how idiosyncratic. Yet autonomy may not be conducive to democracy, such as in cultures that subordinate women or, in addition, practice blood feuds.

DEMOCRACY PROMOTION

Foundations want to teach democracy, but missing from their lessons is the consideration of whether massive funding and threatening as election techniques have anything to do with "government by the consent of the governed." Democracy promoters are not very interested in political parties and unions in the United States, but foundations consider them the pure will of the people elsewhere. A leading democracy promoter asserts that the United States and Western Europe did a fine job using political parties and elections to overthrow the Yugoslav government; his major concern is that the techniques might not work so well elsewhere.[10]

The National Endowment for Democracy claims that its funds are only "leveling the playing field" in Eastern Europe, since the Communist and Socialist parties have domestic resources. This view is inconsistent with the U.S. government's contention that *no matter how small* the support the USSR provided to political parties in Nicaragua, Afghanistan, Vietnam, and El Salvador, or to the African National Congress, they were consequently merely agents of the Soviets. On the other hand, U.S. aid makes nations "free," whether it funds parties, cabinet members, newspapers, NGOs, or military.

Also absent from democracy lessons is how corporate power invalidates the rare legislation that is in the average citizen's interest. This happens not merely in Third World countries. In West Virginia, mountaintop removal as a mining technique has not ended, despite much-heralded environmental laws and persistent NGO advocacy and litigation.

Corporations also overpower democratic institutions through the relentless promotion of consumerism. This is not a vice of "shopping addicts" but a necessity for a now-worldwide system that produces more than people need or want. Of course, there are many hungry and homeless who lack access to goods because of poverty. Nevertheless, for the "health" of the economy, most people must be induced to buy, and this pressure starts at age three or so. Consequently, the scarce leisure time not devoted to TV is spent buying and using the latest whatever, not dropping in on city council meetings.

GLOBALIZATION

The globalization of political decision making is yet another threat to democracy. It has long been a project of the Council on Foreign Relations and other agencies of the capitalist avant garde. International bodies such as the World Trade Organization, the European Monetary Union, and the International Monetary Fund restrict policies that countries may adopt, regardless of what their majorities want. Germany is not even permitted to utilize Keynesian economics, although it has massive unemployment. In the same way that USSR troops reduced the autonomy of Eastern Europe, NATO remains an occupying army maintaining capitalism; it was not sitting all over Italy to protect it from a Hungarian invasion. Especially shocking to those who maintain some belief in democracy was the news that the Danish prime minister found out accidentally that nuclear weapons were stationed in Denmark; they are not permitted by Danish laws. The NATO command within each nation dictates to parliaments and prime ministers. Similarly, the military in Indonesia, South Korea, the Philippines, Honduras, Turkey, and other satellite countries take orders from their extraterritorial sponsor and are expected to maintain control over civilian governments. They are sometimes foiled by rebellions, but their role is not questioned by the democracy promoters. The politics of other countries are manipulated also by what Diana Johnstone calls "humanitarian vigilante power."[11] The Carnegie Endowment introduced the doctrine of "humanitarian intervention" in a 1992 report, just in time for Clinton's use.[12]

In accordance with the feudal spirit, the globalization advocates champion networks, which weaken and minimize the nation. Celebrated as nonhierarchical, networks enable the powerful to appear as just another participant, as in the cognate "roundtables" of local politics. This is one way that democratic institutions are quietly being supplanted by the "public-private partnerships," advocated by the *Recent Social Trends* authors. The partisans of globalization eschew national boundaries for corporations (whether profit making or nonprofits). However, their scheme does not open borders for the free movement of people. That might have some revolutionary implications.

INFORMATION

The left and the liberal press frequently decry concentration of ownership in the commercial media; however, little attention is paid to nonprofit information sources. These include university faculties, conferences, publications, and libraries. Can libraries be biased? Who knows? Who researches this? Currently, Eastern European libraries are being redone by the Soros and Mellon foundations. What goes in, and what stays out?

Other nonprofit information sources are the foundations themselves, their reports, and those of the think tanks they fund. The latter would include groups such as the National Governors Association, the International City Management Association, the Brookings Institution, and the American Enterprise Institute. We also might look at reference books, scholarly journals, university presses, Web databases, opinion magazines, and public TV and radio, which showcase think-tank types. The controversy over Pacifica radio indicates the fragility of independent broadcasting. Perhaps the cultural studies people will investigate when they tire of deconstructing vintage clothing and teapots; there is work aplenty here.

The earlier public diplomacy of the Cold War entailed joint CIA-foundation support for foreign media, writers, and artists, and for international periodicals such as *Encounter*.[13] What about the current period? Which foreign news sources and cultural media are owned or supported by foundations? And what difference does it make? A brief experience using the "free trial offers" for Internet databases of Transitions on Line, <www.tol.cz>, one of many such Soros news services, and the U.S. Department of Commerce's World News Connection, <wnc.fedworld.gov>, gave me a whiff of difference. Seeking news of Eastern Europe and Eurasia (former Communist countries), it appeared that Transitions on Line (TOL) uses its own specially trained or retrained journalists, while the U.S. government mostly translates what appears in local news sources.

Universities and individual disciplines have been crucially shaped by foundations. How should higher education curriculum be determined, and who decides when subjects or methods have become obsolete? Are state universities, religious colleges, and the federal Howard University more independent of foundation influence than the mainstream private institutions? What supports the sports-team distortion of higher education, now a driving force at even the most prestigious small liberal arts colleges? Commercial sports frequently are accused of inducing passivity and consent to hegemonic power. What of noncommercial sports? Perhaps the very bowling leagues, and now the teenagers' soccer teams, keep the players, and their parents, away from local political events.[14]

Systematic study might tell us more about how academic disciplines obtain their shape and status within academia. What would political science be like had foundations not intervened? Which people, topics, and paradigms were rejected from grant support and/or inclusion in the discipline in any significant way? The Social Science Research Council archivist, located at the Rockefeller Archive Center in Tarrytown, New York, would not divulge such information. Perhaps the rejectees would be good informants. Probably only a few from the earliest days (1930s) are still alive, but the sooner such inquiries begin, the farther back one will reach. There are some excellent studies of the Cold War and the university, detailing the foundations' role, but a full-scale investigation—the issue that prompted the Caucus for New Political Science—awaits the type of funding and research organizing that is unlikely to be forthcoming from foundations.

We also could use a systematic study of those think tanks considered liberal, conservative, and left wing. Which ones do not receive foundation funding? How has funding affected those that began as severely critical of the system? There are numerous exposés of conservative foundations and think tanks, mostly by journalists, but it is not clear how much they differ from the liberal ones. Clear areas of contention are "social issues," such as abortion, affirmative action, and gay rights. In foreign and economic policy, there seems to be considerable agreement, as between the supposedly hostile ideologies of corporate liberalism and conservatism. We might note that the Brookings Institution has several publications supporting education vouchers, and that the Ford Foundation recommends government funding for religious-based social services. The libertarian Cato Institute does hold a different view, even eschewing "democracy promotion," and it champions extensive privatization. Does it propose dismantling the military-industrial complex and other props to the economic system? On the other side, the "left-wing" and mainstream policy groups seem to share common ground. The Economic Policy Institute, supposedly representing labor and the poor, is heavily foundation funded. The World Social Forum, held in Brazil in opposition to the Davos (or New York) World Economic Forum, also has Ford Foundation sponsorship.

Art and culture are issues of both information and economy. What are the appropriate funding sources in a democracy: markets, corporations, foundations, government and/or communities? Do we adopt a laissez-faire attitude toward commercial entertainment, in which violent video games and pornography are large components? Should we acknowledge the political role of art? Foundations work to increase the supply and demand for certain types of cultural production. Where might public sponsorship fit into the picture?

ECONOMY

The liberal foundations undoubtedly will continue their attempts to fix up the economic system, constructing epicycles if that would prolong capitalism. They, and the World Bank, are well aware of the poverty and inequality that remain even in the richest country. We can expect that nonmarket techniques, such as microcredit, individual development accounts, and subsidized employment, will continue to be piloted by foundations and advocated for full-scale government adoption. It would not be surprising if elites joined the basic income guarantee movement, echoing the "negative income tax" proposal proffered by conservatives in the 1970s.

Ultimately, the 1930s' proposals for economic planning may be revived and the myth of the "free market" gently laid to rest. In that case, whether we would have fascism, socialism, corporatism, or something else would depend on who is framing and creating new institutions. Compassionate liberals often advance solutions to poverty that require more wasteful and polluting production. At one time, it was thought that the military-industrial complex, without actual war, would provide adequate economic stimulus. It may be that permanent war, which burns surplus faster, will be the winner.

A new hegemony would need to transcend multiple crises. Our environment is increasingly degraded not only by weapons production but also from extraction of resources, production of energy, manufacturing, transportation, and disposal of products to accommodate the new purchases from our overproductive economy. Even in poor countries, obesity is becoming more of a health problem than starvation; rich and poor children are being weaned onto junk food everywhere. Agriculture wins all blue ribbons for quantity, but on most other counts, it is a disaster, including the work life of both migrant farm labor and "family farmers" themselves. We also face increasing shortages of teachers, nurses, carpenters, and fishmongers. It seems that the invisible hand does not prod youngsters into, for example, furnace repair careers, even when the wages are good. The aging of the population exacerbates many problems; for example, we may need to institutionalize the elderly because there is no one, or no one affordable, to repair the furnace, fix the roof, or shovel the snow. The declining contribution of the family to nutrition, hygiene, child rearing, or "haven in a heartless world" also begs for some creative alternatives.

Surely there needs to be a serious discussion of these matters in arenas independent of the corporate elite. Is planning a possible solution? Can planning be democratic (or at least more democratic than our current economic system)? How does the foundations' Progressive social engineering ideology relate to socialism? There is a historical connection via the technocratic socialism of Claude-Henri de Saint Simon, the positivism of August Comte, and the revised liberalism of John Stuart Mill. Mill, however, unlike our foundations, believed that dissent was vital to any polity. Progressivism and British Fabian socialism were contemporary ideologies, and they have some similarities, including support for moral "uplift" and economic planning. However, the Fabians hoped to eliminate capitalism gradually, whereas Progressives and corporate liberals want to maintain corporate wealth and power, even if the "free market" must be sacrificed to do so.

What if political science had studied Fabianism instead of behavioralism? This is not such a crazy idea, as the London School of Economics was created for that very purpose, although it quickly met diversionary forces. Academic trends could have blown in the other direction.

Foundations, as institutions, suggest a general question. What is the place, in a democracy, of self-perpetuating, self-governing corporations, subject to minimum public control (other than financial reporting, spending amounts required, etc.)? A related issue arose two centuries ago, in the *Dartmouth College* case decided by the U.S. Supreme Court. The government of New Hampshire believed that democracy required public control of major institutions, and that a charter granted by the former colonial ruler was invalid after a revolution. Furthermore, any self-perpetuating corporation was suspect. New Hampshire lost. In 1886, the U.S. Supreme Court further ruled that corporations have civil rights, just as natural persons do *(Santa Clara County v. Southern Pacific Railroad Company).*

The U.S. Declaration of Independence, although discussing only governments, implied that institutions should be judged by human needs and should be subject to revision or elimination by living citizens. The very size and power of some private institutions, such as the new $21 billion Gates Foundation, threaten democratic control by citizens. On the other hand, incorporation may have creative possibilities; it was used in the nineteenth century for many experiments in living.[15] The histories of these alternative communities may even suggest a way out of our environmental, economic, and family crises, but this world could not coexist with the barons of yore, and is unlikely to be acceptable to their present-day humanitarian counterparts.

Appendix A

Inquiry Letter for Haymarket Research

My home address
Date (1986)

Dear

I am trying to find out about the experience of groups that received grants from Haymarket People's Fund during its first four years. My interest is as a political scientist, local activist, and present member of the New Hampshire Funding Board of HPF. I also have a strong desire to find and record some of the history of progressive organizing in New England, which mainstream media and textbooks ignore or belittle.

I would appreciate it if you could answer the enclosed questionnaire. If there are others associated with the group who would be good sources, please duplicate the questionnaire and pass it along. Newsletters or other printed material would be useful; I can return these if you wish.

While the staff at HPF has been very helpful to me, this study is not a project of HPF itself. The general results may be used by HPF to aid in long-term policy making. Your responses will not be made available to boards considering any future grant application you or your group may make. I will not participate in granting decisions concerning any group I have studied.

Please be frank. In order to be effective in promoting peace and justice, it is necessary to know what works and what doesn't.

If you wish to verify my role in this project, you may call Haymarket at (phone number).

I may be calling you to see if I can have a personal interview or attend a meeting of your group. You may prefer to discuss these issues on the phone; if so please let me know when are some good times to call you.

In solidarity,
Joan Roelofs

Appendix B

Haymarket Research Questionnaire

Date _____

Name of Group:

Name of Person Answering Questionnaire:

Address:

Phone:

Role in Group: (e.g., member, leader, part of minority faction, etc.)

1. Is the group still active?
2. Did it evolve into other organizations and/or join a coalition? If so, which organizations?
3. What were your original goals?
4. Were these goals achieved? Please explain to what extent you feel they were.
5. Did goals change as the group evolved? If so, in what ways?
6. What were the major tactics used?
7. Did the group have an impact on the local, regional, national, or international level? Explain.
8. Did it contribute to consciousness raising among the general public or its own membership?
9. Did it force the public to consider your issues?
10. Did it produce benefits for disadvantaged people, or more general benefits, or both? Please describe.

11. Did it produce leaders for other organizations, and members who continued to be active in other organizations (including electoral politics)?

12. What were your biggest problems?

13. Did you meet with repression?

14. What were your group's greatest strengths?

15. How many members did you have when your organization was largest? How many were active? What size group did you find best for successful activities?

16. How important was Haymarket funding to your group?

17. Other comments:

Appendix C

Selected Groups Funded by Haymarket 1974–1978

Type	Connecticut	Maine	New Hampshire	Vermont	Rhode Island	Massachusetts, non-Boston	Boston
PEACE							! MOBILIZATION FOR SURVIVAL **A, C**
ANTI-IMPERIALIST							★ Haiti Culturelle ! AFRICAN LIBERATION SUPPORT **A, B, C** ! FRIENDS OF FILIPINO PEOPLE **A, C**
PUERTO RICAN SOLIDARITY	★ P.R. Solidarity New Haven					★ PR Solidarity, Springfield ? P.R. Solidarity, Amherst/Nhampton	★ P.R. Solidarity
NATIVE AMERICAN		! PENOBSCOT NATION **A, B, D**		! ABENAKI SUPPORT **A, B**		? W MA Native Americans ? Native American Solidarity, Am/No	
CIVIL RIGHTS	! Nat. Alliance against Racist & Pol. Repression **A, B, C**						

(continued on next page)

Type	Connecticut	Maine	New Hampshire	Vermont	Rhode Island	Massachusetts, non-Boston	Boston
WORKERS	! UFW Support **A, C** ? Assoc. de Trabadores Agricolas					★ Franklin Training Corp. ? 12-1 U. Mass	! N.E. Medical Center Employees ★ NINE to FIVE
TENANTS	★ People Acting for Change	! Lewiston Tenants Union **A, B, C** ! Bangor Tenants Union **A, B**		! PACT, **A, B**			? Ad Hoc. S. End ! J.P. Tenants Action **A, B, C** ★ Simplex Steering ★ Cambridge Tenants
HEALTH		! Feminist Health Project **A**		! Healthy Vt. **A, B**	★ RI Cosh		! Transfusion ★ Urban Planning Aid ! Mental Patients Lib. Front **A, C**
ENERGY			! Upper Valley Energy Coalition **A**				
ANTI-NUCLEAR POWER		! Nuclear Reaction **A, C**	! N.H. Research Project **A** ! Clamshell **A, C**			★ Alt. Energy of Hampden County ★ Nuclear Info. Commune, Montague	

(continued on next page)

Type	Connecticut	Maine	New Hampshire	Vermont	Rhode Island	Massachusetts, non-Boston	Boston
POOR		! H.O.M.E. A, B	? Community Advocacy Center				
WOMEN		(see health)				★ Valley Women's Union	
MISC.	! Public Power Project	? Maine Gay Task Force	★ N.E. Prisoners Assoc.			? Northampton Veterans Coalition	

Code:

★ Questionnaire sent, no reply

? No contact found

! Completed questionnaire and/or interview

Organizations in UPPER CASE were still in existence as of 1986

Goals reported achieved: **A**: Consciousness Raising; **B**: Reforms; **C**: Interest Group Formed; **D**: Social Change

Notes

PREFACE

1. "The Third Sector As a Protective Layer of Capitalism," *Monthly Review* (September 1995): 16–25; "Foundations, Social Scientists, and Eastern Europe" (with Erkki Berndtson), in *The Political Influence of Ideas*, ed. Stephen Brooks and Alain-G. Gagnon (Westport: Praeger, 1994), 163–85; "Foundations and Political Science," *New Political Science* (fall 1992): 3–28; "Foundations and Social Change Organizations: The Mask of Pluralism," *Insurgent Sociologist* 14 (fall 1987): 31–72; "Foundations and the Supreme Court," *Telos* (winter 1984–1985): 59–87; Unpublished work on Haymarket People's Fund and Social Change (my sabbatical project in 1986).

2. Sidney Tarrow, "Aiming at a Moving Target: Social Science and the Recent Rebellions in Eastern Europe"; Adam Przewroski, "The 'East' Becomes the 'South'? The 'Autumn of the People' and the Future of Eastern Europe," (both) *PS: Political Science & Politics* 24:1 (March 1991): 12–23.

3. Zbigniew Brzezinski, *Alternative to Partition* (New York: McGraw-Hill, 1965).

4. Christopher Black, "An Impartial Tribunal? Really?" Available: <http://www.emperors-clothes.com/analysis/Impartial.htm>. Accessed: 7/5/00.

5. Przeworski, "The East," 20.

CHAPTER 1

1. Antonio Gramsci, *Selections from the Prison Notebooks* (New York: International, 1971), 12.

2. Robert Michels, *Political Parties* (New York: Collier, 1962), 188.

3. Crane Brinton, *The Anatomy of Revolution* (New York: Vintage, 1958), 41.

4. Raymond Williams, "Base and Superstructure in Marxist Cultural Theory," *New Left Review* 82 (November–December 1973): 9.

5. G. William Domhoff, *Who Rules America? Power and Politics in the Year 2000*, 3rd ed. (Mountain View, Calif.: Mayfield, 1998), 2.

6. Peter Dobkin Hall, *Inventing the Nonprofit Sector* (Baltimore: Johns Hopkins University Press, 1992), 26.

7. Domhoff, *Who Rules America?*, 2.

8. Robert Arnove, ed., *Philanthropy and Cultural Imperialism* (Boston: G. K. Hall, 1980).

9. Arnove, *Philanthropy*, 1.

10. One of the few exceptions is Irene L. Gendzier, *Development against Democracy: Manipulating Political Change in the Third World* (Hampton, Conn.: Tyrone Press, 1995).

11. Thomas R. Dye, *Top Down Policymaking* (New York: Chatham House, 2001).

12. Barry D. Karl and Stanley N. Katz, "The American Private Philanthropic Foundation and the Public Sphere: 1890–1930," *Minerva* 19 (summer 1981): 243.

13. J. Craig Jenkins, "Foundation Funding of Progressive Social Movements," in *The Grant Seekers Guide*, 3rd ed., ed. Jill Shellow and Nancy Stella (Mt. Kisco: Moyer-Bell, 1986), 11.

14. Zbigniew Brzezinski, *The Grand Chessboard* (New York: Basic Books, 1997), 25.

15. Brzezinski, *Between Two Ages* (New York: Viking, 1970), 59.

16. Brzezinski, *The Grand Chessboard*, 27.

17. Brzezinski, *The Grand Chessboard*, 195.

18. Brzezinski, *The Grand Chessboard*, 210.

CHAPTER 2

1. Barbara Howe, "The Emergence of Scientific Philanthropy 1900–1920," in *Philanthropy and Cultural Imperialism*, ed. Robert Arnove (Boston: G. K. Hall, 1980), 29.

2. Merle Curti and R. Nash, *Philanthropy in the Shaping of American Higher Education* (New Brunswick: Rutgers University Press, 1965), 215.

3. Leonard and Mark Silk, *The American Establishment* (New York: Basic Books, 1980), 126.

4. Allen, *The Rockefeller File* (Seal Beach, Calif.: '76 Press, 1976), 42.

5. U.S. Congress, Commission on Industrial Relations (Walsh Commission) *Report* (Washington, D.C.: Government Printing Office, 1915), 118–25.

6. "This foundation was essentially a $10 million trust which financed pensions for aging college and university professors in a number of elite private east coast institutions. . . . Similar arrangements were demanded by faculty and supported by trustees at other leading public and private universities. Once established, the plan worked to insure loyal service from grateful faculty and thus encouraged stability, compliance, and conservatism on the part of the academic labor force. . . . By 1931 . . . Carnegie financial advisors shifted the program to a contributory plan administered by the Teachers Insurance and Annuity Association (TIAA)." David E. Weischadle, "The Carnegie Corporation and the Shaping of American Educational Policy," in Arnove, *Philanthropy*, 364–66.

7. David Kennedy, *Birth Control in America* (New Haven: Yale University Press, 1970).

8. U. S. Congress, House, *Hearings before the Select Committee to Investigate Tax-Exempt Foundations and Comparable Organizations*, 83rd Cong., 2nd Sess., 1954 (Reece Committee).

9. Wormser, *Foundations: Their Power and Influence* (New York: Devin-Adair, 1958), 81.

10. But the Ford Foundation did give a grant to critical legal theorist Roberto Unger of $104,400 for the development of A New Social Theory. Ford Foundation, *Annual Report*, 1979.

11. Waldemar Nielsen, *The Big Foundations* (New York: Columbia University Press, 1972), 45.

12. Ford Foundation, *Report of the Study for the Ford Foundation on Policy and Program* (Detroit: Ford Foundation, 1949).

13. Horace Coon, *Money to Burn* [1938] (New Brunswick: Transaction, 1990).

14. Ferdinand Lundberg, *America's Sixty Families* (New York: Vanguard, 1937): *The Rich and the Super-Rich* (New York: Lyle Stuart, 1968); *The Rockefeller Syndrome* (Secaucus: Lyle Stuart, 1975).

15. David Horowitz, "Sinews of Empire," *Ramparts* (October 1969): 32–42. Also see, with David Kolodney, "The Foundations," *Ramparts* (April 1969): 38–48.

16. Ben Whitaker, *The Foundations* (London: Methuen, 1974).

17. Whitaker, *The Foundations*, 168. See also Edward Berman, *The Influence of the Carnegie, Ford and Rockefeller Foundations on American Foreign Policy* (Albany: State University of New York Press, 1983).

18. Lawrence Shoup and William Minter, *Imperial Brain Trust* (New York: Monthly Review Press, 1977).

19. U. S. Congress, House, *Hearings on Exempt Foundations and Charitable Trusts before the Subcommittee on Domestic Finance of the House Committee on Banking and Currency*. 93 Cong., 1st Sess., 1973 (Patman Committee), 15.

20. John Stormer, *None Dare Call It Treason* (Florissant: Liberty Bell, 1964).

21. Capital Research Center Web Site: <http://www.capitalresearch.org>.

22. Domhoff, *Who Rules America?*, 255.

23. Burton Weisbrod, "Conceptual Perspectives on the Public Interest: An Economic Analysis," in *Public Interest Law*, ed. Weisbrod, Joel Handler, and Neil K. Komesar (Berkeley: University of California Press, 1978), 25.

24. Barry D. Karl and Stanely N. Katz, "The American Private Philanthropic Foundation and the Public Sphere: 1890–1930," *Minerva* 19 (summer 1981): 238.

25. Barry D. Karl, "Philanthropy and the Maintenance of Democratic Elites," *Minerva* 35 (fall 1997): 207–20.

26. Karl Polanyi, *The Great Transformation* (Boston: Beacon Press, 1957), 3.

27. Jon Van Til, "Shifting Boundaries of the Nonprofit Sector in a Changing Social Economy: An Experience in Theory Construction," Discussion Paper, January 1996. Available: <http://crab.rutgers.edu/~vantil/papers/CWRU-THEORY.html>. Accessed: 3/02/01.

28. James A. Joseph, president of the Council on Foundations, in John A. Edie, *Congress and Private Foundations: An Historical Analysis* (Washington, D.C.: Council on Foundations, 1987), v.

29. Cited in Edie, *Congress,* 3.

30. U.S. Congress, Senate Committee on Finance, *Hearing before the Committee on Finance on Improper Payments by Private Foundations to Government Officials,* 91st Cong., 1st Sess., 1969 (Russell Long, chair).

31. Manning Pattillo, president of the Foundation Center, in Senate, *Improper,* 74.

32. Senate, *Improper,* 50.

33. Philip Shenon, "House Votes Haunt Retreat Meant to Spur Collegiality," *New York Times,* March 10, 2001, p. NE 17.

34. U.S. Congress, Staff of the Joint Committee on Internal Revenue Taxation, *General Explanation of the Tax Reform Act of 1969* (Washington, D.C.: Government Printing Office, 1970), 49.

35. U.S. Congress, *General,* 54.

36. U.S. Congress, *General,* 58.

37. Filer Commission, *Research Papers of the Commission on Private Philanthropy and Public Needs,* 5 vols. (Washington, D.C.: U.S. Department of the Treasury, 1977).

38. Peter Dobkin Hall, *Inventing the Nonprofit Sector* (Baltimore: Johns Hopkins University Press, 1992), 247.

39. Jon Van Til, *Growing Civil Society: From Nonprofit Sector to Third Space* (Bloomington: Indiana University Press, 2000), 203.

40. Peter Dobkin Hall, "Abandoning the Rhetoric of Independence: Reflections on the Nonprofit Sector in the Post-Liberal Era," in *Shifting the Debate,* ed. Susan A. Ostrander and Stuart Langton (New Brunswick: Transaction Books, 1987), 14.

41. See <http://www.independentsector.org>.

42. Robert Putnam, *Bowling Alone* (New York: Simon and Schuster, 2000).

43. Van Til, *Growing,* 212.

44. Independent Sector, *Nonprofit Almanac in Brief: 2001,* 7. Available: <http://www.independentsector.org>. Accessed: 1–3–02.

45. Independent Sector, *Nonprofit,* 7.

46. Foundation Center, *Highlights of Foundation Yearbook: 2001.* Available: <http://fdncenter.org>. Accessed: 1/2/02.

47. Foundation Center, *Highlights of Foundation Yearbook: 2000.* Available: <http://www.fdncenter.org>. Accessed: 3/17/01.

48. Gates Foundation Web Site. Available: <http://www.gatesfoundation.org>. Accessed 12–31–01; The Foundation Center. Available: <http://fdncenter.org/research/trends_analysis/top100assets.html>. Accessed 1–2–02.

49. Foundation Center. Available: <http://fdncenter.org/research/trends_analysis/top50assets.html>. Accessed 1–2–02.

50. Foundation Center, *Highlights: 2001.*

51. Reynold Levy, "Corporate Philanthropy Comes of Age," in *Philanthropy and the Nonprofit Sector in a Changing America,* ed. Charles Clotfelter and Thomas Ehrlich (Bloomington: Indiana University Press), 99.

52. Gerard Colby and Charlotte Dennett, *Thy Will Be Done: The Conquest of the Amazon: Nelson Rockefeller and Evangelism in the Age of Oil* (New York: HarperCollins, 1995), 482.

53. Guidestar Web Site <http://www.guidestar.org>.

54. Shelley Feldman, "NGOs and Civil Society: (Un)stated Contradictions," *Annals of the American Academy of Political and Social Science* 554 (1997): 46–66.

55. Joseph Schumpeter, *Capitalism, Socialism, and Democracy* (New York: Harper and Brothers, 1950), 143.

56. Whitaker, *Foundations,* 171.

57. Robert McKay, *Nine for Equality under Law: Civil Rights Litigation* (New York: Ford Foundation, 1977), 12.

58. Study Commission on U.S. Policy Toward Southern Africa, *South Africa: Time Running Out* (Berkeley: University of California Press, 1981).

CHAPTER 3

1. One of the exceptions is Donald Fisher, *Fundamental Development of the Social Sciences* (Ann Arbor: University of Michigan Press, 1993).

2. Samuel Hays, *The Response to Industrialism: 1885–1914* (Chicago: University of Chicago Press, 1957), 142.

3. Robert Arnove, ed., *Philanthropy and Cultural Imperialism* (Boston: G. K. Hall, 1980), 18.

4. Sheila Slaughter and Edward T. Silva, "Looking Backwards: How Foundations Formulated Ideology in the Progressive Period," in Arnove, *Philanthropy,* 59.

5. G. William Domhoff, *The Powers That Be* (New York: Random House, 1978), 155.

6. Daniel Rodgers, *The Work Ethic in Industrial America: 1850–1920* (Chicago: University of Chicago Press, 1978).

7. Adolph Berle and Gardiner Means, *The Modern Corporation and Private Property* (New York: Macmillan, 1933).

8. Berle and Means, *The Modern Corporation*, 27.

9. Ford Foundation, *Report of the Study for the Ford Foundation on Policy and Program* (Detroit: Ford Foundation, 1949), 46.

10. Ford Foundation, *Report*, 1949, 59.

11. Thomas Dye, *Who's Running America?* (Englewood Cliffs: Prentice Hall, 1983), 259–62.

12. Council for Public Interest Law, *Balancing the Scales of Justice: Financing Public Interest Law in America* (New York: CPIL, 1976), 8.

13. Stanley Katz, "Grantmaking and Research in the U.S., 1933–1983," *Proceedings of the American Philosophical Society* 129 (1985): 1–2.

14. See Joan Roelofs, "Foundations and Social Change Organizations: The Mask of Pluralism," *Insurgent Sociologist* 14 (1987): 31–72.

15. Thomas Dye and Harmon Zeigler, *The Irony of Democracy* (Pacific Grove: Brooks/Cole, 1990).

16. Jon Weiner, "Dollars for Neocon Scholars," *The Nation* (January 1, 1990): 12–14.

17. Gabriel Almond, in *Political Science in America: Oral Histories of a Discipline*, ed. Michael Baer, Malcolm Jewell, and Lee Sigelman (Lexington: University Press of Kentucky, 1991), 127.

18. Baer et al., *Political Science*, 129.

19. Charles Lindblom, "Another State of Mind," *American Political Science Review* 76 (1982): 9–21.

20. Barry Karl, "Philanthropy and the Social Sciences," *Proceedings of the American Philosophical Society* 129 (1985): 14.

21. Donald Fisher, "Philanthropic Foundations and the Social Sciences: A Response to Martin Bulmer," *Sociology* 18 (1984): 584.

22. Raymond Seidelman and Edward Harpham, *Disenchanted Realists: Political Science and the American Crisis: 1884–1984* (Albany: State University of New York Press, 1985), 99.

23. Peter Seybold, "The Ford Foundation and Social Control," *Science for the People* (May–June 1982): 29.

24. Robert Dahl, "The Behavioral Approach in Political Science: Epitaph for a Monument to a Successful Protest," *American Political Science Review* 55 (1961): 765.

25. Roger Geiger, "American Foundations and Academic Social Science: 1945–1960," *Minerva* 26 (1988): 329.

26. U. S. Congress, House, Special Committee to Investigate Tax-exempt Foundations and Comparable Organizations, *Tax-Exempt Foundations*. 83rd Cong. 2nd Sess., 1954.

27. Andrew Hacker, "Political Behaviour and Political Behavior," *Political Studies* 7 (February 1959): 39–40.

28. David Truman, in Baer et al., *Political Science,* 148.

29. David Easton in Baer et al., *Political Science,* 210.

30. Baer et al., *Political Science,* 212.

31. Cited in Albert Somit and Joseph Tanenhaus, *The Development of American Polit-ical Science* (Boston: Allyn and Bacon, 1967), 200.

32. David Horowitz and David Kolodney, "The Foundations," *Ramparts* (April 1969): 40.

33. See Theda Skocpol and Morris P. Fiorina, eds., *Civic Engagement in American Democracy* (Washington, D.C.: Brookings Institution, 1999), 62.

34. David Horowitz, "Sinews of Empire," *Ramparts* (October 1969): 33.

35. Victor Marchetti and Jon Marks, *The CIA and the Cult of Intelligence* (New York: Dell, 1980), 237.

36. Bruce Cumings, "Boundary Displacement: Area Studies and International Studies during and after the Cold War," in *Universities and Empire: Money and Politics in the Social Sciences during the Cold War,* ed. Christopher Simpson (New York: New Press, 1998), 166.

37. Simpson, *Universities,* 40.

38. Simpson, *Universities,* 40.

39. Edward Berman, *The Influence of the Carnegie, Ford, and Rockefeller Foundations on American Foreign Policy* (Albany: State University of New York Press, 1983), 113.

40. Berman, *The Influence,* 80–81.

41. Berman, *The Influence,* 86.

42. For a critic of these theories, see Irene Gendzier, in Simpson, *Universities,* 61; for a supporter, see Ricardo Hausmann, "Prisoners of Geography," *Foreign Policy* (January–February 2001): 44–53.

43. Gendzier, in Simpson, *Universities,* 61; and Kenneth Prewitt, "Social Science and the Third World," *Society* (May–June 1984): 84–89.

44. Charles Beard, "Neglected Aspects of Political Science," *American Political Science Review* 42 (April 1948): 218.

45. Donald Fisher, "American Philanthropy and the Social Sciences: The Reproduc-tion of a Conservative Ideology," in Arnove, *Philanthropy,* 240.

46. Arnove, *Philanthropy,* 233.

47. Raymond Fosdick, *The Story of the Rockefeller Foundation* (New York: Harper, 1952), 198–99.

48. K. Paakkunainen, "A Periphery in Search of a Center," in *Political Science between Past and Future,* ed. Dag Anckar and Erkki Berndtson (Helsinki: Finnish Political Science Association, 1988), 31–32.

49. Cumings, "Boundary Displacement," 168.

50. Social Science Research Council, *Annual Report: 1987–1988* (New York: SSRC, 1988), 84.

51. V. Volkov, "Facts, the Air History Breathes," *Sofia News* (November 2–8, 1989): 8–9.

52. Seymour Martin Lipset, "Politics and Society in the USSR," *PS* 23 (March 1990): 20–28.

53. Somit and Tanenhaus, *The Development*, 167.

54. Social Science Research Council Web Site <http://www.ssrc.org>. Accessed: 2/11/01.

55. Cumings, in Simpson, *Universities*, 173.

56. Weiner, "Dollars," 12.

57. Berman, *The Influence*, 31.

58. Gabriel Almond, "Separate Tables," *PS* 21 (1988): 828–42.

59. George Shakhnazarov, *Contemporary Political Science in the USA and Western Europe* (Moscow: Progress, 1985), 142.

60. *Vencermos, Papel del Barrio Las Corras Negras* 1 (July 1971), cited in *Voces Unidas* 11 (spring 2001): 17.

61. Rosa Proietto, "The Ford Foundation and Women's Studies in American Higher Education: Seeds of Change?" in *Philanthropic Foundations: New Scholarship, New Possibilities*, ed. Ellen Condliffe Lagemann (Bloomington: Indiana University Press, 1999), 271–84.

62. Daniel Brandt, "Multiculturalism and the Ruling Elite," *NameBase NewsLine* 3 (October–December 1993). Available: <http://www.pir.org/news03.html>. Accessed: 7/3/00.

63. Eric Schmitt, "Wanted: More Than a Few Good Women," *Ford Foundation Report* (summer 1994): 29.

64. Schmitt, "Wanted," 29.

65. Rachel Marcus, "'Marginal' News with More Impact," *Ford Foundation Report* (fall 1999): 22.

66. David Samuels, "Philanthropical Correctness," *The New Republic* 213 (September 18–25, 1995): 28–29ff. Available: WilsonWeb. Accessed: 12/24/00.

67. Steven J. Rosenstone and John Mark Hansen, *Mobilization, Participation, and Democracy in America* (New York: Macmillan, 1993), 167.

68. Robert Putnam, *Bowling Alone* (New York: Simon and Schuster, 2000).

69. Jeffrey Berry, "The Rise of Citizen Groups," in *Civic Engagement in American Democracy*, ed. Theda Skocpol and Morris P. Fiorina (Washington, D.C.: Brookings Institution, 1999), 391.

70. Theda Skocpol, "Advocates without Members: The Recent Transformation of American Civic Life," in Skocpol and Fiorina, *Civic Engagement*, 481.

71. G. W. F. Hegel, *Philosophy of Right*, tran. T. M. Knox (Oxford: Clarendon Press, 1942), 130.

72. Hegel, *Philosophy*, 150–51.

73. "Who Killed Peggy Sue? Civic Renewal Report Laments the Death of 50s," *Responsive Philanthropy*. Available: <http://www.ncrp.org/articles/rp/peggysue.htm>. Accessed: 2/28/01.

74. Joan Roelofs, "Eco-Cities and Red Green Politics," *Capitalism, Nature, Socialism* 11 (March 2000): 139–48.

75. Bruce Adams, "Building Healthy Communities," *Civic Practices Network Tools*. Available: <http://www.cpn.org/cpn/sections/tools/manuals/pew_healthy_com.html>. Accessed: 4/20/01.

76. David Mathews and Noelle McAfee, *Making Choices Together* (Dayton: Kettering Foundation, 1999), 6–7.

77. Jean Bethke Elshtain, "Civil Society," *Liberal Education* (winter 1998): 9.

78. Ivan Eland, "Robust Response to 9/11 Is Needed but Poking the Hornets' Nest Is Ill-Advised," *Cato Foreign Policy Briefing No. 69*. Available: <http://www.cato.org>. Accessed: 1/1/02.

79. See James A. Smith, *The Idea Brokers: Think Tanks and the Rise of the New Policy Elite* (New York: Free Press, 1991); Joseph Peschek, *Policy-Planning Organizations: Elite Agendas and America's Rightward Turn* (Philadelphia: Temple University Press, 1987).

80. Laurence Shoup and William Minter, "Shaping a New World Order: The Council on Foreign Relations' Blueprint for World Hegemony," in *Trilateralism: The Trilateral Commission and Elite Planning for World Management*, ed. Holly Sklar (Boston: South End, 1980), 151.

81. Peter Thompson, "Bilderberg and the West," in Sklar, *Trilateralism*, 166.

82. "Press Release" (June 3, 2000). Available: <http://www.bilderberg.org/2000.htm>. Not a Bilderberg Web site, but one compiled by Tony Gosling, Bristol, England. Accessed: 7/31/00.

83. Available: <http://www.aspeninst.org/policy/index.html>. Accessed: 4/24/01.

84. Karl Marx, *Capital III*, in *Karl Marx: Selected Writings in Sociology and Social Philosophy*, ed. T. B. Bottomore and M. Rubel (New York: McGraw-Hill, 1956), 190.

85. See Stephen Gill, *American Hegemony and the Trilateral Commission* (New York: Cambridge University Press, 1991); Sklar, *Trilateralism*.

86. Michel Crozier, Samuel P. Huntington, and Joji Watanuki, *The Crisis of Democracy* (New York: New York University Press, 1975).

87. Crozier et al., *The Crisis*, 180.

88. Crozier et al., *The Crisis*, 182.

89. Crozier et al., *The Crisis*, 183.

90. Christopher Lydon, "Jimmy Carter Revealed: He's a Rockefeller Republican," *Atlantic Monthly* (July 1977): 52.

91. World Economic Forum Web Site: <http://www.weforum.org>.

92. "Measuring Globalization," *Foreign Policy* (January–February 2001): 56–65.

93. Mario Vargas Llosa, "The Culture of Liberty," *Foreign Policy* (January–February 2001): 69.

94. Carnegie Endowment for International Peace. Available: <http://www.ceip.org>. Accessed: 5/23/01.

95. Patrick Reilly, "The Mott Family of Foundations: Nurturing a Worldwide Movement of Liberal Activists," *Foundation Watch* 2 (October 1997): Available: <http://www.capitalresearch.org>.

96. Kimberly Pohlman, "The Commercialization of Children's Public Television," *Extra!* (May–June 2000). Available: <http://www.fair.org/extra/0005/pbs-ads.html>. Accessed: 3/12/01.

97. Beth Schulman, "Foundations for a Movement: How the Right Wing Subsidizes Its Press," *FAIR* (March–April 1995). Available: <http://www.fair.org/extra/9503/ right-press-subsidy.html>. Accessed 4/24/01.

98. Ron Curran, "Buying the News," *San Francisco Bay Guardian*, October 8, 1997. Available: http://www.sfbg.com/News/32/02/Features/news.html>. Accessed: 7/28/00.

99. Alicia Shepard, "Press Coverage: How Pew's Civil Journalism Projects Put Newspaper, Radio, and Television Stations on the Payroll," *Foundation Watch* (August 1996): Available: <http://www.capitalresearch.org>.

100. Ron Curran, "Following the Money," *San Francisco Bay Guardian*, October 8, 1997. Available: <http://www.sfbg.com/News/32/02/Features/follow.html>. Accessed: 7/28/00.

101. Iver Peterson, "Media," *New York Times* (February 3, 1997), p. D7.

102. William Hoynes, "The Cost of Survival: Political Discourse and the 'New PBS,'" *FAIR* (June 1999). Available: <http://www.fair.org/reports/pbs-study-1999.html>. Accessed 6/29/99.

103. Hoynes, "The Cost."

104. *The Progressive Review*, ed. Sam Smith (On-line newsletter) (February 13, 2001). Available: <http://prorev.com>.

105. Tara Weiss, "Alarms Ring over Kuwait's NPR Funding," *The Hartford Courant*, March 6, 2001. Available: <http://www.ctnow.com>. Accessed: 5/30/01.

106. Available: <http://www.transitions-online.org/about.html>.

CHAPTER 4

1. Hindy Lauer Schachter, "Reinventing Government or Reinventing Ourselves: Two Models for Improving Government Performance," *Public Administration Review* 55 (November–December 1995): 530.

2. Schachter, "Reinventing," 532.

3. Hindy Schachter, "Settlement Women and Bureau Men: Did They Share a Usable Past?" *Public Administration Review* 57 (January–February 1997): 93.

4. Horace Coon, *Money to Burn* [1938] (New Brunswick: Transaction, 1990), 322. Coon also informs us that Allen wanted studies of what foundations do not fund, and what goes into the wastebasket. This merits a book in itself.

5. Raymond Fosdick, *The Story of the Rockefeller Foundation* (New York: Harper, 1952), 199.

6. Fosdick, *The Story*, 206.

7. Alasdair Roberts, "Demonstrating Neutrality: The Rockefeller Philanthropies and the Evolution of Public Administration, 1927–1936," *Public Administration Review* 54 (May–June 1994): 221.

8. Roberts, "Demonstrating," 225.

9. Bruce Stave, *Socialism and the Cities* (Port Washington: Kennikat, 1975), 5.

10. Richard Childs, *Civic Victories* (New York: Harper and Brothers, 1952), 151.

11. Craig M. Wheeland, "An Analysis of the Legislative Oversight Activity in Council-Manager Muncipalities" (paper presented at the annual meeting of the American Political Science Association, Washington, D.C., 1988), 26.

12. "Newsmakers," *Philanthropy News Digest* (December 2000). Available: <http://fdncenter.org/pnd>. Accessed: 12/28/00.

13. Brigid McMenamin, "Trojan Horse Money," *Forbes* 158 (December 16, 1996): 123. Available: EBSCO Academic Search Elite. Accessed: 1/12/01.

14. Rob Gurwitt, "With Strings Attached," *Governing* 11 (April 1998): 18–20.

15. Two excellent studies are Ellen Condliffe Lagemann, *Private Power for Public Good: A History of the Carnegie Foundation for the Advancement of Teaching* (Middletown: Wesleyan University Press, 1983), and Robert Arnove, ed., *Philanthropy and Cultural Imperialism* (Boston: G. K. Hall, 1980).

16. Barry D. Karl, "The Troublesome History of Foundations: Correcting a Contentious History," *Reviews in American History* 25 (1997): 614.

17. Dennis C. Buss, "The Ford Foundation in Public Education: Emergent Patterns," in Arnove, *Philanthropy*, 342.

18. Buss, "The Ford Foundation," 355.

19. A recent one in this series is Terry Moe, *Schools, Vouchers, and the American Public* (Washington, D.C.: Brookings Institution, 2001).

20. July 29, 1999. Available: <http://www.house.gov/science/bartlett_072999.htm>.

21. Joseph Peschek, *Policy-Planning Organizations: Elite Agendas and America's Rightward Turn* (Philadelphia: Temple University Press, 1987), 19.

22. President's Research Committee on Social Trends (PRCST), *Recent Social Trends in the United States* [1933] , 2 vols. (Westport: Greenwood Press, 1970).

23. PRCST, *Recent*, lxxiv.

24. Barry D. Karl and Stanley N. Katz, "The American Private Philanthropic Foundation and the Public Sphere: 1890–1930," *Minerva* 19 (summer 1981): 268.

25. Karl and Katz, "The American," 268.

26. Juan O. Tamayo, "U.S. Civilians Taking Risks in Colombian Drug War," *Messenger-Inquirer,* February 26, 2001. Available: http://www.messenger-inquirer. com. Accessed: 3/9/01.

27. Raymond Seidelman and Edward Harpham, *Disenchanted Realists: Political Scientists and the American Crisis: 1884–1984* (Albany: State University of New York Press, 1985), 225.

28. G. William Domhoff, *Who Rules America? Power and Politics in the Year 2000,* 3rd ed. (Mountain View, Calif.: Mayfield, 1998), 148.

29. Domhoff, *Who Rules America?,* 278.

30. See Robin Winks, *Cloak and Gown* (New York: Morrow, 1987).

31. Victor Marchetti and John Marks, *The CIA and the Cult of Intelligence* (New York: Laurel, 1980), 237.

32. *Congressional Quarterly Special Report,* "Foundations, Private Organizations Linked to the CIA" (February 24, 1967): 271; David Horowitz, "Sinews of Empire," *Ramparts* (October 1969): 32–42; Frances Stonor Saunders, *Who Paid the Piper?: The CIA and the Cultural Cold War* (London: Granta, 1999), 116, 139.

33. Harvey Brooks, "Sponsorship and Social Science Research," *Society* 21 (May–June 1984): 82.

34. (Reading, Mass.: Addison-Wesley, 1992).

35. "The Role of Foundations in Influencing Public Policy," *National Civic Review* 87 (summer 1998): 117–27. Available: EBSCO Academic Search Elite.

36. David R. Morgan and Robert E. England, *Managing Urban America,* 5th ed. (New York: Chatham House, 1999), 7.

37. *The Blair House Papers,* "National Performance Review" (January 1997). Available: <http://www.npr.gov/library/papers/bkgrd/blair.html>.

38. Schachter, "Reinventing Government," 535.

39. Christopher Reardon, "Faith Matters," *Ford Foundation Report* (spring–summer 1999): 9.

40. Reardon, "Faith Matters," 9.

CHAPTER 5

1. Karl and Katz, "The American Private," 268.

2. Margaret J. Wyszomirski, "Philanthropy and Culture," in *Philanthropy and the Nonprofit Sector in a Changing America,* ed. Charles T. Clotfelter and Thomas Ehrlich (Bloomington: Indiana University Press, 1999), 475.

3. Hiroka Tsuchiya, "'Let Them Be Amused,': The Industrial Drama Movement, 1910–1929," in *Theatre for Working Class Audiences in the United States, 1830–1980,* ed. Bruce McConachie and Daniel Friedman (Westport: Greenwood Press, 1985), 103.

4. Wyszomirski, "Philanthropy and Culture," 474.

5. Possibly because guilt-ridden working parents feel they must spend most of their leisure time with the children. Observers have noted an increasing infantilization of our culture.

6. Wyszomirski, "Philanthropy and Culture," 467.

7. Don Shewey, "The Buck Starts Here," *American Theatre* (March 1991): 29.

8. Christopher Reardon, "Composing in the Key of Life," *Ford Foundation Report* (winter 1998): 25.

9. Christopher Reardon," Unconquered Spirits," *Ford Foundation Report* (spring 1993): 6.

10. "Recent Grants," *Ford Foundation Report* (winter 1998): 51.

11. Christopher Reardon, "Memories in Motion," *Ford Foundation Report* (spring 1994): 8.

12. *Ford Foundation Report* (fall 1998): 40.

13. Saunders, *Who Paid the Piper?,* 139.

14. Saunders, *Who Paid the Piper?,* 134.

15. Kathleen McCarthy, "From Cold War to Cultural Development," *Dedalus* (winter 1987): 99.

16. Saunders, *Who Paid the Piper?,* 140.

17. Saunders, *Who Paid the Piper?,* 142. I have seen no evidence that art or symphonies won any points in the Cold War. Leftists, even Gramsci, often were suspicious of the "dead white male" culture. Gresham's law seemed to be operating: fast food and the strategic use of rock bands probably had a greater effect.

18. Gerard Colby and Charlotte Dennett, *Thy Will Be Done: The Conquest of the Amazon: Nelson Rockefeller and Evangelism in the Age of Oil* (New York: HarperCollins, 1995), 482.

19. McCarthy, "From Cold War," 98.

20. McCarthy, "From Cold War," 101.

21. Suzanne Charlé, "Street Smarts," *Ford Foundation Report* (fall 2000): 16.

22. Charlé, "Street Smarts," 16.

CHAPTER 6

1. Wesley Mitchell, "Introduction," in President's Research Committee on Social Trends, *Recent Social Trends in the United States* [1933], 2 vols. (Westport: Greenwood Press, 1970), xxviii.

2. Mitchell, "Introduction," lxxii.

3. Karl and Katz, "The American Private," 268.

4. G. William Domhoff, *The Power Elite and the State* (New York: De Gruyter, 1990), 47.

5. G. William Domhoff, *Who Rules America?*, 271.

6. Donald Fisher, *Fundamental Development of the Social Sciences* (Ann Arbor: University of Michigan Press, 1993), 150.

7. Meg Jacobs, "Constructing a New Political Economy, " in *Philanthropic Foundations: New Scholarship, New Possibilities*, ed. Ellen Condliffe Lagemann (Bloomington: Indiana University Press, 1999), 103.

8. Jacobs, "Constructing," 113.

9. Jacobs, "Constructing," 103.

10. U. S. Congress, Senate, *Report of the Commission on Country Life*, Senate Document 705, 60th Cong., 2nd Sess., 1909.

11. Domhoff, *Who Rules America?*, 269.

12. Alice O'Connor, "The Ford Foundation and Philanthropic Activism in the 1960s," in Lagemann, *Philanthropic Foundations*, 172.

13. O'Connor, in Lagemann, *Philanthropic Foundations*, 183.

14. Richard Magat, *The Ford Foundation at Work: Philanthropic Choices, Methods, and Styles* (New York: Plenum, 1979), 121.

15. The grant reinforced congressional suspicions that foundations were engaged in partisan activity and led to new foundation regulation in the Tax Reform Act of 1969.

16. Magat, *The Ford Foundation*, 122.

17. "Communities and Neighborhoods—Possible Private Sector Initiatives for the 1980's," cited in Ronald Schiffman and Susan Motley, "Comprehensive and Integrative Planning for Community Development," a discussion paper, 1989. Available: Pratt Institute Center for Community and Environmental Development: <http://www.picced.org>. Accessed 3/7/01.

18. Gregory Raynor, "The Ford Foundation's War on Poverty," in Lagemann, *Philanthropic Foundations*, 223.

19. Harold deRienzo, president of the Parodneck Foundation for Self-Help Housing and Community Development, cited in Mike Miller, *Can the Debate Be Resolved?: The Controversy about Community Organizing and Community Development*. A report sponsored by the Aspen Institute Nonprofit Sector Research Fund, n.d.

20. Scott Cummings and Mark Glaser, "Neighborhood Participation in Community Development," *Population Research and Policy Review* 4 (1985): 267–87.

21. Schiffman and Motley, "Comprehensive," 5.

22. Gary Walker and Jean Grossman, "Philanthropy and Outcomes," in Charles T. Clotfelter and Thomas Ehrlich, eds., *Philanthropy and the Nonprofit Sector in a Changing America* (Bloomington: Indiana University Press, 1999), 451.

23. Christopher Reardon, "Career Ladders," *Ford Foundation Report* (spring 1995): 5.

24. Tony Proscio, "A Double 'Bottom Line,'" (1999), Report available: <http://www.rockfound.org>. Accessed 3/28/01.

25. Schiffman and Motley, "Comprehensive," 5.

26. Angela Bonavoglia, "Women's Work," *Ford Foundation Report* (winter 2000): 10.

27. Lucy Conger, "Think Big, Lend Small," *Ford Foundation Report* (spring–summer 1998): 16.

28. Dana Canedy, "Down Payments on a Dream," *Ford Foundation Report* (winter 1998): 5.

29. Carol Steinbach, "Pragmatic Passion," *Ford Foundation Report* (spring–summer 1999): 18.

30. Richard Magat, "Organized Labor and Philanthropic Foundations: Partners or Strangers?" *Nonprofit and Voluntary Sector Quarterly* 23 (winter 1994): 362.

31. "Lane's Friends," *The Nation* (January 19, 1980): 3–4.

32. Richard Magat, "Unions and Foundations As Public Policy Actors," *Policy Studies Review* 14 (spring–summer 1995): 161–70. Available: Wilson Web. Accessed: 2/07/01.

33. Elena Cabral, "Building Safety Nets for the New Work Force," *Ford Foundation Report* (spring–summer 1999): 4.

34. Peter Dobkin Hall, "The Model of Boston Charity: A Theory of Charitable Benevolence and Class Development," *Science and Society* 38 (1975): 464–77.

CHAPTER 7

1. Abraham Flexner, *Funds and Foundations* (New York: Arno, 1952), 135.

2. U.S. Congress, House Committee on Banking, *Hearings on Exempt Foundations and Charitable Trusts before the Subcommittee on Domestic Finance.* 93rd Cong., 1st Sess. (Patman Committee), 1973, 171.

3. Joel Handler, *Social Movements and the Legal System* (New York: Academic Press, 1978), 233.

4. Thomas Marvell, *Appellate Courts and Lawyers: Information Gathering in the Adversary System* (Westport: Greenwood Press, 1978), 308.

5. Some examples of funded organizations include: American Bar Association Fund for Public Education; American Law Institute; Law Students Civil Rights Research Council; Institute for Local Self-Government; Council on Legal Education for Professional Responsibility; Association of American Law Schools; Educational Testing Service; National Urban League; Center for Community Change; White House Conference of Food, Nutrition, and Health, Inc.; League of Cities/Conference of Mayors; Urban Institute; Metropolitan Applied Research Center; American Political Science Association; American Society for Public Administration; Council of State Governments; Regional Plan Association; National Municipal League; RAND Corporation; Brookings Institution; Citizens' Research Foundation; National Academy of Sciences.

6. Erwin Griswold, "Philanthropic Foundations and the Law," in *United States Philanthropic Foundations*, ed. Warren Weaver (New York: Harper and Row, 1967), 291.

7. Richard Magat, *The Ford Foundation at Work: Philanthropic Choices, Methods, and Styles* (New York: Plenum, 1979), 110.

8. Joel Seligman, *The High Citadel: The Influence of Harvard Law School* (Boston: Houghton Mifflin, 1978), 162.

9. Charles M. Lamb, "Judicial Policy-making and Information Flow to the Supreme Court," *Vanderbilt Law Review* 29 (1976): 45–124.

10. Alexander Bickel, *Politics and the Warren Court* (New York: Harper and Row, 1965), 143.

11. Bob Woodward and Scott Armstrong, *The Brethren* (New York: Avon, 1979), 419.

12. Ford Foundation, *The Public Interest Law Firm* (New York: Ford Foundation, 1973), 39.

13. Council for Public Interest Law (CPIL), *Balancing the Scales of Justice: Financing Public Interest Law in America* (New York: CPIL, 1976), 8.

14. Robert McKay, *Nine for Equality under Law: Civil Rights Litigation* (New York: Ford Foundation, 1977), 12.

15. Ford Foundation-American Bar Association (FF-ABF), *Public Interest Law: Five Years* (New York: FF-ABF, 1976), 14.

16. CPIL, *Balancing the Scales*, 237.

17. Alan Stang, "Foundations Pay the Way," *American Opinion* 20 (1977): 35.

18. Jack Walker, "Origins and Maintenance of Interest Groups in America," *American Political Science Review* 77 (June 1983): 401.

19. Handler, *Social Movements*, 217.

20. David Trubek, "Review of 'Balancing the Scales of Justice,'" *Wisconsin Law Review* 77 (1977): 309.

21. Stephen Halpern, "Assessing the Litigative Role of ACLU Chapters," in *Civil Liberties*, ed. Stephen Wasby (Carbondale: Southern Illinois University Press, 1977), 165.

22. LCCRUL Web Site: <http://www.lawyerscomm.org>. Accessed: 4/11/01.

23. PILI Web Site: <http://www.pili.org>. Accessed: 4/11/01.

24. Joan Roelofs, "The Warren Court and Corporate Capitalism," *Telos* 39 (spring 1979): 94–112.

25. Arthur S. Miller, *The Supreme Court and American Capitalism* (New York: Free Press, 1968), 146.

26. Thomas Reeves, *Freedom and the Foundation* (New York: Knopf, 1969), 30.

27. Reeves, *Freedom*, 284.

28. Samuel Stouffer, *Communism, Conformism, and Civil Liberties* (New York: Doubleday, 1955), 222.

29. Harry Kalven Jr., "Uninhibited, Robust and Wide-Open—A Note on Free Speech and the Warren Court," in *The Warren Court: A Critical Analysis*, ed. Richard Saylor, Barry Boyer, and Robert Gooding (New York: Chelsea House, 1968), 110.

30. Robert Justin Goldstein, *Political Repression in Modern America: 1870 to the Present* (Cambridge: Schenkman, 1978), 406.

31. James Anderson, "Philanthropic Control over Private Black Higher Education," in Arnove, *Philanthropy*, 153.

32. Anderson, "Philanthropic Control," 154.

33. Gerald Horne, *Black and Red: W. E. B. DuBois and the Afro-American Response to the Cold War, 1944–1963* (Albany: State University of New York Press, 1986), 19.

34. B. Joyce Ross, *J. E. Springarn and the Rise of the NAACP: 1911–1939* (New York: Atheneum, 1972), 106.

35. Ben Whitaker, *The Foundations* (London: Methuen, 1974), 171.

36. Joel Handler, George Edgar, and Russell Settle, "Public Interest Law and Employment Discrimination," in Burton Weisbrod et al., *Public Interest Law* (Berkeley: University of California Press, 1978), 272.

37. Kenneth Pye, "The Warren Court and Criminal Procedure," in Saylor et al., *The Warren Court*, 66–67.

38. U.S. Congress, House Committee on Banking, *Hearings on Exempt Foundations and Charitable Trusts before the Subcommittee on Domestic Finance of the House Committee on Banking and Currency*. 93rd. Cong., 1st Sess., 1973, 171.

39. Lewis, "Legislative Apportionment and the Federal Courts," *Harvard Law Review* 71 (1958): 1057–98.

40. Ford Foundation (FF), *The Near Side of Federalism: Improving State and Local Government* (New York: FF, 1972), 10.

41. Robert McKay, *Reapportionment* (New York: Twentieth Century Fund, 1965), 6.

42. Thomas Dye, *Who's Running America?* (Englewood Cliffs: Prentice Hall, 1983), 259.

43. Eva Rubin, *Abortion, Politics and the Courts* (Westport: Greenwood Press, 1982), 20.

44. Lamb, "Judicial Policy-Making," 72.

45. Harrington, *The Other America* (New York: Macmillan).

46. Frank Kelly, *Court of Reason* (New York: Free Press, 1981), 201.

47. Jack Greenberg, *Cases and Materials on Judicial Process and Social Change: Constitutional Litigation* (St. Paul: West, 1977), 591.

48. A. James Lee and Burton Weisbrod, "Public Interest Law Activities in Education," in Weisbrod et al., *Public Interest Law*, 318.

49. Magat, *The Ford Foundation*, 147.

50. Dennis Buss, "The Ford Foundation in Public Education: Emergent Patterns," in Arnove, *Philanthropy*, 356.

51. Timothy O'Rourke, *The Impact of Reapportionment* (New Brunswick: Transaction Books, 1980), 153.

52. Ford Foundation, *1949 Report*, 46.

53. Miller, *The Supreme Court*, 8.

54. O'Rourke, *The Impact*, 153.

55. Ward E. Elliott, *The Rise of Guardian Democracy: The Supreme Court's Role in Voting Rights Disputes: 1845–1969* (Cambridge: Harvard University Press, 1974), viii.

56. Russ Bellant, *The Coors Connection* (Cambridge: Political Research Associates, 1990), 72.

57. Jacqueline Vaughn Switzer, *Environmental Politics*, 3rd ed. (Boston: Bedford, 2001), 48.

58. *Whitman, Administrator of EPA, v. American Trucking Association, Inc. et al.* No. 99–1257. Argued 11–7–00; Decided 2–27–01.

59. Lawrence Soley, "The New Corporate Yen for Scholarship," in Christopher Simpson, *Universities and Empire: Money and Politics in the Social Sciences during the Cold War* (New York: New Press, 1998), 232.

CHAPTER 8

1. Steven Lukes, *Power: A Radical View* (London: Macmillan, 1974).

2. Murray Edelman, *The Symbolic Uses of Politics* (Urbana: University of Illinois Press, 1964).

3. G. William Domhoff, *Who Rules America?*

4. Charles Lindblom, *Politics and Markets* (New York: Basic, 1977).

5. J. Craig Jenkins, "Resource Mobilization Theory and the Study of Social Movements," *Annual Review of Sociology* 9 (1983): 527–53; John D. McCarthy and Mayer N. Zald, "Resource Mobilization and Social Movements: A Partial Theory," *American Journal of Sociology* 82 (1977): 1212–41; Jack Walker, "Origins and Maintenance of Interest Groups in America," *American Political Science Review* 77 (1983): 390–406.

6. Magat, *The Ford Foundation*, 83.

7. As of 9/30/00, Ford's assets were $14,659,683,000. "Top 100 U.S. Foundations by Asset Size," the Foundation Center. Available: <http://fdncenter.org>. Accessed: 12/24/01.

8. Joseph Helfgot, *Professional Reforming* (Lexington: Lexington Books, 1981), 108.

9. Roger Williams, "All in the Family (Well Mostly)," *Foundation News* (July–August 1984): 42–49.

10. Ford Foundation, *Letter* of October 1, 1985.

11. Frank Koch, *The New Corporate Philanthropy* (New York: Plenum, 1979), 5.

12. Robert McKay, *Nine for Equality under Law: Civil Rights Litigation* (New York: Ford Foundation, 1977), 12.

13. Michael Crozier, Samuel Huntington, and Joji Watanuki, *The Crisis of Democracy* (New York: New York University Press, 1975), 9.

14. James Wright, *The Dissent of the Governed* (New York: Academic Press, 1976), 81.

15. U. S. Congress, House Committee on Ways and Means, *Hearings on Tax Reform,* 91st Cong. 1st Sess. 1969, 371.

16. Anthony Oberschall, "The Decline of the 1960s Social Movements," *Research in Social Movements, Conflicts, and Change* 1 (1978): 257–89; Doug McAdam, "The Decline of the Civil Rights Movement," in *Waves of Protest: Social Movements Since the Sixties,* ed. Jo Freeman and Victoria Johnson (Lanham, Md.: Rowman and Littlefield, 1999), 325–48; Herbert Marcuse, "The Failure of the New Left," *Sociological Quarterly* 18 (1979): 3–11.

17. Sidney Tarrow, *Power in Movement,* 2d ed. (New York: Cambridge University Press, 1998), 46.

18. Wini Breines, *Community and Organization in the New Left: 1962–1968* (New York: Praeger, 1982), 133.

19. Emily Stoper, "The SNCC—Rise and Fall of a Redemptive Organization," *Journal of Black Studies* 8 (1977): 13–34.

20. Oberschall, "Decline," 275; Robert J. Goldstein, *Political Repression in Modern America: 1870 to the Present* (Cambridge, Mass.: Schenkman, 1978), xvi.

21. Ken Lawrence, "The New State Repression," *Covert Action Information Bulletin* (summer 1985): 3–11.

22. Richard Flacks, "Making History vs. Making Life," *Working Papers* (summer 1974): 56–71.

23. Todd Gitlin, *The Whole World Is Watching* (Berkeley: University of California Press, 1980), 291; Oberschall, "Decline," 281.

24. William I. Robinson, *Promoting Polyarchy: Globalization, U.S. Intervention, and Hegemony* (New York: Cambridge University Press, 1996), 4.

25. Jenkins, "Resource," 527–53.

26. Howard Dressner, *The Search for the Public Interest* (New York: Ford Foundation, 1969), 47.

27. Mary Anna C. Colwell, "Philanthropic Foundations and Public Policy: The Role of Foundations," Ph.D. dissertation, University of California, Berkeley, 1980.

28. Robert Johnson, "The Community Groups Are Still There, but the Grants Aren't," *Foundation News* (January–February 1984): 36–39.

29. Roger Williams, "All in the Family (Well, Mostly)," *Foundation News* (July–August 1984): 42–49.

30. Robert Johnson, "How to Evaluate a Neighborhood Organization," *Foundation News* (May–June 1984): 33–37.

31. Ben Whitaker, *The Foundations* (London: Methuen, 1974), 160.

32. David Nevin, *Left-handed Fastballers: Scouting and Training America's Grass Roots Leaders* (New York: Ford Foundation, 1981), 5.

33. Nevin, *Left-handed*, 66.

34. Ford Foundation, *Civil Rights, Social Justice, and Black America* (New York: Ford Foundation, 1984), 52–53.

35. Brian Tokar, *Earth for Sale* (Boston: South End, 1997); Mark Dowie, *Losing Ground: American Environmentalism at the Close of the Twentieth Century* (Cambridge: MIT Press, 1996).

36. Gerald Horne, *Black and Red: W.E.B. Du Bois and the Afro-American Response to the Cold War, 1944–1963* (Albany: State University of New York Press, 1986), 235.

37. Horne, *Black and Red*, 76.

38. Herbert Haines, "Black Radicalization and the Funding of Civil Rights: 1957–1970," *Social Problems* 32 (1984): 31–43.

39. August Meier and Elliot Rudwick, *CORE: A Study in the Civil Rights Movement 1942–1968* (New York: Oxford University Press, 1973), 420.

40. Robert Allen, *Black Awakening in Capitalist America* (Garden City: Doubleday, 1969), 133.

41. Haines, "Black Radicalization," 34.

42. Martin Luther King Jr. Center for Non-Violent Social Change, Inc., *Profile* (Atlanta: M. L. King Jr. Center, 1985), 1.

43. Foundation Center, *Grants for Public Policy and Political Science* (New York: Foundation Center, 1984).

44. M. L. King Jr. Center, *Profile*, 2.

45. M. L. King Jr. Center, *Profile*, 6.

46. M. L. King Jr. Center, *Profile*, 10.

47. John Herbers, "Coretta King Struggles with a Weighty Legacy," *New York Times*, January 18, 1986, p. 1.

48. Christine Sierra, "The Political Transformation of a Minority Organization—Council of La Raza," Ph.D. dissertation, Stanford University, 1983.

49. Sierra, "The Political," 269.

50. Craig L. Hymowitz, "The Birth of a Nation," American Patrol News Item. Available: <http://www.americanpatrol.org>. Accessed 4/6/01.

51. Center for Community Change (CCC), *Annual Report: 1984* (Washington, D.C.: CCC), 4–8.

52. Neal Peirce and Carol Steinbach, "Reindustrialization on a Small Scale—But Will the Small Business Survive?" *National Journal* 13 (1981): 105–108.

53. Adolph Reed Jr., Telephone interview (July 14, 1986).

54. Sarah Carey, "Philanthropy and the Powerless," in Vol. II, 1109–64, *Research Papers of the Commission on Private Philanthropy and Public Needs*, 5 vols. (Filer Commission) (Washington, D.C.: U.S. Department of the Treasury, 1977), 1151.

55. The Youth Project, *Annual Report* (Washington, D.C., 1984–1985).

56. Anderson, "Black Belt Counties Organize," *Foundation News* (July–August 1981): 13–16.

57. S. M. Miller, "Challenges for Populism," *Social Policy* 16 (1985): 3–6.

58. Robert Johnson, "How to Evaluate a Neighborhood Organization," *Foundation News* (May–June 1984): 33–37.

59. Lawrence Goodwyn, "The New Populism," *The Progressive* (June 1984): 18–20.

60. John Hall Fish, *Black Power/White Control: The Struggle of The Woodlawn Organization in Chicago* (Princeton: Princeton University Press, 1973), 302.

61. Fish, *Black Power*, 310.

62. David Moberg, "Citizen Groups Seek Effective National Politics," *In These Times* (September 4–10, 1985): 2.

63. Environmental Grantmakers Association. Available: <http://www.ega.org>.

64. Personal communication, October 2001.

65. Kathleen Teltsch, "Filling Big Hopes with Small Grants," *New York Times*, May 1, 1985, p. C1.

66. Talmadge Wright, Felix Rodriguez, and Howard Waitzkin, "Corporate Interests, Philanthropies, and the Peace Movement," *Monthly Review* (February 1985): 19–31.

67. Susan Reed, "Nuclear Anonymity," *Foundation News* (January–February 1983): 42–49.

68. Wright et al., "Corporate Interests," 25.

69. Horace Coon, *Money to Burn* [1938] (New Brunswick: Transaction, 1990), 124.

70. Wright et al., "Corporate Interests," 22.

71. Colwell, "Philanthropic Foundations," 27; Council for Public Interest Law, *Balancing the Scales of Justice*, 237.

72. Gloria G. Samson, *The American Fund for Public Service* (Westport: Greenwood Press, 1996), 220.

73. Samson, *The American Fund*, 223.

74. Scott Nearing, *The Making of a Radical* (New York: Harper and Row, 1972), 49.

75. Samson, *The American Fund*, 220.

76. Samson, *The American Fund*, 224.

77. Alan Rabinowitz, *Social Change Philanthropy in America* (Westport: Quorum, 1990), xv.

78. Maureen T. Hallinan, "The Sociological Study of Social Change," *American Sociological Review* 62 (February 1997): 1–11.

79. Haymarket People's Fund (HPF), *Annual Report: May 1987 to May 1988* (Boston: HPF), 3.

80. Martin Espinoza, "Sleeping with the Enemy," *San Francisco Bay Guardian,* October 8, 1997. Available: <http://www.sfbg.com/News/32/02/Features/sleep.html>. Accessed: 7/28/00.

81. J. Craig Jenkins and Abigail Halcli, "Grassrooting the System," in Lagemann, *Philanthropic Foundations,* 238–39.

82. Marco Giugni, "How Social Movements Matter: Past Research, Present Problems, Future Developments," in *How Social Movements Matter,* ed. Marco Giugni, Doug McAdam, and Charles Tilly (Minneapolis: University of Minnesota Press, 1999), xxi.

83. Charles Tilly, "From Interactions to Outcomes in Social Movements," in Giugni et al., *How,* 268.

84. The Funding Exchange. Web Site: <http://www.fex.org>. Accessed 3/17/01.

85. Peace Development Fund (PDF). "What Is PDF?" *Annual Report: 2000.* Available: <http://www.peacefund.org>. Accessed 4/2/01.

86. PDF, "What?"

87. "Profile," NAYA, in PDF, "What?"

88. Resist, Inc. Home Page: <http://www.resistinc.org>. Accessed: 4/2/01.

89. No evaluations of the long-term effect of grant making on social change were found, although a clue that the Field Foundation had done such a study was pursued fruitlessly.

90. William Foote Whyte, *Learning from the Field* (Beverly Hills: Sage, 1984), 20.

91. Haymarket People's Fund. *Annual Report: 1986* (Boston: HPF), 3.

92. William Gamson, *The Strategy of Social Protest* (Homewood: Dorsey, 1975), 174.

93. Arthur Stein, *Seeds of the Seventies* (Hanover: University Press of New England, 1985).

94. Betty Zisk, *The Politics of Transformation: Local Activism in the Peace and Environmental Movements* (Westport: Praeger, 1992), 63–64.

CHAPTER 9

1. Foundation Center, *International Grantmaking II* (Foundation Center/Council on Foundations, 2000). Summary available: <http://fdncenter.org.>. Accessed: 12/23/2001.

2. James F. Clarke, *The Pen and The Sword* (Boulder: Colorado University Press, 1988), 312.

3. Clarke, *The Pen,* 314–15.

4. E. Richard Brown, "Rockefeller Medicine in China: Professionalism and Imperialism," in *Philanthropy and Cultural Imperialism,* ed. Robert Arnove (Boston: G. K. Hall, 1980), 127.

5. Edward H. Berman, "Educational Colonialism in Africa: The Role of American Foundations, 1910–1945," in Arnove, *Philanthropy*, 179.

6. Kenneth Prewitt, "Social Science and the Third World," *Society* (May–June 1984): 84–89.

7. Lawrence Shoup and William Minter, "Shaping a New World Order: The Council on Foreign Relations Blueprint for World Hegemony," in *Trilateralism*, ed. Holly Sklar (Boston: South End, 1980), 149.

8. Franz Shurmann, *The Logic of World Power* (New York: Pantheon, 1974), 67–68.

9. Ambrose Evans-Pritchard, "Euro-federalists Financed by U.S. Spy Chiefs," *Telegraph* (September 19, 2000). Available: <http://www.telegraph.co.uk>. Accessed 9/24/00.

10. Janet Maughan, "The Road from Rio," *Ford Foundation Report* (summer 1992): 13.

11. For a video, Yakoana, of this unprecedented event, see <http://www.yakoana.com>.

12. "On CIA Disclosures," *Congressional Quarterly* (February 24, 1967): 271.

13. *Mott Foundation 1998 Report* (Detroit: Mott, 1998). Available: <http://www.mott.org.>. Accessed: 2/21/01.

14. Council on Hemispheric Affairs (COHA), *National Endowment for Democracy (NED): A Foreign Policy Branch Gone Awry* (Albuquerque: Inter-Hemispheric Education Resource Center, 1990), 53.

15. Wolf Grabendorff, "International Support for Democracy in Contemporary Latin America: The Role of the Party Internationals," in *International Dimensions of Democratization*, ed. Laurence Whitehead (New York: Oxford University Press, 1996), 217.

16. COHA, *NED*, 12.

17. Michael Pinto-Duschinsky, "The Rise of 'Political Aid,'" in *Consolidating Third Wave Democracies*, ed. Larry Diamond et al. (Baltimore: Johns Hopkins University Press, 1997), 297.

18. Pinto-Duschinsky, "The Rise," 300.

19. Pinto-Duschinsky, "The Rise," 304.

20. COHA, *NED*, 43.

21. David Corn, "Muzzling a Watchdog" *Washington Monthly* 29 (January–February 1997): 26–29.

22. COHA, *NED*, 48.

23. Kai Bird, *John J. McCloy and the Making of the American Establishment* (New York: Simon and Schuster, 1992), 519.

24. David Ransom, "Ford Country: Building an Elite for Indonesia," in *The Trojan Horse: A Radical Look at Foreign Aid*, ed. Steve Weissman and members of the Pacific Studies Center and the North American Congress on Latin America (San Francisco: Ramparts Press, 1974), 96.

25. Ransom, "Ford Country," 106.

26. "Afghanistan Foundation: What Is the Foundation?" Available: <http://www.afghanistanfoundation.org>. Accessed 7/3/00.

27. Interhemispheric Resource Center GroupWatch File: "Afghanistan Relief Committee." Available: <http://www.pir.org/gw/>. Accessed: 7/3/00.

28. See <http://www.rawa.org>.

29. Shelley Feldman, "NGOs and Civil Society: (Un)stated Contradictions," *Annals of the American Academy of Political and Social Science* 554 (November 1997): 46–66. Available: EBSCO. Accessed: 7/6/00.

30. Feldman, "NGOs."

31. Feldman, "NGOs." See also Rajni Kothari, "NGOs, the State, and World Capitalism," *Economic and Political Weekly* 21 (December 13, 1986): 2177–82; Brian H. Smith, *More Than Altruism* (Princeton: Princeton University Press, 1990), 16; Tajudeen Abdul-Raheem, "Impact of Angels," *New Internationalist* 326 (August 2000): 20–21.

32. "Initiative Promotes Economic and Civic Growth in the Gobi Region," *Civnet News* (September 20, 1998): Available: <http://civnet.org/news/news.htm>. Accessed: 7/5/00.

33. Robert Arnove, "Foundations and the Transfer of Knowledge," in *Philanthropy*, 318.

34. Arnove, "Foundations," 321.

35. Claribel Alegria, *They Won't Take Me Alive* (London: The Women's Press, 1987), 61; Jennifer Harbury, *Bridge of Courage* (Monroe, Maine: Common Courage Press, 1994), 251.

36. James Petras, "NGOs: In the Service of Imperialism," *Journal of Contemporary Asia* 29 (1999): 429–40. Available: Wilson Web. Accessed: 2/8/01.

37. Petras, "NGOs."

38. Ken and Richard Anderson, "Limitations of the Liberal-Legal Model of International Human Rights: Six Lessons from El Salvador," *Telos* 64 (1985): 91–104.

39. Petras, "NGOs."

40. Laura MacDonald, "A Mixed Blessing: The NGO Boom in Latin America," *NACLA Report on the Americas* 28 (March–April 1995): 30–35. Available: Wilson Web. Accessed: 8/28/00.

41. James Petras, "Reply to Vilas," *Latin American Perspectives* 20 (spring 1993): 107–11. Available: EBSCO. Accessed 2/8/01.

42. Carlos Vilas, "Between Skepticism and Protocol," *Latin American Perspectives* 20 (spring 1993): 97–107.

43. Petras, "NGOs."

44. Petras, "NGOs."

45. Margaret E. Keck and Kathryn Sikkink, *Activists Beyond Borders* (Ithaca: Cornell University Press, 1998), 171.

46. Yasmine Shamsie, *Engaging with Civil Society* (Ottawa: International Center for Human Rights and Democratic Development, 2000), 14.

47. Shamsie, *Engaging*, 23.

48. Petras, "NGOs."

49. Abdul-Raheem, "Impact," 21.

50. Abdul-Raheem, "Impact," 21.

51. Study Commission on U.S. Policy toward Southern Africa, *South Africa: Time Running Out* (Berkeley: University of California Press, 1981), xi.

52. Study Commission, *South Africa*, xxv.

53. Sam Kauffmann, "Human Rights in South Africa: A Continuing Struggle," *Ford Foundation Letter* (fall 1991): 8.

54. Andrew Nash, "South Africa: Is the Revolution Over?" *New Socialist* 2 (March–April 1997). Available: <http://www.web.ca/~newsoc>.

55. Donald G. McNeil Jr., "Once Bitter Enemies, Now Business Partners," *New York Times* (September 24, 1996), p. D1. Note that this report is from the capitalist- and South African-loving *New York Times*.

56. Joseph Berliner and R. V. Burks, "Introduction," in *Innovation in Communist Systems*, ed. A. Gyorgy and J. Kuhlman (Boulder: Westview Press, 1978), 3.

57. J. F. Brown, "Eastern Europe's Western Connection," in *Eroding Empire: Western Relations with Eastern Europe*, ed. Lincoln Gordon (Washington, D.C.: Brookings Institution, 1987), 41.

58. Brown, "Eastern," 39.

59. Janina Frentzel-Zagórska and Krzysztof Zagórski, "East European Intellectuals on the Road of Dissent: The Old Prophecy of a New Class Re-examined," *Politics and Society* 17 (1989): 89–113.

60. Mayer Zald and John D. McCarthy, "Organizational Intellectuals and the Criticism of Society," *Social Science Review* (September 1975), 345; Crane Brinton, *Anatomy of Revolution* (New York: Vintage, 1958), 66.

61. Laurence Whitehead, "Democracy and Decolonization: East Central Europe," in Whitehead, *International Dimensions*, 388.

62. Christopher Simpson, *Blowback* (London: Weidenfeld, 1988), 268.

63. Social Science Research Council (SSRC), *Annual Report: 1987–1988* (New York: SSRC, 1988), 84.

64. "East Central Europe Program," New School Web Site: <http://www.newschool.edu/centers/tcds/intro.htm>.

65. Soros foundations can be found in these places, as of May 2001: Albania, Lithuania, Armenia, Macedonia, Azerbaijan, Moldova, Bosnia and Herzegovina, Mongolia, Bulgaria, Montenegro, Croatia, Poland, the Czech Republic, Romania, Estonia, Russia, Georgia, Bratislava, Slovakia, Guatemala, Slovenia, Haiti, South Africa, Hungary, Southern Africa, Kazakstan, Tajikistan, Kosova, Ukraine, Kyrgyzstan, Uzbekistan, Latvia, Yugoslavia, and the New York headquarters.

66. William Luers, "The United States and Eastern Europe," *Foreign Affairs* 65 (1987): 980.

67. Gail Lapidus, *Patterns of Daily Life*, IREX Occasional Papers (New York: IREX, 1980), 4.

68. Gerald Creed, *Domesticating Revolution: From Socialist Reform to Ambivalent Transition in a Bulgarian Village* (University Park: Pennsylvania State University Press, 1998), 57.

69. Ralph McGeehee, *Deadly Deceits* (New York: Sheridan Square Publications, 1983), 180.

70. EECF, flyer, London, n. d.

71. Vaclav Havel, *The Power of the Powerless* (White Plains: M. E. Sharpe, 1985), 89.

72. Vaclav Havel, "Between Ideals and Utopias," *East European Reporter* 2 (1987): 13–17.

73. Jan Hus Educational Foundation (JHEF), *Report: 1988–1989* (London: JHEF, 1990), 3.

74. Personal correspondence, February 24, 1990; author's anonymity preserved.

75. John K. Glenn, "Civil Society Transformed: International Aid to New Political Parties in the Czech Republic and Slovakia," *Voluntas* 11 (2000): 164. See also Václav Benda et al., "Parallel Polis or An Independent Society in Central and Eastern Europe: An Inquiry," *Social Research* 55 (spring–summer 1988): 211–46.

76. Roger Cohen, "Who Really Brought Down Milosevic?" *New York Times Magazine* (November 26, 2000): 42. Available: <http://www.nytimes.com>. Accessed: 11/27/00.

77. "The Man Who Moves Markets," *Business Week* (August 23, 1993): 58.

78. Kotaro Kohata, "Birth of a 35-Year-Old Prime Minister in Hungary," Sasakawa Peace Fund Web Site. Available: <http://www.spf.org/spf_e/spffeatures/myturn5.html>. Accessed 5/6/01.

79. Eleanor Smollett, "America the Beautiful: Made in Bulgaria," *Anthropology Today* 9 (April 1993): 11. Smollett also points out that in 1932, the Communists won a majority in the Sofia City Council elections and were prevented from governing.

80. Kohata, "Birth."

81. Tina Rosenberg, "From Dissidents to MTV Democrats," *Harper's* 285 (September 1992): 46–53. Available: EBSCO. Accessed 2/17/01.

82. Rosenberg, "From Dissidents."

83. "The Struggle for Political Pluralism: The First Congress of the Association of Young Democrats (Fidesz)," *East European Reporter* (spring–summer 1989): 20.

84. K. Engelbrekt, "The Waning of Communist Ideology," *Report on Eastern Europe* (July 27, 1990): 5–7.

85. Rosenberg, "From Dissidents."

86. Kevin F. F. Quigley, *For Democracy's Sake: Foundations and Democracy Assistance in Central Europe* (Washington, D.C.: Woodrow Wilson Center Press, 1997), 75.

87. Philippe C. Schmitter, "The Influence of the International Context upon the Choice of National Institutions and Policies in Neo-Democracies," in Whitehead, *International Dimensions*, 29.

88. William Blum, "Bulgaria 1990: Teaching Communists What Democracy Is All About," in *Killing Hope*, ed. William Blum (Monroe, Maine: Common Courage, 1995), 317.

89. Whitehead, "Democracy," in Whitehead, *International Dimensions*, 383.

90. Claus Offe, *Varieties of Transition* (Cambridge: MIT Press, 1997), 37.

91. Kevin F. F. Quigley, "Philanthropy's Role in East Europe," *Orbis* 37 (fall 1993): 581–99. Available: EBSCO: Academic Search Elite.

92. Quigley, "Philanthropy's Role."

93. Quigley, "Philanthropy's Role."

94. Quigley, "Philanthropy's Role."

95. Quigley, *For Democracy's Sake*, 16.

96. Paul G. Lewis, "Party Funding in Post–Communist East-Central Europe," in *Funding Democratization*, ed. Peter Burnell and Alan Ware (Manchester: Manchester University Press, 1998), 140.

97. Stephen Engelberg, "U.S. Grant to 2 Czech Parties Is Called Unfair Interference," *New York Times*, June 10, 1990, p. 8.

98. Henry Kamm, "How to Disarm Hungary (Hamburgers? Tennis?)," *New York Times*, October 4, 1989, p. 4.

99. Larry Diamond, "Promoting Democracy in the 1990s: Actors and Instruments, Issues and Imperatives," A Report to the Carnegie Commission on Preventing Deadly Conflict (New York: Carnegie Corporation, 1995). Available: <http://www.ccpdc.org/pubs/diamond/diamond.htm>. Accessed 7/5/00.

100. USAID, *USAID Political Party Development Assistance* (Washington, D.C.: USAID, 1999), 26.

101. USAID, *USAID Political Party*, 38.

102. Nearer to the West's than mine. I was in Bulgaria in 1989 and have remained somewhat attentive to developments there. When there, I was shocked by a policy announced by the Bulgarian Communist Party. The top dogs (males) had concluded that the Bulgarian cosmetic industry was inadequate because it could not produce 100 new shades of lipstick annually. Therefore, a joint venture with a West German firm had been concluded to alleviate the situation. Bulgaria was the world's leading producer of rose oil and was noted for its natural cosmetics. One might as well say that the Bulgarian yogurt did not meet advanced Western standards of guar gum levels.

103. Roumen Daskalov, "A Democracy Born in Pain: Bulgarian Politics, 1989–1997," in *Bulgaria in Transition*, ed. John D. Bell (Boulder: Westview, 1998), 12.

104. Daskalov, "A Democracy," 12; Luan Troxel, "Bulgaria: Stable Ground in the Balkans?" *Current History* 98 (November 1993): 386–89; Albert Melone, *Creating Parlia-*

mentary Government: The Transition to Democracy in Bulgaria (Columbus: Ohio State University, 1998), 5, 219; Misha Glenny, *Rebirth of History: Eastern Europe in the Age of Democracy* (London: Penguin, 1993), 176.

105. USAID, *USAID Political Party*, 37.

106. Quigley, "Philanthropy's Role."

107. USAID, *USAID Political Party*, 32.

108. Quigley, *For Democracy's Sake*, 53.

109. Patrice C. McMahon, "Building Civil Societies in East Central Europe: The Effect of American NGOs on Women's Groups," Conference Paper, American Political Science Association, 2000. Available: <http://PRO.harvard.edu/>. Accessed: 3/16/01.

110. Boran Koulov, "Political Change and Environmental Policy," in Bell, *Bulgaria*, 158.

111. Institute for Sustainable Communities Web Site: < http://www.iscvt.org/prj-cov3.htm#Bulgaria>. Accessed: 5/15/01.

112. McMahon, "Building."

113. Thomas Carothers, "Aiding Post–Communist Societies: A Better Way?" *Problems of Post–Communism* 43 (September–October 1996): 15–25. Available: EBSCO Academic Search Elite. Accessed 7/6/00. Carothers thinks that the Soros system is better than most democratization programs, as it gives so much responsibility to local people.

114. For allegation of waste, see John Horvath, "The Soros Network," 1996. Available: Nettime Archive <http://www.nettime.org>. Accessed: 11/28/00.

115. Quigley, *For Democracy's Sake*, 97.

116. Quigley, *For Democracy's Sake*, 98–99.

117. Janine Wedel, *Collision and Collusion: The Strange Case of Western Aid to Eastern Europe 1989–1998* (New York: St. Martin's Press, 1998), 12.

118. Wedel, *Collision and Collusion*, 50; Gerald Creed and Janine Wedel, "Second Thoughts from the Second World: Interpreting Aid in Post–Communist Eastern Europe," *Human Organization* 56 (1997): 258.

119. Wedel, *Collision and Collusion*, 72.

120. Michael Dobbs, "Aid Abroad Is Business Back Home," *Washington Post*, January 26, 2001, p. A01. Available: <http://www.washingtonpost.com>. Accessed 2/2/01.

121. Blagovesta Doncheva, "Letter to the Serb 'Democratic Opposition,'" Available: <http://www.emperors=clothes.com/articles/doncheva/donch3.htm>. Accessed: 7/5/00.

122. Edmund L. Andrews, "The Yoke of Capitalism," *New York Times*, January 16, 2001, p. C1.

123. *Information Today* 17 (April 2000): 52. Available: EBSCO Academic Search Elite. Accessed: 1/6/01.

124. Wedel, *Collision and Collusion*, 73.

125. USAID, "Europe and Eurasia Overview," text from 2001 Budget Justification. Available: <http://www.usaid.gov/country/ee>. Accessed: 12/12/00.

126. Creed and Wedel, "Second Thoughts," 257.

127. Margaret E. Keck and Kathryn Sikkink, *Activists Beyond Borders* (Ithaca: Cornell University Press, 1998), 2.

128. Rajesh Tandon and Miguel Darcy de Oliveira, *Citizens—Strengthening Global Civil Society* (Washington, D.C.: CIVICUS, 1994). Excerpt from chapter 1. Available: <http://www.civicus.org/pages/pubs9.html>. Accessed: 5/17/01.

129. Thomas Carothers, "Civil Society," *Foreign Policy* 117 (winter 1999–2000): 18–30. Available: EBSCO Academic Search Elite. Accessed: 7/6/00.

130. Keck and Sikkink, *Activists*, 9.

131. Michel Chossudovsky, "Seattle and Beyond: Disarming the New World Order." Available: <http://www.emperors-clothes.com/articles/chuss/seattle.htm.>. Accessed: 5/22/01.

132. Éva Kuti, "Different Eastern European Countries at Different Crossroads," *Voluntas* 10 (1999): 55.

133. Éva Kuti, "Hungary" (Washington, D.C.: Civicus, 2001). Available: <http://www.civicus.org/pages/hungary.html>. Accessed: 5/17/01.

134. Available: <http://www.wmd.org>.

135. Cohen, "Who Really," 42.

136. The World Bank Group: PovertyNet, "Voices of the Poor." Available: <http://www.worldbank.org/poverty/voices/globcoal/connectivity.htm>. Accessed: 5/1/01.

137. The World Bank Group. Available: <http://www.worldbank.org/poverty/data/trends/index.htm>. Accessed 5/16/01.

138. The World Bank Group, *Poverty Trends and the Voices of the Poor* (Washington, D.C.: World Bank, 2001), 46. Available: <http://www.worldbank.org/poverty/data/trends/index.htm>. Accessed 5/16/01.

139. The World Bank Group, *Poverty Trends*, 53.

140. The World Bank Group, *Poverty Trends*, 14.

141. The World Bank Group, *Poverty Trends*, 53.

CHAPTER 10

1. Brookings Institution, "Government's 50 Greatest Endeavors," Available: <http://www.brookings.edu/GS/CPS/50ge/50greatest.htm>. Accessed: 2/11/01.

2. David Horowitz and David Kolodney, "The Foundations, " *Ramparts* (April 1969): 38.

3. Corey Robin, "The Ex-Cons," *Lingua Franca* 11 (February 2001). Available: <http://www.linguafranca.com/print/0101/cover_cons.html>. Accessed 5/21/01.

4. George Soros, *The Crisis of Global Capitalism* (Washington, D.C.: Public Affairs, 2000).

5. Michael Pollan, "How Organic Became a Marketing Niche and a Multibillion-Dollar Industry. Naturally," *New York Times Magazine* (May 13, 2001): 30–37ff.

6. For an explanation of the tax credit, see the Green Party of Manitoba Web Site: <http://www.greenparty.mb.ca/join.html#donations>.

7. Barbara Rogers, *Men Only* (London: Pandora, 1988), 82.

8. E. E. Shattschneider, *The Semi-Sovereign People* (New York: Holt, Rinehart and Winston, 1960), 31; Kay Lehman Schlozman and John T. Tierney, *Organized Interests and American Democracy* (New York: Harper and Row, 1986), 68.

9. David Rieff, "Civil Society and the Future of the Nation-State," *Nation* (February 22, 1999): 11–16. Available: EBSCO Academic Search Elite. Accessed: 7/24/00.

10. Thomas Carothers, "Ousting Foreign Strongmen: Lessons from Serbia," Carnegie Endowment for International Peace Policy Brief 1 (May 2001). Available: <http://www.ceip.org/>. Accessed: 5/23/01.

11. Diana Johnstone, "Humanitarian War: Making the Crime Fit the Punishment." Available: <http://www.emperors-clothes.com/articles/Johnstone/crime2.htm>. Accessed: 5/22/01.

12. Carnegie Endowment for International Peace, *Changing Our Ways: America and the New World* (1992). Summary Available: <http://www.ceip.org/files/publiscations/changingourwaysummary.asp>. Accessed: 5/23/01.

13. Frances Stonor Saunders, *Who Paid the Piper?: The CIA and the Cultural Cold War* (London: Granta, 1999), 142. Published in the United States as *The Cultural Cold War* (New York: New Press, 1999).

14. I served as a moderator at a community "futures" workshop, to which the whole, perfect New England town of Dublin, New Hampshire, was invited. The turnout was very low; senior citizens predominated. I was told that some of the nonattendees were at a big match of the girls' soccer teams.

15. Carol Weisbrod, *The Boundaries of Utopia* (New York: Pantheon, 1980), 45.

Select Bibliography

Abdul-Raheem, Tajudeen. "Impact of Angels." *New Internationalist* 326 (August 2000): 20–21.

Almond, Gabriel. "Separate Tables." *PS* 21 (1988): 828–42.

Anderson, Ken, and Richard Anderson. "Limitations of the Liberal Legal Model of International Human Rights: Six Lessons from El Salvador." *Telos* 64 (1985): 91–104.

Arnove, Robert, ed. *Philanthropy and Cultural Imperialism.* Boston: G. K. Hall, 1980.

Baer, Michael, Malcolm Jewell, and Lee Sigelman, eds. *Political Science in America: Oral Histories of a Discipline.* Lexington: University Press of Kentucky, 1991.

Beard, Charles. "Neglected Aspects of Political Science." *American Political Science Review* 42 (April 1948): 211–22.

Bellant, Russ. *The Coors Connection.* Cambridge: Political Research Associates, 1990.

Bendaña, Alejandro. "Which Way for NGOs?" *Interhemispheric Resource Center Bulletin* (October 1998): Available: <http:www.irc-online.org>.

Berger, Raoul. *Government by Judiciary.* Cambridge: Harvard University Press, 1977.

Berman, Edward. *The Influence of the Carnegie, Ford, and Rockefeller Foundations on American Foreign Policy.* Albany: State University of New York Press, 1983.

Black, Christopher. "An Impartial Tribunal? Really?" (2000). Available: <http://www.emperors-clothes.com/analysis/Impartial.htm>. Accessed 7/5/00.

Blum, William. *Killing Hope.* Monroe, Maine: Common Courage, 1995.

Brandt, Daniel. "Multiculturalism and the Ruling Elite." *NameBase NewsLine* 3 (October–December 1993). Available: <http://www.pir.org/news03.html>. Accessed: 7/3/00.

Brooks, Harvey. "Sponsorship and Social Science Research." *Society* 21 (May–June 1984): 81–83.

Brzezinski, Zbigniew. *Alternative to Partition.* New York: McGraw-Hill, 1965.

———. *The Grand Chessboard.* New York: Basic Books, 1997.

Capital Research Center Web Site: <http://www.capitalresearch.org>.

Carothers, Thomas. "Aiding Post–Communist Societies: A Better Way?" *Problems of Post–Communism* 43 (September–October 1996): 15–25.

———. "Civil Society." *Foreign Policy* 117 (winter 1999–2000): 18–30. Available: EBSCO Academic Search Elite. Accessed: 7/6/00.

"CIA Funding of Domestic Groups." *Congressional Quarterly* (February 24, 1967): 271–72.

Civic Education Project Web Site. 2000. Available: <http://www.cep.org.hu/proffund.htm>. Accessed 7/3/00.

Civnet News. September 20, 1999. Available: http://civnet.org/news/news.htm. Accessed 7/5/00.

Clotfelter, Charles T., and Thomas Ehrlich, eds. *Philanthropy and the Nonprofit Sector in a Changing America.* Bloomington: Indiana University Press, 1999.

Cohen, Roger. "Who Really Brought Down Milosevic?" *New York Times Magazine* (November 26, 2000): 42. Available: <http://www.nytimes.com>. Accessed: 11/27/00.

Colby, Gerard, and Charlotte Dennett. *Thy Will Be Done: The Conquest of the Amazon: Nelson Rockefeller and Evangelism in the Age of Oil.* New York: HarperCollins, 1995.

Colwell, Mary Anna C. "Philanthropic Foundations and Public Policy: The Role of Foundations." Ph.D. dissertation, University of California, Berkeley, 1980.

Coon, Horace. *Money to Burn* [1938]. New Brunswick: Transaction, 1990.

Council on Hemispheric Affairs (COHA). *National Endowment for Democracy (NED): A Foreign Policy Branch Gone Awry.* Albuquerque: Inter-Hemispheric Education Resource Center, 1990.

Council for Public Interest Law (CPIL). *Balancing the Scales of Justice: Financing Public Interest Law in America.* New York: CPIL, 1976.

Curti, Merle, and R. Nash. *Philanthropy in the Shaping of American Higher Education.* New Brunswick: Rutgers University Press, 1965.

Dahl, Robert. "The Behavioral Approach in Political Science: Epitaph for a Monument to a Successful Protest." *American Political Science Review* 55 (1961): 763–72.

Domhoff, G. William. *The Power Elite and the State.* New York: De Gruyter, 1990.

———. *The Powers That Be.* New York: Random House, 1978.

———. *Who Rules America Now?* Englewood Cliffs: Prentice Hall, 1983.

———. *Who Rules America? Power and Politics in the Year 2000.* 3rd ed. Mountain View: Mayfield, 1998.

Dowie, Mark. *American Foundations.* Cambridge: MIT Press, 2001.

———. *Losing Ground: American Environmentalism at the Close of the Twentieth Century.* Cambridge: MIT Press, 1995.

Dye, Thomas. *Top Down Policymaking.* New York: Chatham House, 2001.

Espinoza, Martin. "Sleeping with the Enemy." *San Francisco Bay Guardian,* October 8, 1997. Available: <http://www.sfbg.com/News/32/02/Features/sleep.html>. Accessed: 7/28/00.

Evans-Pritchard, Ambrose. "Euro-federalists Financed by U.S. Spy Chiefs." *Telegraph* (September 19, 2000). Available: <http://www.telegraph.co.uk>. Accessed: 9/24/00.

Feldman, Shelley. "NGOs and Civil Society: (Un)stated Contradictions." *Annals of the American Academy of Political and Social Science* 554 (1997): 46–66.

Fernando, Jude. "Nongovernmental Organizations, Micro-credit, and Empowerment of Women." *Annals of the American Academy of Political and Social Science* 554 (1997): 150–78.

Filer Commission. *Research Papers of the Commission on Private Philanthropy and Public Needs.* 5 vols. Washington, D.C.: U.S. Department of the Treasury, 1977.

Fish, John Hall. *Black Power/White Control: The Struggle of The Woodlawn Organization in Chicago.* Princeton: Princeton University Press, 1973.

Fisher, Donald. *Fundamental Development of the Social Sciences.* Ann Arbor: University of Michigan Press, 1993.

Ford Foundation. *Annual Report.* New York: Ford Foundation, 1984.

———. *Civil Rights, Social Justice, and Black America.* New York: Ford Foundation, 1984.

———. *Report of the Study for the Ford Foundation on Policy and Program.* Detroit: Ford Foundation, 1949.

Ford Foundation-American Bar Association (FF-ABA). *Public Interest Law: Five Years.* New York: FF-ABF, 1976.

Fosdick, Raymond. *The Story of the Rockefeller Foundation.* New York: Harper, 1952.

Foundation Center. *Highlights of Foundation Yearbook:* 2000. Available: <http://www.fdncenter.org>. Accessed: 3/17/01.

"Foundations Deeply Influence 'the Movement.'" *New Options* (October 24, 1984): 3–4.

Gamson, William. *The Strategy of Social Protest.* Homewood: Dorsey, 1975.

Geiger, Roger. "American Foundations and Academic Social Science: 1945–1960." *Minerva* 26 (1988): 315–41.

Gendzier, Irene. *Development against Democracy: Manipulating Political Change in the Third World.* Hampton, Conn.: Tyrone Press, 1995.

Gill, Stephen. *American Hegemony and the Trilateral Commission.* New York: Cambridge University Press, 1991.

Goldstein, Robert Justin. *Political Repression in Modern America: 1870 to the Present.* Cambridge: Schenkman, 1978.

Gramsci, Antonio. *Selections from the Prison Notebooks.* New York: International, 1971.

Griswold, Erwin. "Philanthropic Foundations and the Law." In *United States Philanthropic Foundations,* edited by Warren Weaver, 287–98. New York: Harper and Row, 1967.

Guidestar Web Site. <http://www.guidestar.org>.

Haines, Herbert. "Black Radicalization and the Funding of Civil Rights: 1957–1970." *Social Problems* 32 (1984): 31–43.

Hall, Peter Dobkin. *Inventing the Nonprofit Sector.* Baltimore: Johns Hopkins University Press, 1992.

————. "The Model of Boston Charity: A Theory of Charitable Benevolence and Class Development." *Science and Society* 38 (1975): 464–77.

Handler, Joel. *Social Movements and the Legal System.* New York: Academic Press, 1978.

Harrington, Michael. *The Other America.* New York: Macmillan, 1962.

Hays, Samuel. "The Politics of Reform in Municipal Government in the Progressive Era." *Pacific Northwest Quarterly* (October 1964): 157–69.

————. *The Response to Industrialism: 1885–1914.* Chicago: University of Chicago Press, 1957.

Horowitz, David. "Billion Dollar Brains." *Ramparts* (May 1969): 36–44.

————. "Sinews of Empire." *Ramparts* (October 1969): 32–42.

Horowitz, David, and David Kolodney. "The Foundations." *Ramparts* (April 1969): 38–48.

Hoynes, William. "The Cost of Survival: Political Discourse and the 'New PBS.'" *FAIR* (June 1999). Available: <http://www.fair.org/reports/pbs-study-1999.html>. Accessed: 6/29/99.

Huntington, Samuel. "One Soul at a Time: Political Science and Political Reform." *American Political Science Review* 82 (1988): 3–10.

International Political Science Association (IPSA). *Synthesis Report on the IPSA.* Paris: IPSA, n.d.

Jenkins, J. Craig. "Foundation Funding of Progressive Social Movements." In *The Grant Seekers Guide,* 3rd ed., edited by Jill Shellow and Nancy Stella, 1–13. Mt. Kisco: Moyer-Bell, 1986.

————. "Resource Mobilization Theory and the Study of Social Movements." *Annual Review of Sociology* 9 (1983): 527–63.

Karl, Barry D. "Philanthropy and the Maintenance of Democratic Elites." *Minerva* 35 (fall 1997): 207–20.

————. "Philanthropy and the Social Sciences." *Proceedings of the American Philosophical Society* 129 (1985): 14–19.

Karl, Barry D., and Stanley N. Katz. "The American Private Philanthropic Foundation and the Public Sphere 1890–1930." *Minerva* 19 (summer 1981): 236–70.

Katz, Stanley. "Grantmaking and Research in the U.S., 1933–1983." *Proceedings of the American Philosophical Society* 129 (1985): 1–2.

Klausner, Samuel, and Victor Lidz, eds. *The Nationalization of the Social Sciences.* Philadelphia: University of Pennsylvania Press, 1986.

Koch, Frank. *The New Corporate Philanthropy.* New York: Plenum, 1979.

Kohata, Kotaro. "Birth of a 35–Year-Old Prime Minister in Hungary." Sasakawa Peace Fund Web Site. Available: <http://www.spf.org/spf_e/spffeatures/myturn5.html>. Accessed 5/6/01.

Kothari, Rajni. "NGOs, the State, and World Capitalism." *Economic and Political Weekly* 21 (December 13, 1986): 2177–82.

Lagemann, Ellen Condliffe. *The Politics of Knowledge.* Chicago: University of Chicago Press, 1989.

———. *Private Power for Public Good: A History of the Carnegie Foundation for the Advancement of Teaching.* Middletown: Wesleyan University Press, 1983.

———, ed. *Philanthropic Foundations: New Scholarship, New Possibilities.* Bloomington: Indiana University Press, 1999.

Laski, Harold. "Foundations, Universities, and Research." *Harper's* (August 1928): 295–303.

Lerner, Max. "The Divine Right of Judges." *The Nation* (January 29, 1936): 379–81.

Lundberg, Ferdinand. *America's Sixty Families.* New York: Vanguard, 1937.

———. *The Rich and the Super-Rich.* New York: Lyle Stuart, 1968.

———. *The Rockefeller Syndrome.* Secaucus: Lyle Stuart, 1975.

Lydon, Christopher. "Jimmy Carter Revealed: He's a Rockefeller Republican." *The Atlantic Monthly* (July 1977): 50–59.

McAdam, Doug. "The Decline of the Civil Rights Movement." In *Waves of Protest: Social Movements Since the Sixties,* edited by Jo Freeman and Victoria Johnson, 325–48. Lanham, Md.: Rowman and Littlefield, 1999.

McCarthy, John D., and Mayer N. Zald. "Resource Mobilization and Social Movements: A Partial Theory." *American Journal of Sociology* 82 (1977): 1212–41.

McCarthy, Kathleen D. "From Cold War to Cultural Development." *Dedalus* (winter 1987): 93–117.

MacDonald, Laura. "A Mixed Blessing: The NGO Boom in Latin America." *NACLA Report on the Americas* 28 (March–April 1995): 30–35. Available: Wilson Web. Accessed: 8/28/00.

Magat, Richard. *The Ford Foundation at Work: Philanthropic Choices, Methods, and Styles.* New York: Plenum, 1979.

———. "Unions and Foundations As Public Policy Actors." *Policy Studies Review* 14 (spring–summer 1995): 161–70. Available: Wilson Web. Accessed: 2/07/01.

Maren, Michael. *The Road to Hell.* New York: Free Press, 1997.

Martin Luther King Jr. Center for Non-Violent Social Change, Inc. *Profile.* Atlanta: M. L. King Jr. Center, 1985.

Marx, Karl, and Frederick Engels. *The Communist Manifesto.* New York: International, 1948.

Miller, Arthur S. *The Supreme Court and American Capitalism.* New York: Free Press, 1968.

Miller, Mike. *Can the Debate Be Resolved?: The Controversy about Community Organizing and Community Development.* A report sponsored by the Aspen Institute Nonprofit Sector Research Fund, n.d.

Mott Foundation. *2000 Grants Database. Civil Society-Central/Eastern Europe, Russia and the Republics-1995-1999.* Available: <http://www.mott.org/cgibin/mottgrants/grantsearch.pl>. Accessed 7/25/00.

Myrdal, Gunnar. *An American Dilemma.* New York: Harper and Row, 1944.

Nagai, Althea K., Robert Lerner, and Stanley Rothman. *The Culture of Philanthropy: Foundations and Public Policy.* Washington: Capital Research Center, 1991.

Nielsen, Waldemar. *The Big Foundations.* New York: Columbia University Press, 1972.

———. *The Golden Donors.* New York: Dutton, 1985.

Oberschall, Anthony. "The Decline of the 1960s Social Movements." *Research in Social Movements, Conflicts, and Change* 1 (1978): 257–89.

Ostrander, Susan. "Upper-Class Women: Class Consciousness As Conduct and Meaning." In *Power Structure Research,* edited by G. William Domhoff, 73–96. Beverly Hills: Sage, 1980.

Ostrander, Susan A., and Stuart Langton, eds. *Shifting the Debate: Public/Private Sector Relations in the Modern Welfare State.* New Brunswick: Transaction Books, 1987.

Peirce, Neal, and Carol Steinbach. "Reindustrialization on a Small Scale—But Will the Small Business Survive?" *National Journal* 13 (1981): 105–108.

Peschek, Joseph. *Policy-Planning Organizations: Elite Agendas and America's Rightward Turn.* Philadelphia: Temple University Press, 1987.

Petras, James. "NGOs: In the Service of Imperialism." *Journal of Contemporary Asia* 29 (1999): 429–40. Available: Wilson Web. Accessed: 2/8/01.

Pinto-Duschinsky, Michael. 1991. "Foreign Political Aid: The German Political Foundations and Their U.S. Counterparts." *International Affairs* 67 (1991): 33–63.

Popper, Karl. *The Open Society and Its Enemies.* Princeton: Princeton University Press, 1971.

Powell, Walter, and E. Clemens. *Private Action and the Public Good.* New Haven: Yale University Press, 1998.

President's Research Committee on Social Trends. *Recent Social Trends in the United States* [1933]. 2 vols. Westport: Greenwood Press, 1970.

Putnam, Robert. *Bowling Alone.* New York: Simon and Schuster, 2000.

Quigley, Kevin F. F. *For Democracy's Sake: Foundations and Democracy Assistance in Central Europe.* Washington, D.C.: Woodrow Wilson Center Press, 1997.

Rabinowitz, Alan. *Social Change Philanthropy in America.* Westport: Quorum, 1990.

Ransom, David. "Ford Country: Building an Elite for Indonesia." In *The Trojan Horse: A Radical Look at Foreign Aid,* edited by Steve Weissman and members of the Pacific Studies Center and the North American Congress on Latin America, 93–116. San Francisco: Ramparts Press, 1974.

Roberts, Alasdair. "Demonstrating Neutrality: The Rockefeller Philanthropies and the Evolution of Public Administration, 1927–1936." *Public Administration Review* 54 (May–June 1994): 221.

Robinson, William I. *Promoting Polyarchy: Globalization, U.S. Intervention, and Hegemony.* New York: Cambridge University Press, 1996.

Roelofs. Joan. "Eco-Cities and Red Green Politics." *Capitalism, Nature, Socialism* 11 (March 2000): 139–48.

————. "Foundations and Political Science." *New Political Science* (fall 1992): 3–28.

————. "Foundations and Social Change Organizations: The Mask of Pluralism." *Insurgent Sociologist* 14 (1987): 31–72.

————. "Foundations and the Supreme Court." *Telos* 62 (1984–1985): 59–87.

————. "Judicial Activism As Social Engineering." In *Supreme Court Activism and Restraint,* edited by Stephen Halpern and Charles Lamb, 249–70. Lexington: Lexington Books, 1982.

Roelofs, Joan, and Erkki Berndtson. 1994. "Foundations, Social Scientists, and Eastern Europe." In *The Political Influence of Ideas: Policy Communities and the Social Sciences,* edited by Stephen Brooks and Alain-G. Gagnon, 163–85. Westport: Praeger, 1994.

Rosenberg, Tina. "From Dissidents to MTV Democrats." *Harper's* 285 (September 1992): 46–53. Available: EBSCO. Accessed 2/17/01.

Rousseau, Jean-Jacques. *Discours sur les Sciences et les Arts. [Discourse on the Arts and Sciences].* Translated by J. Roelofs. Geneva: Barillot and Son, 1750. ATHENA e-text. Available: <http://un2sg4.unige.ch/athena/rousseau/jjr_sca.rtf>. Accessed: 12/12/01.

Saint-Simon, Claude-Henri de. *De l'Organization Sociale.* Translated by J. Roelofs. Paris: National Institute of the French Language, n.d. Available: <http://gallica.bnf.fr>. Accessed: 2/06/02.

Salisbury, Stephan. "Pew Charitable Trusts Develops a Hands-on Role." *Philadelphia Inquirer,* October 13–14, 1996, p. 1.

Samson, Gloria G. *The American Fund for Public Service.* Westport: Greenwood Press, 1996.

Saunders, Frances Stonor, *Who Paid the Piper?: The CIA and the Cultural Cold War.* London: Granta, 1999. Published in the United States as *The Cultural Cold War.* New York: New Press, 1999.

Schachter, Hindy. "Settlement Women and Bureau Men: Did They Share a Usable Past?" *Public Administration Review* 57 (January–February 1997): 93–94.

Seidelman, Raymond, and Edward Harpham. *Disenchanted Realists: Political Science and the American Crisis: 1884–1984.* Albany: State University of New York Press, 1985.

Seybold, Peter. "The Ford Foundation and Social Control." *Science for the People* (May–June 1982): 28–31.

Shoup, Laurence, and William Minter. *Imperial Brain Trust.* New York: Monthly Review Press, 1977.

Sierra, Christine. "The Political Transformation of a Minority Organization—Council of La Raza." Ph.D. dissertation, Stanford University, 1983.

Simpson, Christopher. *Universities and Empire: Money and Politics in the Social Sciences during the Cold War.* New York: New Press, 1998.

Sklar, Holly, ed. *Trilateralism: The Trilateral Commission and Elite Planning for World Management*. Boston: South End, 1980.

Smith, Brian H. *More Than Altruism*. Princeton: Princeton University Press, 1990.

Smith, James A. *The Idea Brokers: Think Tanks and the Rise of the New Policy Elite*. New York: Free Press, 1991.

Smith, Robert. "Black Power and the Transformation from Protest to Politics." *Political Science Quarterly* 96 (1981): 431–43.

Stoper, Emily. "The SNCC—Rise and Fall of a Redemptive Organization." *Journal of Black Studies* 8 (1977): 13–34.

Stouffer, Samuel. *Communism, Conformism and Civil Liberties*. New York: Doubleday, 1955.

Study Commission on U.S. Policy toward Southern Africa. *South Africa: Time Running Out*. Berkeley: University of California Press, 1981.

Tokar, Brian. *Earth for Sale*. Boston: South End, 1997.

U.S. Agency for International Development (USAID). *Democracy and Governance*. Washington, D.C.: USAID, 1991.

———. *USAID Political Party Development Assistance*. Washington, D.C.: USAID, 1999.

U.S. Congress. Commission on Industrial Relations (Walsh Commission). *Report*. Washington, D.C.: Government Printing Office, 1915.

———. House. Special Committee to Investigate Tax-Exempt Foundations and Comparable Organizations. *Tax-Exempt Foundations*. 83rd Cong. 2nd Sess., 1954.

———. House. *Hearings on Exempt Foundations and Charitable Trusts before the Subcommittee on Domestic Finance of the House Committee on Banking and Currency*. 93rd Cong., lst Sess. (Patman Committee), 1973.

———. House Committee on Ways and Means. *Hearings on Tax Reform*. 91st Cong., lst Sess., 1969.

———. Senate Committee on Finance. *Hearings on Improper Payments by Private Foundations to Government Officials*. 91st Cong. 1st Sess., 1969.

Van Til, Jon. *Growing Civil Society: From Nonprofit Sector to Third Space*. Bloomington: Indiana University Press, 2000.

Wagner, David. *What's Love Got to Do With It?* New York: New Press, 2000.

Walsh, Frank. "The Great Foundations." Unpublished manuscript, n.d., cited in James Weinstein. *The Corporate Ideal in the Liberal State*. Boston: Beacon Press, 1989.

Wedel, Janine. *Collision and Collusion: The Strange Case of Western Aid to Eastern Europe 1989–1998*. New York: St. Martin's Press, 1998.

Weiner, Jon. "Dollars for Neocon Scholars." *The Nation* (January 1, 1990): 12–14.

Weisbrod, Burton, Joel Handler, and Neil Komesar, eds. *Public Interest Law*. Berkeley: University of California Press, 1978.

Whitaker, Ben. *The Foundations*. London: Methuen, 1974.

Wormser, René. *Foundations: Their Power and Influence*. New York: Devin-Adair, 1958.

Wright, Talmadge, Felix Rodriguez, and Howard Waitzkin. "Corporate Interests, Philan-thropies, and the Peace Movement." *Monthly Review* (February 1985): 19–31.

Zisk, Betty. *The Politics of Transformation: Local Activism in the Peace and Environmental Movements*. Westport: Praeger, 1992.

Index

sciences and, 34; state and local gov-
ernment, 69; statistics, 19; taxation, 13;
transformation of social change, 148
Friedrich Ebert Foundation, 163
Fulbright fellowships, 43, 176
Fund for the Republic, 102, 109
Funding Exchange, 123, 144, 147

Gaebler, Ted, 77
Gamson, William, 147
Gardner, John W., 70
Garland Fund, 21, 142, 143
Gates Foundation, 19
Gates, Bill, 55
General Education Board, 70, 111
General Electric: public television, 61
Ginsburg, Ruth Bader, 103
globalization, 55, 56, 205
Goode, W. Wilson, 129
government corporations, 73
Grameen Bank, 22, 97, 168
Gramsci, Antonio, 1, 145
Grantmakers in the Arts, 83
Great Society program, 94
Great Soviet Encyclopedia, 177
Green Mountain Fund of Vermont, 145
Griggs v. Duke Power Co, 112
Guadalupe Cultural Arts Center, 84
Guidestar, 21

Hacker, Andrew: behavioralism, 36
Hall, Peter Dobkin, 16
Harrington, Michael: *The Other America,*
94, 115
Havel, Vaclav: *Power of the Powerless,* 178
Haymarket People's Fund, 20, 144; pilot
study, 150
Hays, Samuel, 65
Headstart, 71
Hegel, G. W. F.: civil society, 18, 47
hegemony, 4, 55, 80, 183, 191, 198, 208;
foundations, 2; Gramsci, 1; ideology, 2
Heinrich Böll Foundation, 163
Heintz, Stephen B., 69
Helsinki Accords, 176
Helsinki Watch. *See* Human Rights
Watch

Heritage Foundation, 33, 76, 118;
Mandate for Leadership, 76
higher education, 207; destabilization and,
54
Highlander Folk School, 143
Highlander Research and Education
Center, 62
Hispanics in Philanthropy, 21
Hoffman, Paul, 160, 166
Hoover, Herbert, 89
Horowitz, David, 11
Howe, Harold, 71
Human Rights Watch, 160, 176
humanitarian intervention: Carnegie
Endowment for International Peace, 56
Hungary: Civic Party, 182; FIDESZ, 181;
nonprofit sector, 192
Huntington, Samuel, 43

identity politics, 134, 171; Native
American Youth Association, 148
imperialism: civil society, 47, 203; cultural,
4, 158, 175
Independent Sector, 15, 123
indigenous people, 160
individual development accounts, 98
Indonesia: Ford Foundation, 165
Industrial Relations Counselors, Inc., 90
information, 206
Innis, Roy, 95
Institute for Alternative Journalism, 59
Institute for East-West Security Studies,
177
Institute for International Economics, 98
Institute for International Education, 41
Institute for Public Accuracy, 62
Institute for Sustainable Communities:
Eastern Europe, 187
Institute of Hispanic-American and
Luso-Brazilian Studies (Stanford), 39
Institute of International Education, 177
intellectual, 2, 27, 81, 175, 200; Gramsci,
1
International City Management
Association, 68
International Confederation of Free Trade
Unions, 162

Printed in the United States
84495LV00003B/136-141/A

9 780791 456422